For Sale
by Owner

by George Devine

Legal Editors: Ralph Warner & Mary Randolph
Illustrated by Linda Allison

IMPORTANT: The information in this book changes rapidly and is subject to differing interpretations. It is up to you to check it thoroughly before relying on it. Neither the author nor publisher of this book makes any guarantee regarding the outcome of the uses to which this material is put.

NOLO PRESS • 950 PARKER ST. • BERKELEY, CALIFORNIA • 94710

IMPORTANT

Nolo Press is committed to keeping its books up-to-date. Each new printing, whether or not it is called a new edition, has been revised to reflect the latest law changes. This book has printed and updated on the last date indicated below. Before you rely on information in it, you might wish to call Nolo Press (415) 549-1976 to check whether a later printing or edition has been issued.

PRINTING HISTORY

New "**Printing**" means there have been some minor changes, but usually not enough so that people will need to trade in or discard an earlier printing of the same edition. Obviously, this is a judgment call and any change, no matter how minor, might affect you.

New "**Edition**" means one or more major, or a number of minor, law changes since the previous edition.

FIRST EDITION	March 1987
ILLUSTRATIONS	Linda Allison
PRODUCTION	Stephanie Harolde
BOOK DESIGN & LAYOUT	Keija Kimura
	Toni Ihara
	Jackie Clark
COVER HOUSES	Jackie Clark

Library of Congress Catalog Card Number: 87-60360
ISBN 0-87337-035-X

ACKNOWLEDGMENTS

Like all books, this one is a group effort. Many who helped in its formation were unaware of the extent to which they contributed valuable encouragement, information or advice at important times. I have in mind here several fellow real estate brokers, including Barbara Robinson of Alvarez, Hyland & Young of Beverly Hills, and some brokers who are also attorneys specializing in real estate, especially Daniel F. McHugh of San Francisco and Michael Somers of Novato. Vivien Feyer and Ira Serkes of Berkeley provided valuable reader reactions, as did Cary Fargo, a broker in Sonoma County, Tony and Patricia Dimond, escrow officers Pat Carlin and Helen Dumont, IRS agent Xavier Guerrero, loan officer Karen Cox of Commonwealth Mortgage Corporation of America, Hank and Carla Greenwald, and Hayden Curry, an Oakland real estate attorney who regularly advises people who sell their own houses.

In addition, many people at Nolo Press had a hand in the book. Special thanks to Jackie Clark, Carol Pladsen, Keija Kimura, Stephanie Harolde, Julie Christianson, and Steve Elias.

The most helpful individuals in making this project possible were Nolo's editors, Jake Warner and Mary Randolph, who, from start to finish, were involved in improving, clarifying and polishing this book in truly significant ways.

On a regular basis, the project was kept going by the encouragement and empathy of my wife Joanne, my son George and my daughter Annemarie.

Finally, no successful real estate agent exists or endures without loyal clients. Many of these good people provided me with the experience necessary to write this book: the Kranzke family, and the late Telesforo Batara; the Etcheber family; all the Clisham family, Julie Koppich and Della Hall; the late Caterina Machi; Saul and Barbara Kitchener; Tony Bila and Lisa Hamburger; Ted Raabe and Jenny Hess; and the late Francis J. Donohue, Sr., who probably got me into real estate in the first place.

UPDATE SERVICE
· Introductory Offer ·

Our books are as current as we can make them, but sometimes the laws do change between editions. You can read about law changes which may affect this book in the NOLO NEWS, a 16-page newspaper which we publish quarterly.

In addition to the Update Service, each issue contains comprehensive articles about the growing self-help law movement as well as areas of law that are sure to affect you. (regular subscription rate is $7.00)

To receive the next 4 issues of the NOLO NEWS, please send us $2.00:

Name _____

Address _____

_____

Send to: NOLO PRESS, 950 Parker St., Berkeley CA 94710

fsbo 3/87

Recycle Your Out-of-Date Books & Get 25% off your next purchase!

Using an old edition can be dangerous if information in it is wrong. Unfortunately, laws and legal procedures change often. To help you keep up to date we extend this offer. If you cut out and deliver to us the title portion of the cover of any old Nolo book we'll give you a 25% discount off the retail price of any new Nolo book. For example, if you have a copy of TENANT'S RIGHTS, 4th edition and want to trade it for the latest CALIFORNIA MARRIAGE AND DIVORCE LAW, send us the TENANT'S RIGHTS cover and a check for the current price of MARRIAGE & DIVORCE, less a 25% discount. Information on current prices and editions is listed in the NOLO NEWS (see above box). Generally speaking, any book more than two years old is of questionable value. Books more than four or five years old are a menace.

OUT OF DATE = DANGEROUS

This offer is to individuals only.

TABLE OF CONTENTS

CHAPTER 10: THE BIDS COME IN

CHAPTER 11: AFTER THE CONTRACT IS SIGNED: CONTINGENCIES, TITLE INSURANCE, AND ESCROW

CHAPTER 12: WHAT IF SOMETHING GOES WRONG?

GLOSSARY

APPENDIX

INTRODUCTION

Who can sell your house in California?

You can!

Without a real estate broker?

Sure. And you can save many thousands of dollars if you do.

Yes, there are a number of procedures to follow and rules to learn, but if you're already something of a "do-it-yourselfer," you won't find selling your own house any more difficult than many of the tasks you have already successfully accomplished. Of course, doing any reasonably involved task without resorting to the often traumatic trial and error approach means locating and paying close attention to good, tight step-by-step instructions. That's where this book comes in.

As an experienced real estate broker and educator, I take you through the steps commonly involved in selling a single family residence in California. Perhaps surprisingly, none of these is difficult to carry out on your own, assuming you are willing to dedicate yourself to the mastery of a reasonable amount of detail. To briefly summarize, selling a California house using this book involves:

- determining an advantageous time to sell;

- accurately pricing your house;

• telling the maximum number of potential purchasers your house is for sale;

• dealing with potential purchasers and making sure they are financially qualified to purchase your house;

• receiving an offer (or offers) to purchase your property and, if necessary, making a counter-offer (or offers);

• signing a sales contract with a purchaser, which complies with California law and meets the needs of the purchaser to inspect the house, arrange financing, etc.; and

• completing the escrow process to actually transfer title of the house to the purchaser and the money to you.[1]

How much money can you save by selling your own house? This is obviously an important question to ask before you decide whether or not to go to the trouble. If you're selling the typical California house, the sales price will be between $100,000 and $200,000. The most common real estate commission on a home sale is 6%. The rest is easy arithmetic. Just in case your calculator isn't handy, this works out as follows:

Sales Price	Amount Saved
$100,000	$6,000
$150,000	$9,000
$200,000	$12,000
$200,000 and over	$12,000 +[2]

Of course, selling your own house does involve a considerable investment of your own time. While I know people who have sold their house in a matter of a few hours, this is obviously atypical. Depending on the size, price, location and condition of your house, it's probably realistic to figure that it will take between 75 and 200 hours of your time to sell it on your own. If you value your time at $20 per hour, and it takes 100 hours to sell your house, this means that you

---

[1]This book is directed primarily at persons selling single-family detached homes. If you want to sell a condominium or co-op unit, or your house is part of a subdivision that has a homeowners' association, special legal requirements apply. For example, condominium sellers must provide buyers with documents disclosing financial and organizational information about the condominium development. I alert you to these special rules in the appropriate chapters, but this book does not focus on the special problems associated with condos, co-ops and planned unit development sales.

[2]Commissions on sales over $200,000 are typically renegotiated to an amount less than 6%. While there is no firm rule here, it is typical for brokers to charge a commission of 6% on the first $150,000-200,000, 5% on the next $50,000-100,000, and 2.5% on the balance. See Chapter 4, Section A, for more details on commissions.

have invested $2,000 of your own labor in the sale. For most people, this is probably a reasonable investment, but if you are already extremely busy or harried, it may not be.

Does deciding to sell your own house mean that you need to do everything yourself? Absolutely not. If you decide somewhere along the line that you need the help of a real estate broker, or the advice of a lawyer, you will find that it is possible to hire either or both by the hour. For example, you might want a broker to review all the paperwork you and your buyer prepare before you begin the formal escrow process. Similarly, although lawyers are not normally involved in the routine sale of residential real estate in California, legal questions may well develop which you want answered. The help of a broker is typically available for between several hundred and a thousand dollars, depending on what you want the person to do. I explain in Chapter 4 how you can work with real estate professionals on your terms—not theirs. Of course, saying you may need some help isn't the same thing as saying you will. Many readers of this book will find that they can handle their entire house sale transaction themselves.

I DID IT MYSELF

We wanted to sell our home in the East Bay suburban area near Walnut Creek and move into San Francisco. Since both of us have been to business school we felt we could sell our own home. We knew we had to buy through a broker in San Francisco, since the home we wanted had been listed with an agency there, but we hoped we could save on the commission in selling our home. We followed carefully the steps of appraising our home in terms of comparables, put a price on our house and then held "open houses" for several weekends. Each time we put a roast in the oven, played music on the stereo, and handed out attractive statements describing the house. Frankly, it took several weekends more than we'd expected, but we did sell for close to our asking price. Again following logical steps, and with an attorney charging only a few hundred dollars to review everything, we saved an estimated $12,000. We can appreciate how brokers earn their commissions, but we were glad to earn it for ourselves.

There are other advantages to selling your house yourself. First, it gives you flexibility. You aren't bound by a written commitment to a broker. You can decide not to sell at all, at any time. In addition, you get valuable feedback—in the form of actual offers—on the price you ask for your house. If the market response indicates you've set the price too low, you can raise it overnight.

Selling your house yourself will also help you when you go to buy and eventually sell the next house. You'll not only understand how buyers, sellers and brokers go about the house sale process and what matters to them, but you'll figure out how to use this information to maximize your profit.

Now, before you read further, I have a favor to ask of you. Please read the entire book at least once before you begin any of the formal actions necessary to sell your house. I ask that you do this despite the fact that the book is written in a "first-this-step-then-the-next" style, which may tempt you to delay reading the later chapters until you have completed the steps covered in the earlier ones. The reason I make this request is simple: to successfully sell your own house, you not only have to master and apply, in logical order, a lot of information. You also need a good overview of the whole process. Think of it this way. If you're driving from Los Angeles to Mendocino, it helps not only to know what road you should start on, but also to have a good idea of the overall journey—its length, condition of the road, and logical stopping places.

Finally, a few words about personal pronouns. Because it's as boring to repeatedly write "he and she" and "his and hers" as it is to read them, I attempt to arrive at a reasonable level of gender equality in this area by randomly sprinkling masculine and feminine references throughout the book.

CHAPTER 1

SO YOU WANT TO SELL YOUR HOUSE

▛▞▞▞▞▞▞▞▞▞▞▞▞▞▞▞▞▞▞▞▞▞▞▞▞▞▞▞▞▞▞▞▞▞▞▞▞▞▞▞

My job is to show you how to sell your house. Before I do, however, let me at least suggest that selling your house right now may not be wise. You will rarely hear a real estate agent say this, of course, because brokers typically get a commission only when a house changes hands. Just the same, if you can get most brokers to speak frankly, they will tell you that a great many people end up selling houses for too little because they sell at the wrong time or are in too much of a hurry.

A. TAKE TIME TO PLAN YOUR SALE

Put bluntly, there are times when it's unwise to put a house on the real estate market. Why? Because virtually no one will want to, or be able to, buy it at fair market value. Sometimes the market is flat and getting a fair price is extremely difficult. I've seen hundreds of houses sold for considerably less than they would have brought if they had been sold a year or two earlier or later. Indeed, in recent years, with fast changes in interest rates and consumer confidence, a few months one way or the other can mean a difference of thousands of dollars in the price of a house.

My point is simple. When it comes to selling your house, you are in the driver's seat, if you really want to be. If you plan properly, you have the opportunity to choose a good time to sell, set a fair price and wait until you get it. Unfortunately, as I discuss in this chapter, the reverse of this simple rule is also true; if you don't take the time to really understand how the real estate market works, you can lose your shirt, or at least your collar and cuffs.

These are some typical reasons for wanting to sell your house:

• **Job change:** You can't commute to your new job from your old house.

• **Lifestyle change:** You get married, move in with someone (or someone moves in with you), you move out (or the other does), you have a new child, your children grow up and take wing, your spouse dies, your health argues against continuing to live in a house with stairs or a neighborhood with a certain kind of weather, or you've always wanted to try living in Hawaii.

• **Investment upgrade:** You are doing better financially and want to put some of your financial assets into a home as an investment and because you get to live in a nicer home. You're selling your existing home to "move up."

• **Lifestyle upgrade:** Your old house isn't that bad, but now you can afford something you like better (because it's bigger, closer to work, in a nicer neighborhood, has a pool, an office, or provides something else that's important to you).

• **Financial crisis:** You can't afford to keep up the payments on your home, and hope to sell it and move into a less expensive residence before an actual foreclosure.

• **Tax planning:** When tax laws change, it may be worthwhile to sell quickly or to delay the sale.

Only the first and last reasons are urgent reasons to sell now, and even in these situations it may make economic sense to wait (see Section C below). All of the other situations clearly fit into the "the sale can wait if it needs to" category. That is not to say you don't need more room if you have another child, or that in some instances it wouldn't be better for your health or pocketbook to move, but it also means that selling your house next week, or even next month, isn't essential if by doing so you are not likely to get a fair price.

Another way to think about time pressure when it comes to buying and selling a house is to learn these two basic axioms of the real estate business:

• A buyer who is under abnormal pressure to act ("I have to be moved in so as to have the kids enrolled in school here before the term begins!") almost always pays too much;

Clearly, people who are both buyer and seller (selling their present home and buying another) absolutely want to avoid creating a situation under which they are under abnormal pressure to act on both ends of the deal. Sellers who allow themselves to be maneuvered into this sort of "squeeze play" (and lots do) can lose twice by paying too much and selling for too little. This sort of double loss can easily amount to thousands or even tens of thousands of dollars.

I DID IT MYSELF

When I sold my own house and purchased a larger one, I realized immediately that I didn't have to be under time pressure to sell. Accordingly, the first thing I did was to work out my finances so that I had enough money to close on the new house without needing to sell the old one immediately. This involved arranging a short term loan from a friend. When I did find the house I wanted to buy, it was priced fairly , but at least $30,000 more than I could afford.

When I got friendly with the seller, I learned that she was extremely anxious to sell quickly so as to avoid losing a deal to purchase her custom- built dream house. As it was just after Christmas and houses weren't selling, I decided to make what I thought was a ridiculously low offer. As soon as she saw that I had the money and that my offer was not contingent on selling another house, she accepted. I held on to my old house until March and priced it at $15,000 over the highest amount recommended by my broker friends (at least $20,000 over the current market). I figured that since I wasn't in a hurry, why not test the market for a while and hope that a little spring sunshine would cause a general price increase. The happy result was that the house sold for $100 over my asking price at my first open house.

In short, by planning ahead to have money in hand to buy my new house at the same time I was mellow about the time needed to sell the old one, I estimate that I saved close to $50,000.

B. The Best and Worst Times to Sell a House

What goes into determining how to identify the "best" and "worst" times to sell your house? You may think most of what follows is obvious, but I urge you to slow down and think it through. In my experience, large numbers of otherwise intelligent consumers who should know better make serious errors when it comes to timing the sale of their houses. Here are some things you need to think about:

1. When interest rates are low at banks and savings and loan associations, the pool of potential buyers obviously goes up. This is especially true when you remember that there are a huge number of people who have been prevented from buying a house in the past because of high interest rates and have been anxiously awaiting more affordable rates. Thus, even a relatively small drop in interest rates can mean a huge increase in the number of people who may qualify to buy your house. (I talk about "qualifying a buyer" in Chapter 8.) As the number of existing houses is finite, at least over the short term, this means that when a greater number of potential purchasers chase the same number of houses, prices inevitably rise, sometimes quickly.

2. When the economic climate of your region is healthy, lots of people feel confident about the future, and the pool of potential buyers widens. Many farm communities became economically unattractive places to live in in the mid-1980's because of falling prices for many agricultural products. This caused many homes to be put up for sale at a time when a relatively small pool of buyers were interested in, or qualified to, purchase them. The result, of course, was that supply exceeded demand and prices dropped. Similar depressed housing markets have occurred recently in areas of California dependent on energy and high technology. The moral of all this is simple. In a regional economic slump, it's often best to hold on to your home until conditions improve. Especially in California, no downturn ever seems to last very long.

3. At times when your area is considered especially attractive for any number of reasons, the pool of buyers widens and prices go up. For example, not long ago tourism jumped 17% in the Boston area. Simultaneously, for lots of economic

reasons, the whole area experienced a boom. The result was that suddenly lots of people who had all but written off New England as a desirable place to live and work a few years before began to think about the Boston area as an attractive, exciting and even a romantic place to reside. Not surprisingly, homes began to sell briskly and at sharply higher prices.

Closer to home, for all sorts of reasons, the popularity of geographic areas, cities and neighborhoods can change quickly. For example, Sacramento and a number of other cities in California's Central Valley and foothills are far more popular now than they were just a few years ago. On the downside, there have been soft housing markets in Silicon Valley and in oil producing areas such as Kern County. And of course, significant changes in the desirability of particular areas can and do happen at the neighborhood level, as well as by state, region and city. Recently, for example, a number of particular older semi-rundown neighborhoods in major California cities, such as San Francisco, Los Angeles, San Diego, Oakland, and San Jose, to mention just a few, have become very desirable places to live, and home prices have increased, sometimes dramatically. The point of all this is that you should do some strategic thinking of your own. If you conclude that better times are just around the corner in your area or neighborhood, hold on if you can.

4. At the times of the year when most people are more apt to make a move, prices usually increase, sometimes significantly. Here's a brief home sale calendar that may help:

January: Many people make a New Year's resolution to move, but they're not likely to do it while the Christmas tree is still up.

February: Often, people beset by a hard winter find fault with their present homes (too many leaks, bad drainage, too far to walk to school or the bus, etc.) and start looking to move into a new home. Some of the homes that went on the market in January or have been held over from the fall begin to sell in February.

March: Depending on your part of the state and yearly weather patterns, things may suddenly become beautifully spring-like in your neighborhood, making your house look far more attractive than it did a month before. Homes put up for sale in January and February often sell in March because suddenly they seem to be very reasonably priced. And don't forget, lots of folks are doing their state and federal income tax returns in March, and those who do not enjoy the tax benefits of home ownership may decide that it's silly not to take advantage of the tax deduction for mortgage interest.

April-May: Families with children start to buy so they can move "when the school term ends." Also, yards, decks, pools, etc. begin looking great and everyone is in a better, more expansive mood. Traditionally this is a good time to sell. Prices often take a jump at this time if economic conditions are good.

June-July-August: Families with school-age kids want to be moved in for the new school year. A pool of anxious buyers is always good news for sellers. If you are eager to sell, cancel your vacation and get to work. Also remember, as I mentioned earlier, an anxious buyer is likely to pay top dollar.

September through mid-November: Don't write off the last third of a calendar year, but realize that prices usually stabilize in the fall as the pool of people wanting to move tends to shrink. This is a time when the lookers can often outnumber the buyers, and a seller needs to be patient.

November-December: This is usually a down time for sellers. Most people don't think about buying a new house from Thanksgiving until after the first of the year. However, if economic conditions are strongly on the positive side (interest rates are headed down fast), people have been known to buy a house between opening their presents and carving the turkey.

Needless to say, the above seasonal review is a generalization, and all generalizations are just that. There can easily be good reasons for anyone to pay top dollar for your house at any time of year. Just the same, remember that the trick to selling anything, from donuts to jewelry to a single-family house, is to market your property when most folks are apt to buy. And when it comes to houses, at least, seasonal considerations play a part in making this determination.

C. DON'T SELL YOUR HOME UNDER PRESSURE

Here now are several situations where I've learned that people tend to be stampeded into selling their houses and often make serious mistakes:

1. It's often unwise to make major moves or decisions within at least a year or so of a serious emotional shock (sudden death, divorce, job loss, etc.), providing the move can possibly be avoided or deferred.

2. When a new baby is on the way, people often give in to the normal human urge to quickly create a nest, or trade the old nest in on a better one. In fact, I've noticed that there is usually close to nine months' notice before the new nestling trades womb for room. And it is another two years before he must have a separate bedroom. . .maybe even longer. So again, you can afford to take your time.

3. When people are broke and can't make monthly payments, many panic and sell quickly at a low price to avoid foreclosure. This is almost always a mistake. Foreclosure by trust deed with power of sale takes a minimum of 111 days from the notice of default (recorded when a payment is missed). It can take a good deal longer, especially when lenders are willing to work with people with financial problems to ultimately get their loan paid instead of having to grab the property and sell it. Most lenders would rather have your money than your house and will work with you if they believe that by so doing it will eventually be forthcoming. So, even if a notice of default has been recorded against your home, see if you can work out a part-payment or interest-only arrangement with the lender before you resort to a panic sale. You may be surprised at how accommodating the lender can be.

4. When a homeowner is transferred because of a job change, she often sees no alternative to selling quickly. In fact, employers will, if asked, frequently, assist relocating employees with loans during the transition period.

Here are a few examples of how people I know who managed to delay the sale of their house profited from this strategy:

1. Jon was transferred by his company in the middle of a school year (November to be exact). His new job was a thousand miles away. Jon and his wife Penny realized that houses often sell for less in the winter and thought that because the economy was stagnant interest rates were likely to fall in the spring. They guessed that they might get as much as $15,000 to $20,000 more for their house in May or June and also felt it would be better if their kids didn't

have their schooling interrupted. Accordingly, Jon and Penny decided to try to put off the sale as long as possible. Fortunately, when Jon explained the problem, his employer was willing to help, including putting him up in a company-owned condominium for a very reasonable rent in the new city, and agreeing to pay for his airfare to visit his family on alternate weekends. This not only allowed Jon and Penny time to pick out a home in the new city, but also allowed them to wait to put the existing home on the market until March. When the house sold in April, with a June closing, Jon and Penny got a very good price. Although not everyone has an employer as cooperative as Jon's, your boss will usually be willing to help take some pressure off you.

2. Ann was widowed suddenly. Her first impulse was to sell the home she and her husband had lived in happily for many years. "I just wanted to get out of there!" she said. Ann talked to a good personal counselor and learned that making a major decision like the sale of a house within at least a year of such a shock is usually a mistake. Her counselor even showed her one of a number of studies indicating that human beings' decision-making abilities seem to be short-circuited by grief and shock. But because living in the house was too much for Ann to bear, she rented it to a friend's son and lived elsewhere for several months. Then, when she was ready to cope with business details, she sold the house and got at least $20,000 more than she would have had she sold immediately after her husband's death.

3. Paul wanted to move to a bigger, more expensive house. He had a non-assumable loan at a low interest rate on his existing house. Unfortunately, Paul wanted to move during a time when interest rates were exceedingly high. This meant relatively few people could afford to buy his home, even though it was a desirable one. Paul couldn't carry back the loan (lend the money himself), or even part of it, because he needed all the cash he could get out of his present home in order to buy the new one. Even though all signs signalled caution, Paul was impatient and committed himself to buying the new house, putting down a substantial nonrefundable deposit. When his existing house wouldn't sell at a decent price, Paul found himself in a desperate situation. The end of this sad story was that Paul had to sell to a buyer who could pay cash even though the

offer was for 15% less than a conservative appraiser had told Paul the property was worth. If Paul had continued to live in his house until the market improved, he could surely have sold for at least $10,000 more.

ALTERNATIVES TO TRADITIONAL SALES

Here are several flexible ways you can deal with a real estate market that isn't to your liking, short of selling your house for too little, or deciding not to sell your house at all. I do not show you how to accomplish any of these approaches in this book, but you should know about them.

1. Option

If you've agreed on a sales price, but the buyer cannot raise the cash down payment and/or financing now, you can sell him an option. An option is a contract that binds you to keep open the offer to sell to him at an agreed price, for a certain period of time in exchange for a sum of money, often several thousand dollars. If the buyer doesn't exercise the option within the agreed-upon period, you are no longer obligated to sell the property to him, but you get to keep the option money in exchange for providing the extra time to purchase. There are some complications in options, so I don't normally encourage them, or discuss them in further detail.

2. Lease With Option to Buy

This is similar to the option just discussed except that under this arrangement the prospective buyer leases the house while she determines whether or not she can raise the money to buy it at the agreed-upon price. In addition to paying a reasonable amount of rent, the prospective buyer usually pays something for the option. Of course, the option to purchase at the established price is limited to a specific period of time.

3. Sale-Leaseback

Although this strategy is usually used with commercial property, it is sometimes possible to use it to advantage with a house sale. It works like this: you raise money you need by selling your home to someone else, but you lease it back as a tenant. This way you enjoy the financial benefits of a sale but you don't have to move, at least not right away. It is appropriate if you receive an offer on your house you can't refuse, but can't move for six months.

4. Exchange

You can swap your home for someone else's. If they are of equal value, it's a straight trade. If they're not of equal value, the party "trading up" evens out the deal by throwing in something "to boot." This "boot" can be cash, or anything worth money (notes, stock, personal property such as a car, etc.). This swap technique is typically used with commercial or rental property (Internal Revenue Code Sec. 1031), but it can also be used with a personal residence (IRC Sec. 1034). It may sometimes provide tax benefits compared to an outright sale.

Tax Note: The tax considerations involved in selling homes are briefly considered in Chapter 3.

CHAPTER 2

LEGAL REQUIREMENTS
OF SELLING YOUR
OWN HOUSE

▰▰

Can you legally sell your own California house without professional help? Yes. There is no legal requirement that you deal with a broker, attorney or anyone else as part of selling your house. As long as you (and all other owners) are at least 18 years old[1] and sane, you can do it yourself. You must, however, be aware of some of the legal rules that govern real estate transfers. The most important of them are California's community property and joint ownership laws, which are discussed in Section. A of this chapter.

Note: As discussed in Section B below, in unusual situations, lawsuits, judgment liens or other claims by third parties may make it hard to sell a home without professional help. This is very rare and nothing the average home-owner need worry about.

---

[1]In a few instances, people who are under 18 can also sell their own house. If you're under the age of 18, but have been validly married (even if you're not married now), are on active duty in the armed forces, or have received a declaration of emancipation from a court, you are an adult as far as selling your own house is concerned.

A. Property Sales Rules

1. Single Homeowners

If you are an unmarried adult and have title to your home in your name alone (that is, the deed is in your name alone) with no joint tenants, co-tenants or partners, you can sell it using this book as long as the price you receive is more than enough to pay off all existing debts, mortgages, liens, etc. (see Section B below).

2. Married Homeowners

If you are married and own a house, you must almost always have the consent of your spouse to sell it. This is true even if you are no longer living with your spouse, but not yet divorced. The reason for this rule is that under California community property laws both spouses usually have an ownership interest in real property and therefore both must consent in writing to any sale.[2]

Often community property ownership of real property is reflected on the deed by the words "as community property" after the names of the owners. However, sometimes spouses take title together as "tenants in common" or "joint tenants," and occasionally title to real property owned by a married couple is in one spouse's name alone. The important thing to understand is that no matter what the deed says, the real property of the great majority of married couples is a community property asset. Why? Because at least some of the money used to pay the down payment and/or the mortgage and/or for improvements is almost sure to be community property, which means that at least a portion of the house is also community property.

But suppose you are a married homeowner yet are nevertheless absolutely convinced that your home is your sole and separate property. Perhaps this is because you owned the house outright prior to a very recent marriage (or received it by gift or inheritance after marriage) and have used no community property money for payments or improvements. Do you still need your spouse's signature even though you are sure that he is not legally a co-owner? Yes. Escrow companies and financial institutions have no good way to be sure of your sole ownership status short of your obtaining a court order establishing it. They protect themselves by always requiring the signatures of both spouses. The spouse's consent may be given by signing a sales contract, escrow instructions, or a

---

[2]Civil Code Sec. 4800. If you want to read the statutes themselves, you can get a copy of the California Civil Code at a law library or through Nolo Press (see back of this book for order information).

quitclaim deed that gives complete ownership to the other spouse. This quit-claim deed approach is usually appropriate when the spouse (the person who signs the deed) really doesn't have any interest in the house and wants to remove herself from the sales transaction completely.

A quitclaim deed which releases all claims to ownership by the person who signs it is shown below. A tear-out blank deed is included in the Appendix.

What if your spouse won't consent to your plan to sell the house? See a lawyer; this book won't help you until that problem is resolved.

3. Joint Tenants, Tenants in Common and Partners

In addition to the community property of married couples, there are several other common legal devices by which two or more people co-own title to a piece of real property. The most common of these are joint tenancy, tenancy in common and partnership.

Joint tenancy allows two or more people to own property in equal but undivided shares, with the right of survivorship. This means if one joint tenant dies, the other(s) automatically become the title holder(s).

Tenancy in common occurs when two or more people own an undivided interest in property, without the right of survivorship. In other words, when one tenant in common dies, the other(s) do(es) not automatically own her share; the share of the deceased person passes under the terms of her will or living trust, or by intestate succession if she has executed neither. Another difference between joint tenancy and tenancy in common is that tenants in common can own a piece of property in unequal shares, while joint tenants must own it in equal shares.

You are probably asking what difference it makes whether title to a house is held by joint tenants or tenants in common when it comes to selling it. For our purposes, the answer is "not much." If you want to sell jointly owned property you need the signature of all joint owners and their spouses. If one or more won't sign, you are limited to selling your share only, not the whole property. The mechanics of doing this vary somewhat, depending on how the property is owned, and are always considerably more complicated than simply selling the entire property. Because there is a very limited market for the sale of a part interest in real property, I do not provide how-to details in this book.

Recording requested by
    Thomas Hammond
    3942 Wale Lane
    Rosamond, CA 98309

and when recorded mail this deed
and tax statements to:
    same as above

For recorder's use

QUITCLAIM DEED

☐   This transfer is exempt from the documentary transfer tax.

☒   The documentary transfer tax is $ 438.50   and is computed on
        ☐   the full value of the interest or property conveyed.
        ☒   the full value less the value of liens or encumbrances remaining thereon at the
            time of sale.

The property is located in   ☐ an unincorporated area.
                               ☒ the city of   Rosamond, CA   .

For a valuable consideration, receipt of which is hereby acknowledged,

    Michael Hakim

hereby quitclaim(s) to

    Thomas Hammond

the following real property in the City of   Rosamond   ,
County of   Kern   , California:

        Lot 357 as shown on the map entitled "Map of
Green Acres Subdivision No. 2, Kern County, California,"
recorded January 15, 1976 in Volume 3 of Maps, at page
89, Kern County Records.

Date: March 1, 1987   *Michael Hakim*
                             Michael Hakim

State of California
County of Kern   } ss.

On March 4 , 19 87 ,   Michael Hakim   , known
to me or proved by satisfactory evidence to be the person(s) whose name(s) is/are subscribed
above, personally appeared before me, a Notary Public for California, and acknowledged that
  he   executed this deed.

        [SEAL]   *Susan Barker*
                             Signature of Notary

Another way to own real property is via a partnership. Partnerships are of two basic kinds. The first, the general partnership, is a legal agreement by which all partners participate in the business and have equal and full liability for the partnership's debts. The second, the limited partnership, is primarily an investment device, featuring at least one general or managing partner with unlimited liability for debts and one or more limited partners, whose only role is as a passive investor. Limited partners are not liable for partnership debts in excess of the amount they have invested in the partnership.

Partnerships, whether limited or general, normally are ruled not only by statutory law, but also by complicated written partnership agreements. When it comes to selling real property, many general partnership agreements, particularly, require that detailed procedures be followed. Typically, this involves the first right to purchase the share of the departing partner by the non-selling partner(s), at an agreed-upon price or at its currently appraised value. Because I have no way of anticipating the many different types of possible partnership agreement provisions that can affect the sale of real property, I do not attempt to show you how to sell partnership property under all circumstances. However, the practical steps of marketing a piece of real estate outlined in this book are the same whether property is owned by a partnership or not. They work well for people owning property in general partnerships as long as all partners agree that the property should be placed on the market and sold to a third party, and for limited partnerships if the managing partner has the authority to sell the property, which he normally does.

4. Conservators, Guardians and Trustees

If you're a conservator, guardian or trustee for somebody who can't act for himself because he is insane, legally incompetent or a minor, or if you are an executor for someone who is deceased and you wish to sell real property, you must act under a number of detailed provisions of California law and in many instances have your acts approved by the proper court. I do not cover sales by people in these groups.

5. Examples of Joint Ownership Sales

Because joint ownership rules can be confusing, let's look at a series of examples to clarify when joint property owners can and cannot safely sell their own property using this book.

• Mr. and Mrs. C. own their home "as community property." Both must consent to any sale by signing the escrow instructions and the deed. As long as they agree to do this, they can use this book to help with the house sale.

• Naomi and Ken wish to sell a house they own as joint tenants (or as tenants in common). Both agree to sign all necessary papers. They can do it themselves with the help of this book.

• Evelyn owns the home she and her husband live in. It is in her name alone because she inherited it as sole and separate property. She wants to sell. She learns that both the title company and the bank want her husband David to sign escrow papers to indicate his consent to the sale. Evelyn questions the need for this because she knows she owns the house as her separate property. The financial and insurance institutions won't budge, however, claiming that they have no way of being sure that David does not own at least a portion of the house as community property. They point out that if David had invested any of his earnings in house payments or improvements he would have a community property interest. To sell their own home with the help of this book, Evelyn must get David's signature on the sales agreement or have him transfer any interest he might have in the house to her using a quitclaim deed.

• Jim and Bob are brothers who own a home in joint tenancy which is valued at $200,000. Both are married. Jim wants to sell. Bob does not. Jim can legally sell his one-half interest, worth $100,000, if he has the consent of his spouse. (This is required because of her possible community property interest in his share.) The buyer would then become a tenant in common with Bob. Since both tenants in common would have equal rights of possession, this could become sticky if a dispute arose as to which one was to live in the property and pay rent to the other, unless both agreed to live there together or both wanted to rent it and split the profits. In a dispute, the parties would probably wind up in a partition action, to separate their interests (probably involving the sale of the property), under authority of the court. Because these facts of real estate life are well known, trying to sell one portion of jointly owned property is sufficiently involved that we do not cover it here. Jim would be better off calling a family meeting and talking Bob and his wife into agreeing to the sale. If they do, the two couples should have no problem using this book to help them sell the house.

• Jon is awaiting a decree dissolving his marriage to Marcia. Marcia has already given him a quitclaim deed to their home as part of a financial settlement. Jon may sell the home using this book without further signatures or cooperation from Marcia.

• Sam and Janet have decided to stop living together as husband and wife and to sell the house they own together. They are not sure about many things, such as:

✔ whether or not either has invested separate property funds in the purchase of the home or the payoff of the mortgage principal;

✔ whether the legal presumption in favor of community property applies in their case;[3]

✔ whether they should agree to sell their half as part of a formal court property settlement agreement when they divorce.

Sam and Janet have a basic choice to make. They can either sell the property cooperatively, and after doing some homework as to their respective rights under California community property laws (Nolo's *California Marriage and Divorce Law*, by Ihara, Warner and Elias, is an excellent source), agree on what they consider to be a fair division of the proceeds, or they can wait to sell

---

[3]Property owned jointly by a married couple is presumed to be community property at divorce. (Civil Code Sec. 4800.1)

the house until after they divorce, retaining lawyers to help them work out their respective shares.

B. Encumbrances on the Title to Your House That May Impede Sale

What does it mean, in practical terms, to have a lien or other encumbrance recorded against the title to your house? Generally speaking, an encumbrance is something that slows down or impedes motion. Since we say, in a real estate transaction, that title passes or moves from one party to another, an encumbrance on title is anything that slows down, impedes or blocks this passage or movement. For example, if someone has sued you for $1 million and has properly filed notice of the suit in the county where your property is located, title to that property is encumbered.

Without giving you a course on real estate law, suffice it to say that certain types of encumbrances are routine and easy to cope with yourself as part of selling your own house, while others are neither. For example, money encumbrances (e.g., liens, deeds of trust) simply need to be paid off or taken over by a new owner who agrees to be responsible for them as part of the sale. Most people owe money on their houses in the form of a mortgage or deed of trust. Some have more than one mortgage. There is no problem dealing with this type of encumbrance as long as the sales price is more than enough to cover the total amount owed (or you come up with the difference from another source).

Other simple encumbrances include:

• property taxes (due and payable each year in two installments, November 1 and February 1 of a July 1-June 30 fiscal year),

• unpaid special assessment district bond liens (due on the same dates),

• liens filed by contractors. These often result from a situation where contractors (often called "mechanics," in legalese) work on your home, aren't paid, and record mechanic's liens against the property.

• judgment liens. If you are sued for any reason and lose, an abstract of judgment may be placed as a lien against the title to your property.[4]

Non-money encumbrances, including easements and restrictions of use, are often far more troublesome if they severely restrict the use of the property. For example, in rare instances another party may claim the right to possession or use of the property. A couple of the more common ways are:

• **Prescriptive easement.** This involves someone using property (e.g., to gain access to other property) for five years or more, without your permission. If no one stops them during this period, and certain other conditions have been met, they may have gained a right to keep using the property for this purpose.

• **Adverse possession.** We used to refer to this as "squatters' rights." To oversimplify, if someone occupies property of another without permission (lives there, collects rent on it, fences or posts it, etc.) for five consecutive years, in a reasonably obvious fashion, and pays taxes for each of the five years in succession, he owns it. As you might guess, this seldom happens these days.

• **Encroachment.** This occurs when someone builds on your property, i.e., crosses your property line.

To deal with these encumbrances usually requires the assistance of an attorney.

How can you be sure that no encumbrances on your property exist other than the ones you know about? As part of the escrow process (see Chapter 11) a title company will do this for you, but at this preliminary stage you may want to check things out for yourself. Start by looking at your deed. If you have lost or can't locate it, go to the recorder's office in the county in which the property is located. You can find this office by looking in the county government section of your phone book. Look up your name in the "Grantee Index"; this will enable you to find the recorded deed that transferred title to you in the first place. In addition, it will tell you whether any judgment liens or mechanic's liens have been posted against your property. The deed will show you how you hold title (e.g., in your name alone, as a tenant in common, joint tenant, etc.).

---

4 Even prior to judgment in a lawsuit, a lien may be placed against your real property. This takes place by means of a "writ of attachment," a document which makes your property security for an eventual judgment lien that will be placed on your property if you lose the lawsuit. A judgment lien is, technically, a general lien against all your property in any county in California in which it is recorded; an attachment makes a specific piece of property security for such a lien. Sometimes a notice of a pending lawsuit (*lis pendens*) is filed against the record of a particular piece of property. (Generally speaking, property with *lis pendens* on it cannot be sold, unless the court agrees to lift the *lis pendens*—which it may do if the defendant posts a bond sufficient to ensure eventual payment of a judgment.) If you are in one of these situations, you will need to consult an attorney.

Next, look up your name again in the "Trustor" or "Mortgagor" index. Here you will find a record of any mortgage or trust deed liens against the title to your property. If you wish, you can request a copy of any of these recorded documents. They will cost you a few dollars. For more information about checking and interpreting escrow records, see the excellent book, *All About Escrow*, by Gadow (Express Publishers, El Cerrito, CA—available from Nolo Press).

Note: When you actually sign a deposit receipt contract to sell your house and proceed to escrow, a title company will search your title and issue a preliminary title report (see Chapter 11). If you know how you have title to your house, you are sure that all your taxes are paid, no one has sued you, and you are current on your mortgage, you will probably not want to bother checking for encumbrances yourself, but will prefer to wait for the title company's report.

C. Dealing With Brokers and Other Third Parties

The fact that you decide to sell your own house doesn't mean that you should never deal with a real estate broker. In Chapter 4, I explain several approaches to getting professional help at a very reasonable cost, far less than the usual 5%-7% real estate commission you are undoubtedly trying to avoid. Some of these approaches are so cost-effective that you may decide to combine doing a lot of your own work with paying for some professional help. For this reason, let's briefly examine the California legal rules as to who can and cannot sell your house for you.

Basically, any person in California may sell his own real property, or buy real property for his own account, without having any real estate or other license. However, with a few exceptions, California law requires that anyone who helps you sell your real property in California (or assists you in buying real property), must have an active real estate broker's license (or a salesperson's license placed under the license of an active supervising broker).

What if you pay someone who does not have a real estate license (or conform to one of the legal exceptions described below) to act for you as a real estate agent? You can be liable for a fine of $100; your "friend" can be liable for a fine up to $1,000 and/or a sentence of six months in county jail. Who would be likely to discover such an illegal arrangement and turn you over to the district attorney? Most likely a distressed real estate agent who spots an unlicensed "agent" cutting into his licensed activities. Since there are so many real estate licensees in California (one to every 50 adults or so), it's best to assume that many such vigilant individuals exist and are ready to holler.

1. Power of Attorney

As mentioned, there are a few exceptions to the brokerage license requirement. One of these involves people who have been entrusted with a power of attorney to carry out all or part of a particular real estate transaction by the owner(s), and who receive no compensation for doing so. You can legally give a trusted friend or relative a power of attorney to sign papers or otherwise act on your behalf to sell a house if you are ill or will be out of town during a critical stage of selling your house, or for any other reason. For example, a power of attorney is often used when someone handles a sale for an ill family member or friend.

Perhaps you currently face a situation where your sister says, "We've got to take care of Dad's house right away, before he's unable to make any decisions legally!" Assuming Dad really does want assistance with the transaction and is willing to entrust the details to you, he should sign a durable power of attorney authorizing you to sell his home for him. Once a power of attorney is signed, you should be able to sell the house with the help of this book without problems. If you're interested in pursuing this subject further, see Denis Clifford,

The Power of Attorney Book (Nolo Press) which contains tear-out durable power of attorney forms.[5]

The real estate license requirement is also considered satisfied, or waived, in the following exceptional situations. It will be unusual if any of these affect you, but in the interest of thoroughness, here they are:

2. Attorney at Law Acting As Such

A member of the State Bar of California who does not have a real estate license may legally act as a real estate agent in a transaction (although he must charge a "fee," not a "commission"). However, since there are blurred lines of demarcation in the longstanding turf battle between the real estate industry and the legal profession, many attorneys who deal in real estate on a regular basis get a broker's license.

3. Court Order

If the court orders you to act for another in a real estate matter, that's all the license you need, period. An example is a person named as conservator for an incompetent. Again, unless you're fairly experienced in this area, you will probably need the help of an attorney if you face such a situation.

4. Power of Sale Under a "Trust Deed"

The trustee (not the borrower or lender, but a third party "stakeholder" under a trust deed provision in a real estate loan) may sell the property (which equitably belongs to the borrower, not the trustee) without a real estate license if the borrower defaults. Individuals (as distinct from corporations) seldom are stipulated as trustees. Again, see a lawyer if this affects you.

---

[5]A "durable" power of attorney continues to be valid even if a person is no longer competent to make decisions. This should be distinguished from a regular powe of attorney which automatically lapses should the person granting it (in this case Dad) no longer be mentally competent. See *The Power of Attorney Book*, by Denis Clifford (Nolo Press). See Civil Code Sec. 2400.

Real Estate Broker, Agent, and Salesperson Defined

If you decide to get help from a real estate professional, you will run into several bewildering labels. What's the difference between a real estate agent, a broker, and a salesperson? You need to know before you hire someone.

Brokers or agents. A real estate broker is legally allowed to act for someone else in the sale or purchase of real property in the hope of receiving compensation for doing so. This is often referred to as acting as an agent or real estate agent. To become a broker in California, one must pass a two-part test given by the Department of Real Estate. In order to take this exam, the candidate usually must have completed specific real estate courses on the college level, as prescribed by the Department of Real Estate, and must have two years of full-time experience as a real estate salesperson (or certain equivalents allowed by the state). A broker must also complete a continuing education requirement every four years as a condition of license renewal.

Realtors: A realtor is a licensed broker who belongs to the National Association of Realtors, a private trade organization. A salesperson may be a Realtor-associate.

Salespersons. A real estate salesperson may not represent a buyer or seller of real property (e.g., act as a real estate agent) except under the direct supervision of an actively licensed real estate broker. One may apply for an active salesperson's license upon completing some coursework and passing an examination. The license application must be signed by a broker who agrees to employ and direct the salesperson. For example, if Joe Doakes is a licensed salesperson, he can only represent you as the agent and employee of a real estate broker. Your contractual relationship is with the licensed broker, not the salesperson. Put another way, it is not legal to hire a real estate salesperson to represent you or help you sell your house, or consult with you for a fee, independent of his affiliation with a broker's office.

D. Legal No-No's When Selling Your Own House

When selling your own property, there are also several big legal no-no's. Among the things you can't do are:

 • State or imply that you have a real estate license or membership or partnership in a real estate firm. In other words, when you put up your property for sale, don't call yourself a real estate agent if you're not. Frankly, you have no incentive to do this anyway. If you're a private party selling your own property, advertising that fact makes you more, not less, attractive for most prospective purchasers to deal with.

• Engage in certain "real estate paper" transactions. If you're selling or buying trust deed or mortgage notes on a regular basis, your activities are limited by law. As this is far beyond the scope of this book, I do not go into detail except to suggest that if you wish to deal with "real estate paper" as a business, consult an attorney. Good books on this subject are *Real Estate Law* and the *Reference Book* issued by the California Department of Real Estate (916-739-3758, P.O. Box 16009, Sacramento, CA 95818). Also take a look at Coats, *Smart Trust Deed Investment in California* (Barr-Randol Publishing Co., West Covina, CA). This latter book, which is available from Nolo Press, is an excellent guide for investors anxious to achieve the high yields that are possible by buying trust deeds but minimize the risk of being burned by what can be a very speculative type of investment.

CHAPTER 3

THE TAXMAN COMETH

▀▄▀

Fortunately, the federal and California tax status of profits from the sale of a single-family owner-occupied residence is relatively simple.

Here is a summary of current tax law basics:

• There is normally no tax due if you sell your home at a loss;[1]

• There is no tax due now if you reinvest the proceeds of the sale of an owner-occupied house in another of equal or greater value within 24 months.[2]

• Some tax is due now if you reinvest the proceeds of an owner-occupied house you sell at a profit in an owner-occupied house of lesser value (but less than if you did not purchase another house);[3]

---

[1]In certain circumstances, you may actually have to pay tax even if you lose money on the deal—for example, if your mortgage is bigger than your "basis" (see Section A in this chapter for a definition of this important term) in the property or if you have depreciated income-producing property. See a tax consultant or attorney if your situation is similarly complicated.

[2]You must use both houses as your principal residence. If you used part of either as an office or as rental property, you may not be able to "roll over" all the profit from the sale.

[3]Reinvesting the proceeds does not mean you have to take all the cash you get from the sale of the first house and put it into the second one. You can put part of that money down and finance the purchase.

• There is available a once-in-a-lifetime exclusion from federal tax of $125,000 in profit if you sell an owner-occupied home you have lived in for three of the past five years, providing you or your spouse is at least 55 years of age and neither has used this exclusion before.

• If you sell your owner-occupied house at a profit and do not buy another within 24 months, and do not qualify for the once-in-a-lifetime federal tax exclusion (or qualify but realize a profit of more than $125,000), you are obligated to pay tax now.

A. SELLING YOUR HOME TO BUY ANOTHER OF EQUAL OR GREATER VALUE

If you sell an owner-occupied house and buy a more expensive one, you are in a favorable tax position. As noted above, you pay no federal or California tax now, providing the sale of home #1 and the purchase of home #2 occur within 24 months of each other.[4] This is not the same thing as saying you will never pay a tax on your gain. Eventually you will be liable for tax if you sell your home and do not buy one of equal or greater value, unless you qualify to take the once-in-a-lifetime $125,000 federal tax exclusion (see Section C below). This delayed tax treatment is often colloquially referred to as the "roll over" provision of income tax law because it allows you to "roll over" your gain on the sale of the first home into the new home, and defer your obligation to pay tax. This may be done as many times as you wish. In order to take advantage of this provision of tax law, remember these points:

• It doesn't matter if the home you sell is your first home or fifth. You may use these "roll over" advantages in federal and California tax codes every time you sell a home and buy another within 24 months.

• It doesn't matter if the purchase of your next house occurs before or after the sale of the first one, so long as the two events are not more than 24 months apart.[5]

• Your profit on the sale of a house is computed by subtracting your adjusted cost basis in the property from your adjusted sales price, less costs of sale. Let's discuss those terms now.

---

[4]However, you still must report the sale to the IRS on Form 2119, under the provisions of Sec. 1034 of the Internal Revenue Code.

[5]The important dates, for tax purposes, are when the deeds are signed.

1. Figuring Your Adjusted Cost Basis

To figure profit made on the sale of your house, you start with how much you paid for it. That figure is the tax "basis." You arrive at your adjusted cost basis by adding the cost of any capital improvements you make to your original cost basis. At the risk of oversimplifying slightly, capital improvements are additions to your property that increase its value, that you cannot remove, and that have a useful life of more than one year. For example, a swimming pool, carport or new kitchen is a capital improvement. Less obvious examples include upgrades to components of the property, such as replacing galvanized pipe with copper, putting in new insulation, and installing circuit breakers to replace a fuse box.

Ordinary repairs and maintenance costs do not qualify as capital improvements. Repairs that do not constitute capital improvements include fixing a broken pipe (even if you patch galvanized pipe with a small piece of copper), painting, replacing linoleum, etc.

Obviously, there are situations in which deciding whether a particular expenditure qualifies as a capital improvement can be difficult. In doubtful cases, check with a tax expert or the Taxpayer Assistance Service of the Internal Revenue Service. Or, if the do-it-yourself spirit is abundant within you, you may want to do a little of your own research. For this purpose, I suggest you consult the U.S. Master Tax Guide published by Commerce Clearing House (Chicago, IL) and available in most libraries.

The basis is also automatically adjusted by law under certain statutes. For example, when one spouse dies and leaves a community property house to the other, the basis (for federal tax purposes) of the entire property (the one-half community property shares of both the deceased and surviving spouse) is increased from the original purchase price to its fair market value as of the date of the deceased spouse's death.

2. Costs of Sale

As noted, the costs of selling your house are subtracted from your sales price as part of arriving at your profit. Repair costs for things which do not qualify as capital improvements can be subtracted from your sales price if they are made in order to prepare your house for sale. The figure you get when this is done is called your "adjusted sales price." To qualify as a cost of sale, repairs must be made during the 90 days before the contract to sell the real property was signed, and must be paid for no later than 30 days after the sale takes place (after escrow closes). For this reason, it is often wise to delay ordinary repairs (pest control work, fresh paint, etc.) until shortly before you sell your house. Other costs of sale include broker's and attorney's fees and transfer taxes.

Example: Assume you sell your house for $179,000 and have costs of sale of $5,926.90. Your adjusted sales price is $173,073.10. Here is this same information in chart form.

Gross sale price	$179,000.00
Documentary transfer tax*	- 196.90
Document fees (estimate)**	- 30.00
Repairs necessary (to make sale)	- 5,700.00
Adjusted selling price	$173,073.10

[* The documentary transfer tax (discussed in more detail in Chapters 5, 10 and 11) is a local tax paid when the new deed is recorded. This assumes no existing loans taken over by the buyer, so the tax is calculated on the full sale price of the property, using the general statewide rate of $1.10 per $1,000.]

[** Usually a reconveyance deed must be recorded when you pay off your existing loan. As this is a document that benefits the seller, she generally pays the recording fees for it.]

3. Figuring Profit

To calculate your profit on the sale of a house, whether or not you roll it over into a second house, you subtract your adjusted cost basis in the house from the adjusted sales price. As we learned above, your cost basis is the amount you paid for the house plus the cost of any capital improvements. To continue the example stated above, let's assume that your original purchase price was $71,000 and that you made $9,000 worth of capital improvements.

1. **Figure adjusted selling price**

Gross sale price	$179,000.00
Documentary transfer tax	- 196.90
Document fees (estimate)	- 30.00
Cost of Repairs	- 5,700.00
Recording fees	- 30.00
Adjusted selling price	173,073.10

2. **Figure adjusted cost basis**

Original purchase price	$71,000.00
Capital improvements	+ 9,000.00
Adjusted cost basis	$80,000.00

3. **Figure gain**

Adjusted selling price	$173,073.10
Adjusted cost basis	- 80,000.00
	$93,073.10 Gain

B. SELLING YOUR HOME TO BUY ANOTHER OF LESSER VALUE IF YOU'RE UNDER 55

This is an unusual combination of circumstances. Most folks under 55 don't sell a home to buy a less valuable one. But some, of course, do. A classic instance involves people who are moving out of California to another state with lower property values, or from a high-priced urban metropolitan area, such as the Los Angeles Basin or the San Francisco-Oakland Bay Area, to "the country." If you face this situation, keep in mind the rules concerning the calculation of your tax basis and adjusted selling price, mentioned above. Obviously you want to claim every cost of sale and capital improvement you can, so as to reduce the amount of your taxable gain, because you cannot defer payment of the tax on all your profit.

Example: To continue the above example in which a house was sold for an adjusted sales price of $173,073.10, assume now that the seller purchased a new home within 24 months for $70,000. The taxable gain, which must be reported to federal and California tax authorities, would be $93,073.10 (see example above). However, the seller would pay tax on only $23,073.10, because the cost of the second home can be subtracted from the gain. In chart form it looks like this:

Gain from sale of first house:	$93,073.10
Sale price of second house:	70,000.00
Gain taxable now:	$23,073.10

C. Selling Your Home, Not to Buy One of Equal or Greater Value if You Are 55 or Older

If you or your spouse is over 55 and you sell one home and either don't buy another or buy another of lesser value, you may elect to exclude up to $125,000 of your gain from taxation, providing the following are true:

• You've lived in the house as your principal residence for any three of the past five years (it's not necessary that these are the last three of the five, or that they are consecutive years).

• Neither you nor your spouse has used the exclusion before; it is a "once-in-a-lifetime" opportunity. (Neither spouse may use the exclusion again at a later date—even in another marriage.)

• In the case of a married couple, only one of the spouses must be 55 or older.

• You specifically elect to use the exclusion; it is not automatic.

Note: You may not use part of the exclusion now and part later. You may use it only once, even if you don't use the whole $125,000.

While the once-in-a-lifetime exclusion is of real benefit to many people, not all people who sell a house after age 55 and don't roll the gain over into a new house within 24 months will want to use it. Why? Because in some instances, the tax savings from using this exclusion may be relatively small and the eligible people may foresee that in the future one of them is likely to sell another house at a greater profit and thus want to save the exclusion for use then. However, if you are elderly and don't plan to buy again, it makes sense to use the exclusion now, even though the gain you shelter is relatively small. Or, to make this point in a different way, it makes more sense to use the $125,000 exclusion when you are selling the most expensive home you will ever own and are buying either a very inexpensive home or none at all to replace it.

Example: Assume that Frank and Esther, both age 60, sell their large home and rent a condominium near the beach, planning to use much of the money they pocket on the deal to travel. Their home had appreciated considerably in value, but needed many repairs that had been put off over the years. They had little money for such repairs, but knew they would likely need to be made as a condition of selling the home, so once Helen offered to buy their home for $575,000—$475,000 more than the $100,000 they had paid for it years ago—they accepted her contract with the contingency that Frank and Esther pay in escrow for $40,000 worth of repair recommended by inspections. Assuming they elect to take the $125,000 one-time exclusion, Frank and Esther's tax situation figures out as follows:

1. **Figure adjusted selling price**

Gross selling price on Home #1	$575,000.00
Documentary transfer tax	632.50
Cost of repairs paid as condition of sale	40,000.00
Recording fees	30.00
Adjusted selling price	534,337.50

2. **Figure adjusted cost basis**

Original purchase price	$100,000.00
Capital improvements	+35,000.00
Adjusted cost basis	135,000.00

3. **Figure gain**

Adjusted selling price	$534,337.50
Adjusted cost basis	-135,000.00
Total gain	399,337.50

4. **Figure gain taxable now**

Gain	$399,337.50
Once in a lifetime exclusion	-125,000.00
Gain taxable now	$274,337.50

Now let's assume that Frank and Esther both use the $125,000 exclusion and buy another home--a condo for $200,000--within the 24-month rollover period to increase their tax benefits. To figure gain taxable now, the $125,000 exclusion and the price of the second home are subtracted from the adjusted selling price of the first home.

5. **Figure gain taxable now if another house purchased**

Adjusted selling price of home #1	$534,337.50
Exclusion	-125,000.00
Cost of home #2	200,000.00
Gain taxable now	209,337.50

Note: As you can see from step 5, if Frank and Esther had bought a more expensive new home, they could defer tax on even more gain.

D. Installment Sales

In general, you don't pay tax on income until you receive it. One way to delay paying tax when you don't roll over your gain into another house or don't use the $125,000 exclusion is to string out the gain over a number of years. You are eligible to do this if you receive at least one payment after the tax year in which the sale occurs. The tax advantages of an installment sale are automatic under the Internal Revenue Code unless you specifically elect the contrary. However, the complications of making an installment sale warrant the attention of a knowledgeable tax accountant. Still, to get some idea of what goes on in an installment sale, consider the following example.

Example: Let's return to the story of Frank and Esther with a few changes. Assume that they have lived in their home for many years. It's too big for them now that the children have all grown up and moved away. Besides, because they have put off maintenance, many repairs are needed. If they make all the repairs necessary for them to continue living comfortably, it will cost them more than they can reasonably afford. Neither person has yet reached age 55. To spread their taxable income over several years, they decide to make an installment sale under the Internal Revenue Code (Sections 1245, 1250, 453, and 483). To help sell the house, they also decide to finance the sale themselves and to make the repairs as a condition of sale and pay for them from the proceeds of the sale.

The tax savings come because only the gain they actually receive is taxed that year. To figure out how much of the money they receive is gain, the percentage of profit on the entire sale is figured. Then, that percent of what they receive each year is treated as taxable gain that year.

Let's see how the numbers look:

1. **Figure Adjusted Selling Price**

Gross selling price	$575,000.00
Documentary transfer tax	-632.50
Cost of repairs	-40,000.00
Recording fees	-30.00
Adjusted selling price	$534,337.50

2. **Figure Adjusted Cost Basis**

Original purchase price	$100,000.00
Capital improvements	+ 35,000.00
Adjusted cost basis	$135,000.00

3. **Figure Gain**

Adjusted selling price	$534,337.50
Adjusted cost basis	-135,000.00
Gain	$339,337.50

4. **Figure percent profit on investment:** $339,337.50/$575,000 = 59%

5. **Figure gain taxable this year:** 59% of amount received this year.

Down payment:	$115,000.00
Principal paid this year:	5,000.00

    $120,000.00 x 59% = $70,800 taxable
    this year

Note: Depending on your taxable income, stringing out the gain over several years may reduce the total net tax by keeping you in lower tax brackets. Remember, though, that when you sell on the installment plan, you charge interest on the unpaid balance, and this is taxed.[1]

Rental Property Note: The 1986 tax law changes reduce the advantages of installment sales for rental property. If you want to sell rental property in installments, get tax advice first.

---

[6]Even if you don't charge interest, as might be the case if you sell to a family member, the IRS will impute interest at what it considers the going rate. This is changed from time to time, but is usually slightly less than the interest rate banks charge for a fixed rate long-term mortgage. (Internal Revenue Code Section 453.)

E. Exchanging Homes

Now and then, instead of selling a home and buying another, people trade one for another.[7] Trading can sometimes have tax advantages for both parties because each can defer taxation on at least part of his gain. However, you should also realize that a tax-deferred exchange of personal residences is not always advantageous. These transactions can be quite complicated from the income tax standpoint; you will definitely need to check with a tax advisor before getting into one.

Trading property of equal value is literally tax-free if the properties are really worth the same amount.[8] This, of course, is almost never the case. Nearly always, one house is worth at least a little more than the other. The person "trading up," of course, is putting less value into the deal in terms of real property, and must therefore balance the scales by throwing in something "to boot." "Boot," in tax terms, means anything which is not of "like kind" in the exchange. In this situation you have a tax-deferred exchange, which defers gain in part for the person trading down and entirely for the person trading up, until the traded-for property is eventually disposed of.

Here is a very simple example, for the purpose of illustration only. There are a number of subtleties in the tax law not mentioned here.

Example: John Acton and Billy Bigelow want to trade houses. Both use their houses as their principal residences.

---

[7] Internal Revenue Code Section 1034. Usually, this trading technique applies to property other than a personal residence, e.g., property held for investment or the production of income or used in a trade or business. (I.R.C. Section 1031).

[8] Of course, should these homes subsequently be sold at a profit, there will be a tax due at that time.

	ACTON	BIGELOW
Present Fair Market Value	$185,000	$200,000
Difference (to be equalized)	$15,000	
Adjusted basis (purchase price plus capital improvements)	80,000	$100,000
Realized or actual gain (exists whether or not taxable at this time	105,000	$100,000
Amount of boot that must be paid (by Acton to Bigelow) is also the amount of gain Bigelow recognizes and therefore pays tax on now. Acton pays no tax now because he is trading up.	-0-	15,000 *
Amount of gain deferred	105,000	85,000

[* Acton will pay the boot to Bigelow by giving him cash, stock, notes, a boat or car, or any other assets worth $15,000.]

CHAPTER 4

HOW TO WORK WITH
REAL ESTATE AGENTS

Undoubtedly, one reason you picked up this book is that you don't want to pay a real estate broker a large sum of money for doing things you can quite easily do for yourself. This makes excellent sense. However, it makes far less sense to conclude that you will never wish to consult a broker under any circumstance. Why? Quite simply, because there are a number of ways an experienced real estate broker can help you sell your house by yourself. While arranging for a broker to help you sell your own house will typically cost something, the amount will be very reasonable, certainly thousands of dollars less than the typical real estate commission.

Note on Aggressive Real Estate Brokers: You're almost sure to be approached by at least one real estate broker who wants to list your house. Sometimes he'll "highball" you—tell you he can sell the house for more than it's really worth. If this doesn't persuade you to retain him, he may next try to scare you by telling you that if you do it yourself, you'll never sell the house, or won't get a good price, or won't handle the paperwork correctly. Obviously, I wouldn't have written this book if I thought that were true. If you follow the instructions in the this book, there's no reason why you can't sell your house without a real estate broker. Remember, though, that you may still need or want to get some assistance from a broker—on a less expensive hourly basis, as discussed later in this chapter.

Let's start with the basics of what brokers normally charge by way of commissions to sell residential property.

A. Is There a Standard Real Estate Commission?

California law makes it illegal for brokers to establish a state-wide or region-wide commission rate. By common practice, however, most real estate brokers individually act as though a standard commission rate did exist. They charge between 5%-7% of the sales price of most types of residential property, up to a value of about $200,000. For more expensive homes, a sliding scale for commissions is commonly negotiated: 6% of the first $150,000-$200,000, 5% of the next $50,000-100,000, and 2.5% thereafter, or some similar arrangement, is typical. In most situations, the majority of brokers won't represent you for less, despite the fact that California law requires brokers to tell prospective clients (property owners) that commissions are negotiable. As I discuss in more detail below, a few brokers advertise and charge lower rates.

Most sales in an Exclusive Authorization and Right to Sell situation discussed in this chapter involve two brokerage offices in a "cooperative" sale. The "listing broker" (the broker who represents the seller) and the "cooperating broker" (the broker who provides the buyer) split the 5-7% commission. Incidentally, this custom may be important to you even if you sell your own house. You may be confronted with a broker who claims to have a buyer for your house, but will only produce that person if you agree to cooperate, that is, pay half a commission. More on this in Section C below.

HOW REAL ESTATE SALES PEOPLE EARN COMMISSIONS

Does a 6% commission sound like a lot? It certainly does if you have to pay it—6% of $200,000, for example, is $12,000. In fairness, however, you should realize that it seems like a lot less to the people who sell houses. Here's why. First, on a cooperative sale where two brokers participate—with one advertising and showing the property and another procuring a buyer—the total commission is usually divided equally. Next, the person who actually receives each half of the commission is the broker (or brokerage firm, e.g., Merrill Lynch, Coldwell Banker, or one of the franchisees of Century 21, ERA, etc.).[1] The agent who actually procures the sale (or lists the property) is usually a licensed salesperson working under the broker. (See Chapter 2, Section C on the distinction between broker and salesperson.) Salespersons' commissions are typically 50% of the brokerage office's commission, or—in a cooperative sale—one-fourth of the total commission. This means the salesperson typically receives 1.25-1.50% of the gross sale price of the property. On a home sold for $175,000, this means the salesperson earns a gross commission of $2,187.50 - $2,625.00 before out-of-pocket business expenses for auto use, advertising, business entertaining, supplies, etc. And, of course, if a worked-for sale doesn't close, the salesperson earns nothing. Keep that in mind before you take your frustration out on the average real estate salesperson.

B. THE STANDARD BROKER'S CONTRACT

Usually, a broker asks a person with a house to sell to sign a listing, called an Exclusive Authorization and Right to Sell.

EXCLUSIVE AUTHORIZATION AND RIGHT TO SELL
THIS IS INTENDED TO BE A LEGALLY BINDING AGREEMENT—READ IT CAREFULLY.

1. **Right to Sell.** I hereby employ and grant _____ hereinafter called "Agent," the exclusive and irrevocable right commencing on _____, 19_____, and expiring at midnight on _____, 19_____, to sell or exchange the real property situated in _____ County of _____, California described as follows:

_____
_____
_____

2. **Terms of Sale.** The purchase price shall be $_____, to be paid in the following terms:

_____
_____

(a) The following items of personal property are to be included in the above-stated price:
_____

It obligates the owner to pay a commission if her house sells during the period of time agreed to in the contract. Even if she finds a buyer herself, or if the broker brings in a full price offer that meets her terms and she changes her mind and doesn't sell, she must pay a commission as long as the contract is in effect. This type of contract is frankly designed to protect the earned commission of a real estate broker who is saying, in effect, "If you put me in charge, you have to pay me if your house sells or even if it doesn't, if I produce a full-price offer."[2]

A property owner who is genuinely motivated to sell usually accepts an offer on somewhat different terms than those in the listing contract (e.g., the price is lower, or the seller has to provide some financing, or pay for repairs). If he does, he is legally liable to pay the full commission on the sales price. But if the broker produces an offer with less favorable terms than the listing contract, which the seller does not accept, then the seller has no obligation to pay a commission. In other words, no full price offer on the seller's terms, or no voluntary sale on different terms, means no commission. It's as simple as that.

I DID IT MYSELF

I decided to sell my own house to save what seemed to be the exorbitant real estate commission. I checked prices in my area and figured my house was worth between $140,000 and $125,000. To test the market, I asked for $152,000. As soon as my listing appeared in the paper, real estate brokers began calling and asking if I would "cooperate." I didn't even know what the term meant.
Finally, someone explained it to me. After thinking about it, I decided why not agree to pay a 2.5% commission if a broker brought me a full- price offer. As it developed, that's exactly what happened. It turned out to be a pretty good deal for me, as the broker ended up doing all the paperwork for both the buyer and me. True, I ended up paying a commission of a little over $3,000, but since I got a great price for my house and had to do very little work to sell, I was pleased.

Incidentally, one thing I learned was that brokers didn't seem to resent my acting as my own broker at all as soon as they learned that I would cooperate on full-price offers. At my first and only open house, at least a dozen real estate people brought customers by.

C. Modifying the Standard Contract and Commission

Suppose now that you decide not to sell your own house but consider a 5%-7% commission too high. Here are two ways you can have your cake and eat it too.

1. Find a broker who will not charge the full commission unless there is a cooperating broker.

The Exclusive Authorization and Right to Sell contract discussed in Section A above usually allows a broker who both represents a seller and finds a buyer to keep the entire commission. In other words, if you list with ABC Realty and it produces a buyer, it keeps the whole 5%-7% commission. However, there are some brokers in California who do not charge 5%-7% if they do not have to split this commission with a cooperating broker who procures a buyer. Instead, when they find a buyer themselves, these brokers only charge 2.5%-3.5%. The problem with this sort of contractual arrangement from your point of view is obviously that you have no guarantee that the broker you list with will produce a buyer himself. If he doesn't, you end up paying the entire commission.

2. Find an independent broker who charges a lower commission

Some independent brokers not associated with a large company or franchise will agree to a total commission in the 4%-5% range (allowing for half to go to a cooperating broker) if you will sign the Exclusive Authorization and Right to Sell contract with them. The disadvantages here are that you still pay a pretty good-sized commission and that other brokers will be less likely to show your house, since the commission is less. Also, some small independent brokers provide less service than you need. Many others, however, do a great job. If you call around and find such a broker, you should also assure yourself that she is reasonably equipped to sell your house at a fair price in a reasonable time. The best way to do this is to ask for references from satisfied sellers and check them.

D. ALTERNATIVE REAL ESTATE CONTRACTS

There are several types of contracts with brokers in use in California other than the Exclusive Authorization and Right to Sell contract discussed above. Here are the principal ones:

1. Exclusive Agency Agreement

The Exclusive Agency Agreement allows you to sell the property yourself, while the broker also tries to sell it. Under this agreement, if you sell it yourself you pay no commission. In one sense this allows you to get the best of both worlds, including the broker's newspaper ads (if you wish), the broker's signs on the house (if you wish), and the broker's listing of the property in the appropriate multiple listing service, inviting cooperative brokers to bring buyers with offers.[3] At the same time, if you produce your own buyer you pay no commission. Sounds good, doesn't it? Unfortunately, it probably sounds better than it is. There is still a very good chance that you will end up paying a full commission. Because the broker can draw on the entire resources of the real estate business and you are on your own, chances are pretty good either he or a cooperating broker will sell your house before you do.

If you do decide to try this arrangement, be sure to set up a mechanism so you will be absolutely clear as to whether you or the broker has procured the purchaser. One way to avoid a dispute is to request that the broker periodically give you a list of the potential buyers with whom he has begun negotiations. You, of course, should give the broker a similar list of parties you have begun negotiations with.

2. Single Party Listing Agreement

Sometimes a broker will call a person who is selling her own house and say, "I have a qualified buyer for your property. Will you cooperate by paying a commission?" The broker may then ask for a commission of anywhere between 2.5%-6%. If he asks for a commission at the low end of this range, you may be interested, especially if the prospective buyer is willing to pay top dollar for your house. If you are, be sure to insist on disclosure of the name of the interested purchaser, in writing, as part of signing a Single Party Listing Agreement with the broker. Brokers have been known to use this "I have a buyer" technique when, at best, they have a few potential buyers and are really just trying to back-door you into giving them an exclusive listing. Also, in this situation you can afford to be fairly aggressive about negotiating the commission rate you are willing to pay. For example, if you tell a broker with a buyer that you won't pay more than 2%-2.5%, chances are she will accept if there really is a good prospect. After all, since you are selling the house yourself and there is no other broker involved, this broker still makes out very well. And remember, you are in a good negotiating position; if the broker doesn't agree to your terms, she gets nothing. And who knows? The buyer may even contact you later without the broker.

3. Low-Commission Listing

Another approach to selling your house with the help of a broker at the same time you pay a commission of moderate size is to refuse to pay any commission to a cooperating (or buyer's) broker. In other words, you agree to pay your broker a commission in the range of 2.5%-3.5% to help you find a buyer and handle the necessary paperwork. Because your broker has no authority to cooperate directly with a broker who brings in a buyer, this may reduce the number of people who will be shown your house, and it will be important for you to help publicize the availability of the house widely.

A distinct possibility is that a cooperating broker will surface with an offer and ask for a commission from you—rather than from your broker—as compensation for presenting it. If it's an offer you can't refuse, you may even wind up agreeing to pay the cooperating broker almost as much as you would have paid had you signed an Exclusive Authorization and Right to Sell contract in the first place. This isn't inevitable, however, since these days some brokers do business specifically as buyer's brokers: their job is to find a suitable house for a buyer, with their commission paid directly by that buyer. Thus, if you firmly stick to the position that you will not pay more than your own broker's commission and it's up to the buyer to pay her broker, you will probably sell your house eventually and have help doing it.

4. "Permission to Show" Agreement

Under a "permission to show" agreement, all you are saying to the broker is, "You can show my house to your buyers, but I won't sign a listing. If you can procure from your buyers an offer acceptable to me, then I'll pay you a commission." This sort of deal gives the broker no protection at all, but nevertheless, some brokers are willing to agree to it.

5. Flat Rate Agreements

Some real estate brokers, too, offer certain services on a flat rate basis. For example, one in the Fresno area offers to assist a seller by providing signs and helping with the paper process (e.g., reviewing a contract similar to the one in Chapter 9) and holding your hand through the escrow process described in Chapter 11. Although this type of broker usually advertises a flat fee, their charges often amount to about 2.5-3% of the selling price of the average home in the area. In other words, many flat fee agreements turn out to be not substantially different from the standard low-commission situation mentioned above.

E. Paying a Broker By the Hour

As the purchaser of a book on how to sell your own house, it's safe to assume that you will probably prefer not to list your house with a broker at all. Still, you may want or need to get at least some help from someone experienced in the field of selling houses. It is not hard to do this. Many brokers are glad to provide advice for an hourly consultation fee to people who are handling their own sales. This sort of help usually ends up costing far less than a typical commission and somewhat more than this book.

Independent brokers are usually the best candidates for a "help by the hour" arrangement. If you know a broker you like, ask her. If she doesn't do work by the hour, she can probably suggest the name of someone who will. If you don't know anyone to ask for a recommendation, call several real estate offices. Hourly fees vary widely, but $50 to $75 an hour is common. Here is a contract you may want to use should you wish to hire a broker by the hour (a tear-out copy is in the Appendix). It does a good job of protecting both your interests and the broker's.

AGREEMENT WITH BROKER

_____ , the seller(s) of the real
property located at _____in
the City of_____ , County of _____ ,
California, hereby engage _____ , a licensed real estate broker
in the State of California, to advise them as to the mechanics involved in selling their own house,
with the intention that the broker shall act as needed as an advisor as to typical sales procedures,
the preparation of routine forms, comparable sales prices, information on available financing, and
suggestions as to competent professionals, such as attorneys, accountants, pest control
inspectors, general contractors, etc. as needed.

Broker shall not receive a commission but shall be compensated at $_____ per
hour, not to exceed a total amount of $_____ , based on the broker's estimate that
the advice required shall not call for more than _____ hours of the broker's labor.
Broker shall be paid as follows: _____
_____ .
If the seller and broker agree that more of the broker's time is needed, an additional written
contract will be prepared.

It is understood that sellers are handling their own sale and are solely responsible for all
decisions made and paperwork prepared. In addition, it is expressly agreed that broker will not
provide any legal direction or tax or estate planning advice, and shall make no representation
concerning the physical condition of the property or the legal condition of title to any party. Broker
expressly recommends that sellers seek the appropriate professional advice offered by attorneys,
tax accountants, pest control inspectors and/or general contractors as needed.

Agreed this _____ day of _____ , 19___, by:

_____

_____

Seller(s)

_____

Broker

By _____

Now let's slow down for a moment and examine how a typical for sale by owner deal might work in a situation where some help from a broker is desired.

Example 1: Tomas and Keija Crane want to buy the home they live in as tenants for $140,000. Their landlord, Bill Wilson, is ready to sell. Since both parties are interested in making a deal, it is not necessary for a broker to bring them together. As a result, Bill Wilson has no need or desire to list his property with a real estate broker and wants to avoid any commission expense. He is willing to pass half of his commission's savings on to the Cranes. The Cranes think this sounds great but want to make sure that the "bargain" being offered them by Bill is real and that he is not overpricing the home while pretending to give them a great deal. Having little experience with real estate transactions, they also want some assurance that they understand their rights and obligations. They hire an independent broker on an hourly fee basis to help them as needed. They want to consult the broker in three areas:

• To provide information on sales of comparable homes in the neighborhood, to help them determine the fair market value of the property;

• To review the practical steps involved in buying real property;

• To review all paperwork to be sure it meets reasonable industry standards. This means making sure deposit receipt and escrow instruction contracts are in order. It also means being available to advise them on the various steps involved in escrow, such as getting title insurance, inspecting the property, etc. (I discuss how to handle all of these items yourself in detail in Chapters 10 and 11.)

As it turns out, the Cranes pay the broker/advisor $400 to meet with them three times and discuss matters by phone on several other occasions. Compared to a commission of 6%, Bill saves $8,400. In addition, since the Cranes plan to obtain a loan from a bank for 80% of the property's value, and because Bill charged less since no broker was involved, the Cranes will save another $134.40 in loan origination fees (which are based on the purchase price) because the sale price of the house is $8,400 less than it would be with the commission. Thus, under what amounts to a "split the commission saved" deal with Wilson, the out-of-pocket savings to Mr. and Mrs. Crane amount to $4,267, less the $00 paid the broker. By the time the lower cost of the title insurance premium, homeowners' insurance premiums and property tax are considered, these savings will grow even larger, not to mention the additional savings over the years in terms of lower insurance premiums, taxes, mortgage payments, etc. because of the lower sale price. Of course, Bill benefits too, as under the deal with the Cranes, he gets half of the savings.

Example 2: Steve and Catherine plan to sell their home, without using a broker, for $200,000. They tell a number of friends and neighbors of their plan and advertise the house in the paper. Within a few days, Denis comes by and likes what he sees. But because this will be his first house, he asks for some advice from Susan, a broker friend. Denis wants Susan to take him through the steps involved in considering comparable prices, making an offer, and different financing options given his cash position, income and debts. When Steve and Catherine hear about Susan, they realize that she can also help them with the paperwork involved in the sale and agree to pay half of Susan's fee, which is $50 an hour. The result is that Susan provides valuable handholding to both buyer and seller. She provides basic information, but doesn't act as anyone's agent. Her total fee is $1,000, based on 20 hours' work—only one-half of one percent of the sales price.

---

[1]The brokerage office expenses— including rent, telephone, secretarial, personal legal advice, insurance, and the supervision of salespeople—all are taken out of this share.

[2]This highlights one of the advantages of selling your house yourself. If the broker brings you an offer for your asking price, you must pay a commission, even if you don't go through with the sale. If you're not using a broker and get several offers indicating you can get more than your asking price, you are free to raise the price. In some of California's growing areas, this happens more often than you may expect.

[3]Multiple listing is the device through which brokers share listings information. Your broker lists your house, all the other brokers see it, and one of them may bring you a buyer (and usually, split the commission with your broker).

CHAPTER 5

HOW MUCH TO ASK FOR YOUR HOUSE

By now you've decided on the best time to sell your house. Does this mean you're ready to put up a "For Sale By Owner" sign? Not quite. There is still the little matter of deciding how much to charge.

First, let's take a minute to discuss whether there are some things you can do to give your home added "sales appeal" and justify a higher price than you might otherwise have charged. One obvious way is to make repairs and renovations. The question, of course, is whether money spent to do this will really be recovered in an increased sales price.

A. ARE REPAIRS AND REMODELING ECONOMICALLY JUSTIFIED?

The only honest answer to the question of whether you should put money into a house before selling it is: "It depends."

Short of looking at your house, neighborhood, and the particular market you face, the best thing I can do is to give you a few of the rules of thumb I normally follow when counseling people as to whether pre-sale expenditures are likely to pay off:

• If there are glaring defects that take away from your home's value, and it is feasible to fix them at a reasonable cost, do so. In other words, take care of the leaky gutter over the back door and the broken front step. Replace cracked windows, broken tiles and badly-worn linoleum. Repairing very obvious defects at a low or moderate cost almost always pays for itself. Incidentally, such repairs, made within 90 days of a sale, are considered by the IRS to be deductions from your gross selling price when you calculate your gain (see Chapter 3). Some title companies will provide a checklist of repairs that make a house easier to sell.

• Large-scale improvements and repairs are usually unwise unless you do them yourself at a very low cost. Given today's prices, it's usually hard, and often impossible, to immediately recover the amount you lay out to make major renovations. Even if your house badly needs major work, it's not always wise to do it. Why? Because bargain-hunting buyers often search for a "fixer-upper," planning to do the work themselves. Examples of particularly unwise repairs include interior painting and wallpapering. It's almost always best to let the buyers select a paint job and color rather than to pass your taste off on them. If their taste varies from yours, they may not value your work at all. If painting is so badly needed that you feel you just have to do it, off-white is always the safest.

• Look for ways a good impression can be made inexpensively. For instance, I once listed a home with faded paint on the dining room walls exposed by a glaring overhead light fixture. I advised the owner not to repaint, but to replace the chandelier's flipswitch with a dimmer, at a cost of about $10. Obviously a paint job was still needed (and we didn't try to hide that), but the room certainly looked a lot better. Similarly, while it may not pay you to repaint the outside of a dingy stucco house, surely it is worthwhile to hose it down.

• Make sure the house and everything in it is spotless. While this might seem obvious, I assure you it isn't. I have been asked to sell many dirty houses. If there are rugs, have them shampooed. Similarly, hardwood floors should be waxed, windows washed, tiles polished, etc. Especially if, for some reason, you are in the unfortunate position of having to sell a vacant house, little touches are important, because the house already looks less than its best. Even a vase of flowers on the mantelpiece can make a big difference. In other words, don't be afraid to invest a few dollars in making the house look as inviting as possible.

While the general rule that major renovations just prior to sale don't pay off is a good one, like all rules, there are exceptions. Depending on what your house looks like now, a couple of types of improvements can pay off in some circumstances. These include adding a bathroom, improving a kitchen, or converting a garage to another bedroom. And, since this type of upgrade usually qualifies as a capital improvement for income tax purposes (see Chapter 3 for more on this), the seller can do this at any time and eventually receive at least some tax benefit from it.

The experience of knowledgeable real estate agents suggests that the main room that "sells" a house is the kitchen (with bathrooms and bedrooms next). Remodeling a kitchen if it is not up-to-date can cost anywhere from $15,000 to $50,000 or more. You can normally expect to get 80% of your investment (and sometimes more) later on when you sell. In addition, you can add the cost of this capital improvement to your basis when your calculate profit (discussed in Chapter 3).

Other types of improvements, including the cost of replacing the roof, upgrading a foundation, or fixing plumbing or wiring—no matter how necessary—almost never come close to paying for themselves when you sell your house. Buyers tend to take things like roofs and foundations for granted. They may be delighted to know that you have just fixed or upgraded them, but normally will not want to pay you extra for doing so.

How can you know in advance if an extra bedroom or a remodeled bathroom or kitchen will pay for itself by allowing you to increase the price of the house more than your out-of-pocket cost to do the work? The key is obviously to tightly figure how much the addition or improvement will really cost and then how much more the improved house is likely to be worth. This latter task should be approached following the instructions for determining the prices of comparable houses provided later in this chapter.

Warning: In computing the cost to remodel or add a room, remember that this type of work almost always ends up costing more than you think it will.

WHAT ABOUT APPLIANCES?

Is it wise to include appliances in the sale of your home? There is no ironclad answer, but the following criteria usually apply:

• Built-in appliances should always be included. Indeed, as I discuss in more detail as part of discussing the sales contract in Chapter 10, they are considered to be part of the real property ("fixtures," in real estate lingo). If you want to remove them, you will have to modify this contract.

• When it comes to free-standing appliances such as a stove, or refrigerator, if the home you're moving to has the appliances you'll need, why not leave the ones in your present home, providing the buyer wants them? Even if they add only a little to your home's value, that's better than nothing. (If the appliances are out of warranty, disclose this fact, as well as any defects, recent problems and repairs, as part of the disclosure form in Chapter 7).

• Don't include free-standing appliances just to make your home more valuable, unless there is something special about them (brand new, top-of-the-line, etc.). In other words, if you have run-of-the-mill ten-year-old appliances, including them is not likely to allow you to increase the sale price of your house. A buyer will normally only want them if they are free, and even then may ask you to take them with you. One good strategy is not to list the appliances initially. Save them for use as bargaining chips to throw in when you're negotiating price with a buyer.

B. HOW MUCH IS YOUR HOUSE WORTH?

Your next task is to determine how much your property is actually worth on the market. While no one can ever predict to the penny what a buyer will pay, there are several realistic and reliable methods to arrive at a good estimate of what your house should sell for. Let's look at these.

1. Hire an Appraiser

A real estate appraiser can give you a documented opinion as to your home's value. Remember that no matter how experienced the appraiser, she only gives you an opinion; a buyer is the only one who can really validate that opinion in a way that puts money in your pocket. In my experience, if an appraisal you order is off a little, it's more likely to be too high. That is, the appraiser will overstate the value of your home more often than she will understate it. One reason is that appraisers want to please you. Another is that appraisers, who often do considerable work for insurance companies, sometimes unconsciously use replacement cost (e.g., the amount it would cost to replace the improvements to the property in the event of a casualty loss such as a fire) instead of sales value as an appraisal criterion. While the replacement cost approach usually works well for insurance companies, many of which sell policies based on replacement value, it often tends to overstate a home's value on the real estate market. So if you hire an appraiser, emphasize that you are interested in a realistic estimate of what a reasonable buyer would pay to own the property in its present condition.

For your purposes, you simply need a ballpark estimate of what the property is worth. You don't need the kinds of photographs and detailed work sheets that normally accompany an appraisal presented in court or to the Internal Revenue Service. Once the appraisal is made, the result is transmitted to you orally or by a brief "letter appraisal" in which the appraiser states her opinion as to the house's value and her reasons for arriving at it.

A slightly more detailed approach is known as a "check sheet" or "short form" appraisal, in which the appraiser prepares a form that sets forth information about recent documented sales prices of similar properties within a few blocks of your property. This approach is frequently used by lending institutions and for Veterans Administration (VA) and Federal Housing Administration (FHA) appraisers, and can be helpful to the self-help seller in "proving" the property's value to a potential buyer as part of the negotiating process.

If you have had any physical inspections of your house recently, be sure the appraiser has copies. Without this information, any appraisal is bound to be something of a guess. For example, a house appraised at $250,000 that later turns out to have serious hidden foundation problems will probably sell for considerably less unless corrective work is done.

Make sure to establish the appraiser's fee in advance. This naturally raises the question of how much you should expect to pay an appraiser for a good ballpark appraisal. For a letter or check sheet appraisal on a medium-priced single-family home, $250, or less if possible, is fair. Luxury homes with pools, outbuildings, etc., are harder to appraise and might fairly cost twice as much.

How do you find a qualified appraiser? Let's start by briefly discussing qualifications. Because lending institutions are increasingly fussy about the backgrounds of their appraisers, professional certification is becoming fashionable, although it is not yet required by California law. The qualification that probably tells you the most is whether the appraiser is a Residential Member (RM) of the American Institute of Real Estate Appraisers (AIREA) and therefore considered qualified to appraise single-family homes. AIREA also designates appraisers as MAI (Member of the Appraisers' Institute). This means the appraiser is considered qualified to appraise commercial properties and businesses as well as single-family homes. This is more experience than you need, but if the price is right it doesn't hurt. Use an appraiser who is approved by the FHA. That way, any FHA or conventional lender can use the appraisal when it's deciding whether or not to finance the sale of your house.

You can find appraisers in your local telephone directory under "Appraisers," or you can call the local office of the AIREA in Los Angeles or San Francisco and get a list of appraisers in your area. A bank officer in the branch where you do your business or an attorney who handles real estate matters may also be able to recommend a good appraiser.

2. Do Your Own Appraisal

One good alternative to hiring an appraiser is to do your own. Essentially, this means finding several houses in your immediate area which have sold in the past six months or less that you can honestly say are comparable to yours, and learning their actual selling (not asking) prices. In subdivisions this is usually not hard to do, since so many homes are similar in size, age, construction and layout. In older cities or areas where homes are different from their neighbors, this approach is considerably more difficult.

How do you find out what comparable properties have sold for? Real estate offices normally won't help the self-help seller unless they're campaigning for a listing on your property. Why not simply ask sellers in your area what they got? There is no reason not to do this, as long as you take the answers with a grain of salt. The reason I say this is simple: in my experience, sellers commonly exaggerate what they received, sometimes more than a little, to make themselves look smart.

Another way some people learn selling prices is to get a hold of the multiple listing "comp" book for their area. This paperback volume lists both the asking prices and recent sales prices of residential properties. Real estate brokers aren't supposed to show this to people outside the profession, but with tens of thousands of brokers in the state, it has been known to happen.

Another approach is to check the public record. The easiest way to do this is to ask a local title company for a "property profile," which is almost always free if you've done business with them or they think you will soon, and shows lots of information about a particular parcel. For example, it shows the grant deed, deeds of trust, and recent sales. They sometimes contain inaccuracies, however. Some title companies also have microfiche copies of county records, which they will let you look at.

You can also go to the county recorder's office and look up recorded deeds to comparable properties in your area which have sold recently. Once you find the correct deed, you arrive at the sales price from the amount of the documentary transfer tax. The tax is based on the amount of equity transferred from seller to buyer. The top of the deed shows the tax and indicates whether the tax reflects a sales price with or without the buyer taking over existing loans.

The basic documentary transfer tax is $.55 for each $500 (or part thereof) of the selling price or, in shorthand, $1.10 per $1,000 of the price, except in some cities, such as Vallejo, San Jose, Oakland, San Francisco and several others, which impose their own surtax. In San Francisco, for instance, the total rate is $5.00 per $1,000. Ask at your county assessor's or tax collector's office what the net documentary transfer tax rate in your area is.

Important: Remember, the tax does not reflect the value of any loans assumed by the buyer. Thus, if a house sells for $150,000 and the buyer assumes an existing loan of $30,000, the deed will show a documentary transfer tax of $132, calculated on the value of the property minus the assumed loan ($120,000).

Example 1: The documentary tax is shown as $240.90. Since the county is Marin, which has a documentary transfer tax rate of $1.10 for each $1,000 of the sale price, and since the deed shows that the tax was calculated on the whole price, we know, by dividing $240.90 by $1.10 to get 219 and then multiplying 219 by $1,000 that the price was $219,000.

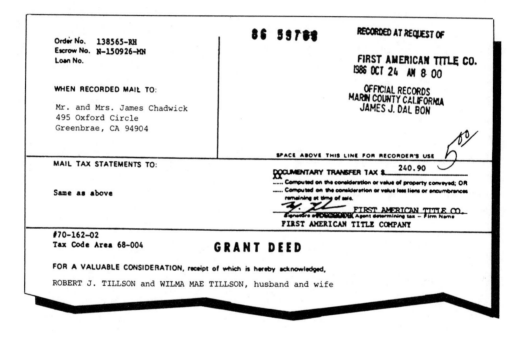

Example 2: The documentary tax is shown as $920. In this case, however, the County and City are San Francisco, with a documentary transfer tax rate of $5 for each $1,000 of the sale price. Since the deed shows that the tax, once more, was calculated on the whole price, we know that the price was $184,000 by dividing $920 by $5 to get 184 and then multiplying 184 by $1,000.

Order No.
Escrow No. N-150900
Loan No.

WHEN RECORDED MAIL TO:

MR. AND MRS. GREGORY RANDOLPH
1635 Bradley Street
San Francisco, CA 94117

RECORDED AT REQUEST OF
FIRST AMERICAN TITLE CO. OF S.F
AT 8:00 AM 10/16 1986
D 884872
City & County of San Francisco, California

SPACE ABOVE THIS LINE FOR RECORDER'S USE

MAIL TAX STATEMENTS TO:

same as above

DOCUMENTARY TRANSFER TAX $ 920.00**
XX Computed on the consideration or value of property conveyed; OR
...... Computed on the consideration or value less liens or encumbrances
remaining at time of sale.

_____ FIRST AMERICAN TITLE CO.
Signature of XXXXXXX Agent determining tax – Firm Name

38/1707   **GRANT DEED**

FOR A VALUABLE CONSIDERATION, receipt of which is hereby acknowledged,
PETER M. MORIWAKI and LINDA T. MORIWAKI, husband and wife

hereby GRANT(S) to
GREGORY RANDOLPH and FRIEDA RANDOLPH, husband and wife

An added bonus of checking with the recorder is that you may wind up receiving help in making up your list of comparable sales. When you call (or, better, go to) your recorder's office, tell the employees you are dealing with exactly what your purpose is. These public employees are commonly hassled and hustled by the "pros" who are always in a hurry. If, by contrast, you go out of your way to be nice, you can often engender a good deal of extremely valuable help for no other reason than that you are a citizen, taxpayer, and, at least as important, a voter, who really does need help to make his way through the labyrinth of county records. In some instances, a county assessor's office employee may even short-cut the whole deed checking system I have just described by showing you to a commercially published book that contains a list of property transactions and sales prices. These are published under a trade name like REDI, Larwood, or Realdex. Such books are also in real estate broker's offices and title insurance company offices. A title company may let you consult its book once you indicate that you plan to do your escrow and insurance business with it (see Chapter 11).

I DID IT MYSELF

As part of selling our small two-story house, my wife and I checked around the neighborhood to see what similar houses had sold for. Two identical houses that were in less good shape had sold for $128,000 and $134,000 respectively, four and six months before. We then asked several real estate friends what they would price our house at. They said $139,000 and $142,500 .

We were a little disappointed to hear this, as we had done a lot of work on our kitchen and yard (we even had a small fish pond full of koi). We decided to wait for a few months to sell the house, as interest rates were dropping. Two months later, we put it on the market for $154,000. Interest rates had dropped dramatically and we quickly sold it for $152,000.

Why did we so so much better than the experts thought we would? The drop in interest rates was part of it; there were lots more potential buyers as a result, and prices went up. But in addition, we had worked hard for three years to get our house into perfect condition. Doing this had cost money, of course, but we looked at it as an investment (a way to put aside money). Some lookers didn't seem to care that the place was perfect, but a fair number (especially older people and couples where both people worked) really did. They were willing to pay a little extra for a house they could move into with no need for fixing anything up.

3. Ask a Broker to Help

A third approach to figuring out what your house is fairly worth is to ask someone in the real estate business. This is both easy to do and (often) free. Many brokers offer a free "market analysis," "property profile" or "appraisal" (a rose by any other name...) to get to know you and to get you to list your house with them. This service is almost always offered with no cost or obligation on your part. Don't feel guilty about accepting this help, even though you don't intend to sell your property through a broker. Even though you plan now to do everything yourself, you may end up hiring the broker to provide at least some help in one or more of the ways discussed in Chapter 4.

Brokers are required to make appraisals (free or not) in writing, using professionally-accepted appraisal techniques.[1] The reason for this is that if the appraisal isn't in writing, the broker can too easily wind up changing it if

---

[1]Code of Ethics of the Real Estate Commissioner (Commissioner's Regulation 2785),

the original amount doesn't seem to meet with your approval. ("Well, maybe it is worth $159,000 instead of $149,000; lemme see....") This practice of telling homeowners what they want to hear is disparagingly referred to as "buying the listing" and happens with appalling frequency.

Even if you get an appraisal in writing, you can't be sure that the broker isn't trying to romance you a little by stating that your house is worth more than it really is. The best way to guard against this is to get several appraisals. That way if one is way too high it will probably be easy to spot.

4. Make Your Final Price Calculations

Let's suppose, now, that you are an extremely thorough person and have come up with a variety of "appraisals" as follows:

Fee appraiser you pay	$195,000
Real estate agent A	$205,000
Real estate agent B	$195,000
Real estate agent C	$198,000
Your own appraisal (from public record)	$190,000
Asking price of comparable home next door (interesting, but mostly irrelevant)	$229,000
What owner with a comparable house down the block says she got (not very relevant unless you really trust her)	$224,000

Note: Another factor that you will want to consider in pricing your home is the cost of complying with any local ordinances requiring a house that changes hands to have energy efficiency devices, smoke detectors, etc. I list the most common types of local requirements in Chapter 9. It's up to you to check with your local title company to find out if any of these apply to you and if they do, whether they will be expensive to comply with. Of course, it's possible to negotiate with a buyer to get that person to pay these costs, but in my opinion, it's usually easier to find out what the financial damage will be in advance and add the cost to your price.

Given all the above data, at what price should you offer your property for sale? If you're in a real hurry, keeping the price below $200,000 will probably move it within a week in most markets, assuming the house is in good physical shape and financing is available to the average buyer. However, given these appraisals, pricing the house under $200,000 probably means you will sell too quickly, for too little. In this situation, the preponderance of evidence argues for a price of slightly more than $200,000. Your next question is surely how much more. Since a comparable home is still for sale for $229,000 next door, and is still on the market, you know you probably won't get that much without a long wait. In this situation, my guess is that asking $214,900 would be about right. Remember, just because you've listed a price, there's nothing to prevent you from accepting a lower one. And, especially if you've not listed with a broker, you can raise your asking price if you receive a number of offers at full price or more and conclude that you underpriced it. However, in my experience it's usually harder psychologically to raise your asking price than it is to lower it. Remember that your asking price should not be too far out of line compared to other similar properties, even though you think you absolutely need to get a certain amount. If the price is unrealistic, even if you get a buyer she won't be able to get financing if the financial institution's independent appraisal shows the price to be seriously inflated.

A WORD ABOUT NEGOTIATING

In Chapter 10 I discuss the actual process of negotiating with a potential buyer. This, of course, involves all sorts of factors, including the buyer's needs for inspection, financing, etc. However, the most important point of departure for negotiation with potential purchasers is the price you set.

This raises questions about how best to negotiate. For example, should you set a very high price and be ready to come down, or a realistic price and stick to it like a bulldog with a hambone? Should you throw in appliances from the start and say you will pay for all work that needs to be done as the result of physical inspections of the property, or should you negotiate each of the points separately?

There is no one answer to any of these questions. Good negotiating strategies honestly reflect the personality of the negotiator. In other words, if you hate bargaining, don't overprice your home and plan to engage in a heavy-duty bargaining session. You are almost sure to end up hating the whole process and, as a result, are unlikely to be successful at it.

What you do want to do is to decide your rock bottom sales price and then adopt a strategy to get at least that much. If you are a small business person or someone else who has daily experience in negotiating, doing this will come easily to you. If you dread buying a new car because of the haggling that's inevitably involved, why not pay a broker for a few hours of time to help you adopt a negotiating strategy and, as part of doing this, to price your home? (See Chapter 4 for information on hiring a broker by the hour.)

CHAPTER 6

HOW TO TELL THE WORLD YOUR HOUSE IS FOR SALE

To sell your house for top dollar, you want as many potential buyers as reasonably possible to know about it. Since you've decided to sell your house yourself, your property won't appear in the "inventory" of any real estate office or the multiple listing service for your area.[1] In other words, it's up to you to do your own publicity. Fortunately, it isn't hard.

A. FORGET EXPENSIVE ADS

Before I tell you how to inform people that your house is for sale, let me point out that many real estate ads placed by brokers engage in what I call "advertising overkill." Perhaps you have seen residential real estate advertised on TV or promoted through radio spots. Certainly you have seen good sized display ads for expensive homes in exclusive magazines. Obviously, this

---

[1]Several courts have held that multiple listing services, both those affiliated with Boards of Realtors and those which are not, may refuse "for sale by owner" listings on the basis that it is reasonable to limit access to members of the real estate profession. *Dersh v. San Mateo/Burlingame Board of Realtors*, 136 Cal.App.3d 534 (1982).

sort of advertising doesn't come cheap, and in most instances, it's hard to see how it can possibly be cost-effective to sell one house, no matter how pricey. The short answer is that it usually isn't. Indeed, what is normally happening when big bucks are spent on advertising is that the brokerage company, not the particular property, is being pushed. In other words, the expensive ads only make sense when seen as part of a campaign to raise the business profile of the particular broker.

What is the message in this for you? Simply that you should forget about purchasing expensive ads, no matter what the medium. You, after all, are trying to sell a house, not a brokerage office.

B. CONCENTRATE ON CLASSIFIED NEWSPAPER ADS

It will probably come as no surprise that your best bet is to advertise your house in the real estate classified section of one or more local newspapers where lots of potential buyers are sure to look. Classified sections offer bargain rates compared with the cost of display ads in the rest of the newspaper. Some current rates are set out below.

HOW MUCH DOES A CLASSIFIED AD COST?

I made some calls in 1987 to check both the prices and circulation figures of various papers. I asked for the private party advertising rate. Where it was available, I also asked for rates for advertising in the open house box in the classifieds. The first thing I learned was that it pays to be persistent in asking for information. I was often put on hold or shuttled between extensions and didn't always get responsive answers to what I thought were straightforward questions until I asked them four or five times.

San Francisco *Chronicle* & San Francisco *Examiner*

(joint advertising daily and joint publication Sundays)

Circulation (est.)   545,000 Daily
706,000 Sunday

2 lines (approx. 48 spaces to a line) for $24.96
This includes Friday and Sunday insertion in a list of open houses.

San Francisco *Progress*

Circulation (est.)   222,000 (3 times/wk)

2 lines (approx. 28 spaces to a line) for $7.50 Fridays only or for $11.25 Friday and Sunday

This means listing in "Open Home Guide" in special Friday Real Estate Guide.

Los Angeles Times

Circulation (est.)   1.35 million Sunday
                      1.10 million Daily

2 lines (approx. 28 spaces each) for a week for $25 for prepaid private parties.

There is no "Open Home Guide" as in the San Francisco papers.

Los Angeles Times, Orange County Edition

Circulation (est.)   177,000 Daily
                      215,700 Sunday

3 lines (approximately 28 spaces each) for a week for $10.50/wk

Anaheim *Bulletin*

Circulation (est.)   10,000 Daily (Does not publish on Sundays)

$1.25/line (approx. 23 spaces)

Orange County Register

Circulation (est.)   340,000 Sunday

$14.25 for real estate ad (3 line minimum, about 54 spaces to a line since double lines are used)

San Diego Union-Tribune

Circulation (est.)   350,000 Daily
                      400,000 Sunday

$4.25/line Sunday, $4.41/line daily (approx. 30 spaces to a line)

1. Deciding Where to Advertise

You'll immediately notice the large price differences between newspapers of small and large circulation. Of course, the more expensive rates of the larger papers reflect the fact that they reach many more people. If you are like most house sellers I know, you will probably conclude that it is better to advertise in the paper that the most people read, and pay the higher rates. This is not necessarily a wise conclusion.

To illustrate this point, let's assume you have a house in San Francisco, where the major metropolitan papers are the *Examiner* and the *Chronicle*. Each is sold throughout northern California. The San Francisco *Progress*, a community-based daily, is available in corner boxes and delivered free to about a quarter-million San Francisco homes. The *Progress*, which contains a real estate section, is seldom read by people outside of its fairly narrow circulation area. Not surprisingly, its classified ad rates are considerably lower than those of the *Examiner* and *Chronicle*.

In which publication would I advise you to advertise a San Francisco home for sale? As with so many other things in life, my answer is that it depends. If the value of your home is $300,000 or more, it's likely to appeal to executives transferring to the Bay Area from elsewhere in the United States, or people in other parts of the Bay Area who may not even know the *Progress* exists. Obviously, in this situation, the slightly higher expenditure for the *Examiner* or *Chronicle* is justified.

On the other hand, suppose the San Francisco home you have for sale is worth $200,000 or less. A home in this price range is not an executive-transfer candidate. It is most likely to be purchased by a first-time buyer who already lives in the area. In this situation, skipping the big paper and advertising in the *Progress*, and perhaps other inexpensive local newspapers, may make better sense. Similarly, in the suburban area around Anaheim and Orange County, it may be more effective, and will cost less, to advertise in the Anaheim *Bulletin* than in the Los Angeles *Times* or even just the Orange County edition of the Los Angeles *Times*.

No matter what newspaper you choose, check to see whether it offers listings in a specific "Open Home Guide" or "Open House" section. If this feature is available, be sure to take advantage of it. Open house sections are an extremely effective marketing tool for owners handling their own sales, and it perplexes me that not all newspapers have caught on to their value. For the uninitiated, an "Open Home Guide" consists of a specially boxed "shopping list" of classified ads for houses that are open on a certain day (almost always Sunday and sometimes Saturday) and can be visited without appointment. The list is typically divided both geographically and by price, allowing readers to quickly zero in on the homes they're interested in. Otherwise, open house section classifieds are the same as any other. They include the features of the house for sale, the address, phone number, and an indication of whether it's for sale by owner or through a broker.

2. How to Write a Good Classified Ad

Many real estate ads written by brokers are terrible. Why? Two reasons. First, they use so much real estate lingo and so many abbreviations you need a Rosetta stone of "real estatese" to understand them. Second, because professionals often exaggerate the features of the house to please the seller, potential buyers are often very disappointed when they actually see the house behind the hype. To avoid both of these mistakes, your ad should truthfully describe the important features of your home, such as its size, condition and location, and be easy to understand.

Here is a brief list of things your ad should mention:

• address

• price

• for sale by owner

• number and type of rooms

• some indication of special charm (e.g., patio, hot tub, big yard, fireplace, view, etc.)

- facts about location, if desirable (e.g., next to a park, near school or rapid transit, etc.)

- financing facts, if noteworthy (e.g., owner will carry a second).

Note: Let me repeat, don't exaggerate or play fast and loose with the truth. One function of your ad is to screen out people who won't be interested. If you describe a small tract home on a busy corner as if it is the first cousin to the Taj Mahal surrounded by Yosemite National Park, you will waste a lot of people's time, including yours.

Here, now, is an example of how to, and then how not to, write an ad for the same three bedroom, two bathroom house. While the good ad will cost a little more, it's worth it.

Good Ad:

BY OWNER, 950 PARKER, 3 BR, 2 BA, $175K.

Hot tub, extra wide sunny fenced yard, Bay view, new kitchen.

Call 549-1976 eves after 6 or leave message on tape. Owner may carry 2nd for 10%.

Poor Ad:

3 BR, 2 BA, $175K, OWNER, 950 PARKER

Ht tb, x-wide yd, bay vu, OWC 2nd?

549-1976 after 6 or lv mess.

---

3. Discriminatory Advertising

I am delighted to report that today virtually nobody advertises property for sale with a stated preference as to the race, color or religion of the buyer. That doing this is illegal needs no repetition from me. However, just because you don't obviously discriminate in your ads doesn't mean you can't be accused of conducting a discriminatory ad campaign. If you advertise a house in a way that ends up discriminating against certain groups by excluding them from even learning that your house is for sale, you may be in violation of the law even though you use no overtly discriminatory language. This might occur, for example, if you only list your house in places where people of a particular group (racial, religious, ethnic, sexual) are likely to see it. Does this imply that you can't advertise in papers such as the *Catholic Voice* or *Jewish Bulletin*, or a newspaper in Greek, Spanish, Tagalog or Cantonese, in order to sell your home? Certainly not. However, I recommend that if you advertise in a newspaper with a religious or ethnic focus you protect yourself from possible charges of discriminatory intent by also placing an inexpensive ad in a newspaper of general circulation in your county.

C. FOR SALE SIGNS

I am sometimes asked, "Which is more effective in marketing residential property: classified advertisements or signs?" My experience suggests that they are of about equal value and that it's usually wise to use both. Certainly, good "For Sale" signs should be a major part of any campaign to sell a house.

RENTAL PROPERTY NOTE

If your home is currently being rented, you should discuss your sale plans with the tenants before you advertise it. While you have a right to show the house for sale, your tenants are entitled to their privacy. This means you must give them reasonable notice of your intent to enter and show the house. Under California Civil Code Section 1954, 24 hours written notice is presumed to be reasonable. I've found that the key to selling a house occupied by tenants is to get the tenants to be at least somewhat cooperative. This is not always easy, as tenants who are about to lose their home are likely to be unhappy. To create an atmosphere of cooperation, I suggest you try to limit the number of times that the house will be shown in a given week. One open house on a Sunday for a couple of hours may be easier for tenants to live with than dragging people through every day.[2] In addition, you may want to offer to reduce your tenant's rent somewhat during the time the house is being shown, in exchange for their cooperation.

If, despite your best efforts to protect their privacy, your tenants are overtly hostile, you will probably want to investigate the possibility of asking (or paying) them to leave. Whether you can legally do this depends on a number of factors, including whether the tenants have a lease or a month-to-month tenancy and whether the city in which the property is located has a rent-control ordinance with a "just cause for eviction" requirement. Dealing with these issues is beyond the scope of this book. They are covered in detail in the *Landlord's Law Book (Vol. 1): Rights and Responsibilities* and *(Vol. 2): Evictions*, both by David Brown (Nolo Press).

---

[2]Make sure that your tenants agree voluntarily that this is a good idea. Under Civil Code Section 1954, you only have the right to show the house during normal business hours after giving reasonable notice.

1. Types of Signs

A flat "For Sale By Owner" sign should be placed on the house itself, placed on a pole in the yard, or tacked to a fence. If you only want to show the house to prospective purchasers during stated hours, prominently list them on the sign, along with your phone number. Some people further try to protect their privacy by only putting up "For Sale" signs during "open house" hours. I recommend that you not follow this silly approach, which obviously limits the effectiveness of your advertising campaign. If you only put up signs on week-ends, none of the people who pass your house during the rest of the week will even know it's for sale. And if they don't know, they can't tell their friends. In my experience, people who leave signs up at all times but indicate that the house is shown only during specific open house times or "by appointment only" are not bothered to any substantial degree by people trying to see the house at other times.

"A-boards" which stand up on their own cost a little more than some other types of signs, but are the best for near-by intersections. I prefer the type that say "For Sale By Owner" and then have a chalk board area to list your address. Remember, signs can be treated as a "cost of sale" for tax purposes, provided the expense is incurred within 90 days of sale.

Obviously, your signs should be easy to read. Use thick chalk and make clear block letters on the chalkboard portion of your A-board signs. If rain is a possibility, use white or yellow adhesive letters instead of chalk. For signs on or in front of your house you need only list the time and day like this: "2-4 PM SUN." For signs farther away from your house, also include the street address: "950 PARKER." Don't clutter your sign by trying to include things like price or terms. The sign is meant to lead people to the property where they will find out the details.

2. Location of Signs

Where should signs be placed? In general, you should include these locations:

• As noted above, at least one sign should be on the side of the house or in the yard, where it's easy to see. If you are on a corner, you will need at least two signs, one or more facing each street.

• On open house days, an A-board with an arrow pointing to the house and listing the hours during which the home is open, should be placed in the yard or on the sidewalk immediately in front of the house.

• A-board signs should also be placed at the two corners of your block. Usually it's best to put them on the same side of the street as your house unless for some reason they would be more noticeable to pedestrian or vehicle traffic on the other side. If you live in a semi-rural area without a conventional street grid, use your common sense to locate signs where the maximum number of passers will spot them.

• A-boards showing your address on the chalkboard portion should also be positioned at the nearest major intersection, or on a major street near your home. Never place signs more than one-third to one-half mile away (once you're more than half a mile away, you're in a different neighborhood).

Play off others' signs. You will observe that other "Open House" showings in your neighborhood may begin as early as 1:00 or even noon. Great. Allow these signs to lead traffic into your neighborhood. Don't duplicate these signs, but play off of them. In other words, you don't need a sign at a main intersection eight blocks away if there are already three there listing houses within a few blocks of yours. What you do need are signs that lead traffic from the other open houses to yours. In this regard, it helps to wait until after 1:00 to put up your signs after you know where the others are. Observe local ordinances and customs as to sign placement, with a view to safety. For example, in some places it's illegal to place signs on pedestrian medians in the midst of wide streets. And obviously, law or no law, it makes sense to avoid cluttering a corner with so many signs that pedestrians can't walk safely and motorists can't see your sign anyway.

Note: Local ordinances in some municipalities—or restrictions in some subdivisions—may limit the size or placement of "For Sale" signs, but may not prohibit them altogether.

3. Where to Purchase Signs

To purchase signs for your house and A-boards for the neighborhood, check in the telephone directory's yellow pages under "signs." You will likely find a number of local sign shops that sell everything you need. As noted, a popular version of the A-board signs is a ready-made signboard that reads "For Sale," "For Sale By Owner," or "Open House" or "Home Open," with a chalkboard portion so you can write in the street address and/or hours for the open house. In addition, some sign shops have prepared signs that say "Open 1-5" (or "1-4" or "2-4"). The shop that sells you these A-board signs will also have signs reading "For Sale By Owner," suitable for tacking on your house or placing in the yard. Small "For Sale" signs are commonly available at hardware and office supply stores, but they rarely have A-boards.

What about custom-made signs? Before you go to the expense of ordering custom-made signs, ask yourself this: which do you want to sell, the property or the sign? In my view, custom signs may be a good idea for a very expensive home. Otherwise, since they are obviously just plain unnecessary, their use may actually narrow your market by frightening people away.

D. Distribute Your Own Printed Statements

You will need to write a complete description of your house to pass out at your open house. Although it's not essential, I recommend that you do this a few weeks ahead. Once your property description is prepared, print it up and distribute as many as you can as widely as you can. They can be left in local stores such as laundromats, coffee shops, and delis, with the owners' permission. They should also be given to friends and co-workers, put into neighbors' mailboxes, and mailed to people you think might be interested. Think of it this way. If you distribute 200 fact sheets, and each person who reads it mentions your house to several friends who are interested in moving, you have reached a large number of potential buyers at a very low cost.

Your sheet should not only give the necessary facts about your house, but should let people know why you have enjoyed living there. If you have a flair with line drawings, a sketch of the house can be a real "grabber."

Your property statement should be designed to achieve two goals:

• Attract people to your showings;

• Give people who come to look at your house all the important facts about it. This not only will save you answering the same questions over and over, it gives potential purchasers something to take away with them for easy referral later. ("Was that a gas or electric range? And how much was the assumable first loan? I thought I'd written down the number of blocks to the elementary school, but . . . ")

After you type your flyer following the samples presented below, take it to an instant printing shop and have it copied on colored paper. Assuming you make 300-500 copies, your cost should be less than three cents each.

Here are some of the items you should cover:

- address (cross streets are helpful)

- type of house

- price

- terms (owner financing, down payment, etc.)

- neighborhood information

- square feet

- lot size

- age

- rooms (bedrooms, baths, etc.)

- garage, if any

- yard

- assumable loans, if any (interest rate, payment amount, balloon payments)

- zoning

- kitchen information, including any appliances that are thrown in

- special features (basement, attic, pool, new roof or carpet, fireplace, sauna, etc.)

- "sex appeal" (list a few items that make your house fun—e.g., sunny yard, wonderful old tree, friendly ghost, famous person used to live there, etc.)

- when shown (days of the week and hours, and if appointments at other times can be arranged)

- phone number for information and best times to call.

Note: If you are a person who sets a price firmly and sticks to it, it will save everyone, including you, a lot of trouble if you say so here. On the other hand, if you are at least willing to consider lower offers, you might also want to indicate this.

Here are three samples. The first was used by the editor of this book when he sold his house without a broker. The second, which I wrote, has a few facts changed to protect the privacy of buyer and seller.

SAMPLE 1:

House For Sale By Owner

1508 Juanita Way (corner of Rose St., three blocks below Sacramento St.)

Small, 2-story Salt Box style, in excellent condition (a cheerful little house)

2 1/2 Bedroom (the one-half is a small but nicely converted garage which is part of the house)

1 Bath with tub and shower (modern and cute)

1 Living room with fireplace and lots of light

1 Dining room (small or cozy, depending on your point of view)

1 Kitchen (includes built-in/brand new gas stove top, wall oven, dishwasher, new counter top, handmade, glass-fronted cupboards, refrigerator)

1 laundry room with washer and dryer

Amenities include deck, Japanese fish pond with four friendly koi, picket fence, edible front yard (strawberries), new shed for garden tools, bikes, etc., refinished wood floors throughout house.

Other facts of interest include:

• Built in 1941 on concrete slab

• Efficient and relatively new forced air heating

• Walking distance to North Berkeley BART, Monterey Market area and Westbrae area (Toot Sweets, Brothers Bagels, etc.— important info for Sunday morning)

• Four houses from Cedar Rose park with kiddie play area and tennis courts

• Two blocks from excellent elementary school and six blocks from middle school

Price: $151,900. Will we negotiate? We wouldn't spoil the drama by telling in advance.

OPEN HOUSE on Sunday, February 16 and subsequent Sundays 1:00 - 5:00 p.m. You can reach us at 549-1976 (day) or 524-0439 (evenings between 6:00 and 8:00 p.m.)

SAMPLE 2:

For Sale By Owner

LUXURY HOME IN SAN FRANCISCO—142 Oak Street

Only $224,900 buys this elegant 3 bedroom, 2 bath home featuring cathedral ceiling, formal dining room, separate breakfast room and attractive low maintenance yard on a 33' x 100' lot.

This pleasant residence features a 30-gallon Rudd Monel water heater. The furnace, tar-and-gravel roof and downspouts are only four years old, and the home has been painted inside within recent months. In addition, a 110,000 BTU gravity furnace has been installed four and a half years ago; all of these features make for trouble-free living and "move-in" condition!

Carpets and window coverings are included in this fine home which offers such distinctive features as a window seat in the living room, mahogany doors and trim in the dining room, hardwood floors throughout the main floor, including random plank flooring in the living and dining area, and even a separate bathroom heater.

The garage accommodates two cars in tandem. Muni bus #43 is at the corner, with easy access to a nearby Metro station. Also at the corner are St. Brendan's Church and School. A shopping center, including Tower Market, is a short couple of blocks away.

For qualified buyers to inspect this home, call 111-1212.

SAMPLE 3:

437 Castenada Avenue
$459,500

This formal architecturally designed **three bedroom+, two and one-third bath** home with a "Tandem Style" **garage** is located in **Forest Hill**, one of the premier residential areas of San Francisco. **Forest Hill** is only a short walk to one of two underground MUNI stations, West Portal shops, and public library.

This is one of the few homes in **Forest Hill** located on a **level street** that also offers a **great view** of Mt. Davidson, St. Francis Woods, San Bruno mountains, the Pacific Ocean, Zoo, Fort Funston, Olympic Golf Course, etc.

With **hardwood or tile floors** throughout, this lovely two-story home has a **sunken living room** with a **barrel ceiling** and woodburning **fireplace**. Many doorways, walkways and windows are **arched**. There's a gracious **formal dining room** with a swinging door passage to an **updated**, bright and cheery **kitchen, breakfast room** and door to the backyard.

A **wide stairway** leads to the upstairs landing from which you can enter one of **three large bedrooms**. The main bathroom on this level has **4 fixtures**, a tub in addition to a large tiled shower. There is a second tile and oak bathroom off the master bedroom.

A **bonus room** (formerly the maid's quarters), located in the basement, functions as a den or office. In the basement you'll also find a new water-heater and electric garage opener; a laundry area with heavy sinks; furnace/storage area and a 3rd bathroom area next to a second walk-out door to a very private **rock patio** and backyard garden.

The front yard has **in-ground sprinklers** for both lawn and plants.

Plumbing and **electrical** systems have been updated.

Call for appointment 555-1652 daytimes or 555-2506 evenings until 9.

E. OTHER TYPES OF ADVERTISING

As noted earlier in this chapter, it's almost never cost-effective to use radio, TV or magazine ads to try to sell your house. However, it may pay to advertise in:

1. A limited-circulation newsletter or small magazine, such as those put out by a consumer group, synagogue or church, which will help spread the word among your acquaintances that your home is for sale at a very reasonable cost. (But remember my cautions about discriminatory advertising in Section B above.)

2. Hobby group newsletters, such as those put out by garden clubs, women's clubs and service organizations. Concentrate on those where you can identify a real tie-in between the interests of the members and your property. For example, if your land is zoned to allow the keeping of a horse, advertising in a local equine journal would make great sense.

CHAPTER 7

AND THIS IS
THE KITCHEN, ED

▼▀▀▀

Now that you've priced your house, circulated your property description, advertised in newspapers and made or purchased signs, you're almost ready to show your house to potential buyers. Here are the final preparations you need to make before putting out the welcome mat.

A. PROTECT YOUR PROPERTY

The unhappy truth is that, while it's rare, there are times when prospective "buyers" are interested in seeing your home for just one reason: they want to "case the joint" so they can efficiently steal your possessions. There is no way to completely prevent this, but you can and should take a few reasonable precautions every time your home is to be shown to strangers, either individually or in larger numbers.

1. Don't display silver, china, or other prized possessions. Sure, they make your dining room look nice, but remember, people are interested in buying the home for its dining room, not your china pattern.

2. Hide all other valuables. Make sure that things like credit cards, ATM-access cards etc., are either on your person or under lock and key. The same goes for small, valuable objects which are easily "lifted"—or broken by accident. This precaution obviously applies to keys, important documents, small antiques, and collectibles. If it's not too inconvenient, it's also wise to remove, from public view, computers, expensive typewriters, stereos, TVs, furs, and any particularly valuable art works.

3. Don't discuss your personal schedule or lifestyle with strangers. Sometimes homeowners try to "sell" the neighborhood and, in doing so, make excessively revealing comments: "It's so safe here we frequently leave the back door open during the day so the children don't need to carry a key!" or "It's only two blocks from church, and every day I can leave at just quarter to twelve and be in my pew for Noon Mass."

4. Be sure people touring your home can enter and leave only through one door, except, of course, when you are escorting them through another, such as to the back yard or garage.

5. Escort and accompany prospective buyers. You needn't be at their side, but do keep them within sight at all times. This is obviously easier to do on a "by appointment" basis than at an open house, but if you can draft a couple of family members or friends to help control traffic, you can handle it even if your house if full of people. Remember, though, that to comply with the real estate license laws discussed in Chapter 2, your friends should not quote or discuss any material facts or terms concerning the sale, and you should not pay them. Simply have them limit their role to directing crowd flow and referring all questions to you. And, if so many people show up at once that it's impossible to deal with them all at once, ask some of them to wait for the next "tour." In other words, don't be afraid to structure the open house so that you feel comfortable.

6. Ask everyone who visits your home to sign a guest register. Position your register, with a pen (attached on a chain or string so it doesn't walk out the door) near the entryway. If anyone refuses to provide this information, don't let them in. Obviously, an experienced thief will simply use a false name, but even so this sort of organized procedure may make them think twice about victimizing you. Besides, you will want names, addresses and phone numbers if you decide to make follow-up calls to see which prospective buyers are really interested in your property, or to get feedback about what they didn't like.

I Did It Myself

After my first open house, I realized it would have been helpful to know, by adding a column to my sign-in list, if people came in response to my San Francisco Chronicle ad, Oakland Tribune ad, Co-op ad, A-boards, word-of-mouth, or what. This would have told me which of my ads was doing the most good, and which to continue. I could have started the first weekend with ads in a variety of places and then cut down in subsequent weeks, after getting feed-back on what worked (and seeing who each ad drew.) Another note on sign-in lists: I got addresses and phone numbers when I made a well-organized form with a designated space for the information I requested. A blank pad didn't get much but names when things got chaotic, despite my instructions on the top of the page and my oral request.

---

7. Consider hiring a private security guard. This costs money, but makes a lot of sense if you own a large luxury home full of valuable objects, and surely impresses prospective buyers with your seriousness of purpose as to the security of your property. And remember, security guards don't all have to look like "Rambo." Many companies provide guards in sportcoat-type outfits.

Again, my emphasis on taking precautions may seem a trifle excessive, but at the risk of adding yet one more bromide to a world already burdened by cliche glut: Better to be careful than to have to shop for a new TV.

B. MAKE YOUR HOME ATTRACTIVE

The desirability of making your house as attractive as possible may seem self-evident. Apparently it isn't, because I've noticed that many sellers don't do much beyond vacuuming the living room rug and maybe cleaning the ring off the bathtub. With a little thought, you can surely do a lot better.

One successful real estate broker I know always insists on having a roast or loaf of bread cooking in the oven because she believes that people react strongly to smell. Another good idea is to leave several magazines, books and record jackets where prospective purchasers can see them. In doing this, think about the typical person you expect to examine your house. In some neighborhoods you might want to display the New York *Times* and the *New Yorker*; while in others, *Sports Illustrated* and *Sunset*. The idea, of course, is to encourage prospective purchasers to fantasize about how pleasant it will be to live in your house.

I DID IT MYSELF

Believe it or not, Catherine Jermany and I almost bought a house in Novato, California in part because it had a variety of interesting reading material in it, including a Nolo Press book.

—Nolo Press editor Steve Elias

Lighting is important. It's usually best to leave window shades up about halfway and turn on a few lights, so there is sufficient—but not glaring—light. Unobtrusive but pleasant background music is also helpful. Do all you can to make the house clean, tidy, airy and attractive. Have flowers in a vase on the kitchen or dining room table, another on the mantel or coffee table in the living room, and perhaps some scented potpourri in an attractive container on the kitchen counter. Remember, short of spending a lot of money to fix up your home, there are always all sorts of inexpensive things you can do to make it show well.

I DID IT MYSELF

Anything that you can do, relatively inexpensively, to make you feel pampered in your home will also help with buyer's fantasies. I bought roses, big plush towels, candlesticks and scented soap and bubbles for a shabby bathroom, along with an opaque rose-colored shower curtain for $3. Everyone commented that they loved the bathroom ,despite the fact that it was in obvious need of extensive structural pest control work.

If you know an experienced decorator, ask him to come by and advise you on how you can improve the look of your house without spending much money. This will mean you have to admit to yourself that your house can use some sprucing up, but the slight dent to your ego that this may entail should not be too hard to bear when you realize that a more attractive house may mean an extra several thousand dollars in your pocket. And while you're adding nice touches, subtract as many detrimental ones as possible. Animal smells, clutter and dust, for example, are all things that detract from the value of your property and can be eliminated fairly easily.

C. PREPARE FOR A SAFE SHOWING

It's important that you take a moment to think about how to protect your prospective purchasers from possible injury, and yourself from lawsuits. Walk through your home, checking for and dealing with everything that might cause injury, especially to someone who is not familiar with every step along the way. At some open houses, 50 or more people can show up at once, and a number of them are likely to be small, so think about safety for kids as well as adults. Here are a few things to check for:

- Slippery throw rugs (take them up);

- Loose steps (fix them);

- Slick areas, such as front steps (put down rubber mats);

- Long electrical and phone cords (make sure they are out of the way);

- Unsafe electrical wires and fixtures (replace them);

- Potentially dangerous areas in yards (block them off);

- Decks and pools (are they childproof?);

- Medicine or household chemicals that children could get into (lock them up);

- Pets (put them in an enclosure people cannot get into, even if they have always been friendly. If they are likely to be noisy, arrange for them to take a brief vacation).

D. Obey Anti-Discrimination Laws

Be courteous to everyone. If you refuse to show your property to or to entertain offers from anyone on the basis of their race, color, religion, sex, marital status, ancestry, national origin, physical handicap, or other similarly arbitrary reason (e.g., sexual preference), you are in legal trouuble. In other words, unless you have a good reason to believe a particular person is a bad credit risk, a thief, or otherwise seriously undesirable (and are prepared to defend that belief), you should show him your house and treat seriously any offer to purchase he makes.

E. Remember That You Are Only Showing, Not Selling

Be cordial to lookers, but don't overwhelm people with energy or enthusiasm. Many prospective purchasers look at hundreds of homes; others check out houses as a hobby and don't ever really plan to buy one. So, if people don't evince obvious interest, just assume it isn't for them and concentrate on the next person. Above all, if you're going to sell your own house, you have to keep your sense of humor. People who don't want to buy your house are not rejecting you. They probably just don't want an all-electric kitchen, or wallpaper in the basement bathroom.

F. Disclose All Material Facts About the Property

If you fail to disclose material facts about the property, you open yourself to the possibility of a lawsuit based on misrepresentation and possibly even fraud. To give you an idea of how strict this legal rule can be, consider the 1983 California Supreme Court decision in the case of *Reed v. King* (193 Cal. Rptr. 130, 145 Cal. App.3d 261), which held that the owner (and real estate agents assisting in the transaction) withheld a material fact by not telling a buyer that a homicide had been committed in the home ten years earlier. Though the murder of a woman and her four children a decade earlier had nothing to do with the foundation, plumbing or roof of the home, the courts considered the plaintiff's argument that the history had "a quantifiable effect on the market value of the premises."

Sellers must, by law, give buyers a statutory disclosure form (see below).[1] A tear-out form is included in the Appendix. I recommend that you have copies of your disclosure material available at your open house. A disclosure sheet form should be given to any prospective purchaser who expresses a serious interest in your property. In all instances, people who sign a contract to purchase your house should acknowledge in writing that they have received your disclosure material.

If you don't give a prospective purchaser a copy of the disclosure statement until she makes an offer, she has three days (five days if the statement was mailed, not personally delivered) to withdraw the offer. Obviously, this introduces considerable uncertainty into the transaction. If someone looks like a serious prospect, go ahead and give him the disclosure statement before he presents you with an offer.

I DID IT MYSELF

When I sold my house, it was before the disclosure law went into effect. Nevertheless, I disclosed everything I could think of and a few things I made up. I even listed things like small rust spots on a gutter. In addition, I had copies of inspection reports available on the dining room table. When anyone seemed sincerely interested in the house, I asked them to read both my detailed disclosures and the inspection reports. A number of people remarked positively that they really appreciated this approach.

You are responsible only for information that is in your personal knowledge—that is, you don't have to hire professionals to answer the questions on the disclosure form. You must, however, fill out the form in good faith—that is, honestly. You must also take "ordinary care" in obtaining the information, which means that you are responsible for including information about the property that you know or, as a reasonable homeowner, should know.

If you don't know and can't find out (by making a reasonable effort) some of the information requested on the form, you may make a "reasonable approxima-

---

[1] Civil Code Sec. 1102.

tion," as long as you make it clear (on the form) that the information is an approximation that is based on the best information available to you.

If an error or omission is carelessly or intentionally made in the statement, the sale is still valid, but the seller is liable for any actual damages the buyer suffers. For example, if you forget to disclose the fact that the roof leaks (and you knew that it did), the sale is still good, but you're responsible for the damage that the leak causes and the cost of repairs.

Please take your disclosure responsibility seriously and err on the side of more, rather than less, disclosure. The point should be simple. Full disclosure of any property defects effectively protects you from any later claim or lawsuit by the buyer based on failure to disclose. This means you should go out of your way to tell people if the roof leaks, the water heater is old, the foundation is not sole-plated, there is dry rot around the windows, appliances are on their last legs, etc. Indeed, even if you have doubts (but not facts) about any important features about your house, don't assume there is no problem. Hire a contractor to "walk through" with you. If problems are discovered, disclose them to all potential buyers.

This is a new requirement (effective January 1, 1987), and no one knows how strictly courts will interpret and enforce its terms. You may, although it is not required by the law, want to hire a general contractor to inspect the house and give you a report which you can both use as a basis for completing your disclosure form and photocopy and give to potential buyers. If a buyer plans to arrange and pay for his own structural pest control report, it may not really be necessary to go to the trouble and expense of doing this, but if for any reason the buyer doesn't plan to have the house checked out, it's particularly wise to protect yourself by arranging for your own inspection.

How much should a home inspection cost and what should you get for your money? Marty Reutinger, a licensed general contractor in Albany, California, charges $245 for an average inspection and detailed written report. He spends about three hours on a typical inspection, evaluating the interior and exterior of the house, the site itself, and the various systems (heating, plumbing, etc.) that operate in the house. His information sheet reads this way:

THE VALUE OF HOME INSPECTIONS

The meteoric rise in the cost of housing has made us all aware of the value of every dollar spent in purchasing and maintaining a home. With a new mortgage and property taxes to pay, the surprise addition of unforeseen maintenance costs could deflate your pleasure in home ownership.

Know as much as you can before you buy! In addition to the information that your realtor can supply, a house inspection by an impartial professional will provide you with detailed information about the physical condition of your future home.

A thorough inspection should cover the property from top to bottom. The inspector will examine the general conditions of the site, such as drainage, retaining walls, fences and driveways; the integrity of the structure and the foundation; the condition of the roof, exterior and interior paint, doors and windows, plumbing, electrical and heating systems.

Accompany the inspector during his examination so that he can give you information about the maintenance and preservation of the house and answer any questions you may have. He should point out any problems that may need attention and tell you which are truly important and which are minor.

The final product of the inspection should be a detailed written report which you can keep for future reference. The report should also give you invaluable information about earthquake protection, general safety measures, insulation and energy conservation. With all this information in hand, you will be more confident of the condition of your house.

Finally, let me put to rest a question that I am often asked. Doesn't disclosing all problems with my house make it harder to sell it? It may surprise you, but my answer is "generally, no." Most buyers suspect that any older house has at least some problems. Some are even paranoid on the subject, suspecting you of covering up all sorts of nasty defects that don't exist. A full and detailed disclosure of problems will go a long way towards convincing these people that, in fact, the house isn't in even worse shape, and will also weed out some problem buyers.

REAL ESTATE TRANSFER DISCLOSURE STATEMENT

THIS DISCLOSURE STATEMENT CONCERNS THE REAL PROPERTY SITUATED IN THE CITY OF _____, COUNTY OF _____, STATE OF CALIFORNIA, DESCRIBED AS _____ _____. THIS STATEMENT IS A DISCLOSURE OF THE CONDITION OF THE ABOVE DESCRIBED PROPERTY IN COMPLIANCE WITH SECTION 1102 OF THE CIVIL CODE AS OF _____, 19___. IT IS NOT A WARRANTY OF ANY KIND BY THE SELLER(S) OR ANY AGENT(S) REPRESENTING ANY PRINCIPAL(S) IN THIS TRANSACTION, AND IS NOT A SUBSTITUTE FOR ANY INSPECTIONS OR WARRANTIES THE PRINCIPAL(S) MAY WISH TO OBTAIN.

I
COORDINATION WITH OTHER DISCLOSURE FORMS

This Real Estate Transfer Disclosure Statement is made pursuant to Section 1102 of the Civil Code. Other statutes require disclosures, depending upon the details of the particular real estate transaction (for example: special study zone and purchase-money liens on residential property).

Substituted Disclosures: The following disclosures have or will be made in connection with this real estate transfer, and are intended to satisfy the disclosure obligations on this form, where the subject matter is the same: _____

_____
_____
_____

(list all substituted disclosure forms to be used in connection with this transaction)

II
SELLERS INFORMATION

The Seller discloses the following information with the knowledge that even though this is not a warranty, prospective Buyers may rely on this information in deciding whether and on what terms to purchase the subject property. Seller hereby authorizes any agent(s) representing any principal(s) in this transaction to provide a copy of this statement to any person or entity in connection with any actual or anticipated sale of the property.

THE FOLLOWING ARE REPRESENTATIONS MADE BY THE SELLER(S) AND ARE NOT THE REPRESENTATIONS OF THE AGENT(S), IF ANY. THIS INFORMATION IS A DISCLOSURE AND IS NOT INTENDED TO BE PART OF ANY CONTRACT BETWEEN THE BUYER AND SELLER.

Seller __is __is not occupying the property.

A. The subject property has the items checked below (read across):

__Range __Oven __Microwave
__Dishwasher __Trash Compactor __Garbage Disposal
__Washer/Dryer Hookups __Window Screens __Rain Gutters
__Burglar Alarms __Smoke Detector(s) __Fire Alarm
__T.V. Antenna __Satellite Dish __Intercom
__Central Heating __Central Air Cndtng. __Evaporator Cooler(s)
__Wall/Window Air Cndtng. __Sprinklers __Public Sewer System
__Septic Tank __Sump Pump __Water Softener
__Patio/Decking __Built-in Barbeque __Gazebo
__Sauna __Pool __Spa__Hot Tub
__Security Gate(s) __Garage Door Opener(s) __Number Remote Controls

Garage: __Attached   __Not Attached   __Carport
Pool/Spa Heater: __Gas   __Solar   __Electric
Water Heater: __Gas   __Private Utility or
Water Supply: __City   __Well
Gas Supply: __Utility   __Bottled   Other _____

Exhaust Fan(s) in _____ 220 Volt Wiring in _____ Fireplace(s) in _____ Gas Starter _____
Roof(s): Type: _____ Age: _____ (approx.)
Other: _____
Are there, to the best of your (Seller's) knowledge, any of the above that are not in operating condition? __Yes __No. If yes, then describe. (Attach additional sheets if necessary.): _____
_____
_____

__Interior Walls __Ceilings __Floors __Exterior Walls __Insulation __Roof(s) __Windows __Doors __Foundation __Slab(s) __Driveways __Sidewalks __Walls/Fences __Electrical Systems __Plumbing/Sewers/Septics __Other Structural Components (Describe: _____
_____
If any of the above is checked, explain. (Attach additional sheets if necessary): _____
_____
_____
_____

B. Are you (Seller) aware of any significant defects/malfunctions in any of the following? __Yes __No. If yes, check appropriate space(s) below.

C. Are you (Seller) aware of any of the following:

1. Features of the property shared in common with adjoining landowners, such as walls, fences, and driveways, whose use or responsibility for maintenance may have an effect on the subject property.................. __Yes __No
2. Any encroachments, easements or similar matters that may affect your interest in the subject property .... __Yes __No

3. Room additions, structural modifications, or other alterations or repairs made without necessary permits . . . . __Yes __No

4. Room additions, structural modifications, or other alterations or repairs not in compliance with building codes . . . . __Yes __No

5. Landfill (compacted or otherwise) on the property or any portion thereof . . . . __Yes __No

6. Any settling from any cause, or slippage, sliding, or other soil problems . . . . . . __Yes __No

7. Flooding, drainage or grading problems . . . . __Yes __No

8. Major damage to the property or any of the structures from fire, earthquake, floods, or landslides . . . . __Yes __No

9. Any zoning violations, nonconforming uses, violations of "setback" requirements . . . . __Yes __No

10. Neighborhood noise problems or other nuisances . . . . __Yes __No

11. CC&R's or other deed restrictions or obligations . . . . __Yes __No

12. Homeowners' Association which has any authority over the subject property . . . . __Yes __No

13. Any "common area" (facilities such as pools, tennis courts, walkways, or other areas co-owned in undivided interest with others) . . . . __Yes __No

14. Any notices of abatement or citations against the property . . . . __Yes __No

15. Any lawsuits against the seller threatening to or affecting this real property . . . . __Yes __No

If the answer to any of these is yes, explain. (Attach additional sheets if necessary.): _____

_____

_____

_____

Seller certifies that the information herein is true and correct to the best of the Seller's knowledge as of the date signed by the Seller.

Seller _____

Date _____

Seller _____

Date _____

III
AGENTS INSPECTION DISCLOSURE

(Please Print)

IV
AGENTS INSPECTION DISCLOSURE

(To be completed only if the agent who has obtained the offer is other than the agent above.)

THE UNDERSIGNED, BASED ON A REASON-ABLY COMPETENT AND DILIGENT VISUAL IN-SPECTION OF THE ACCESSIBLE AREAS OF THE PROPERTY, STATES THE FOLLOWING:

(Please Print)

V

BUYER(S) AND SELLER(S) MAY WISH TO OB-TAIN PROFESSIONAL ADVICE AND/OR INSPEC-TIONS OF THE PROPERTY AND TO PROVIDE FOR APPROPRIATE PROVISIONS IN A CON-TRACT BETWEEN BUYER AND SELLER(S) WITH RESPECT TO ANY ADVICE/INSPEC-TIONS/DEFECTS.

(To be completed only if the seller is represented by an agent in this transaction.)

THE UNDERSIGNED, BASED ON THE ABOVE INQUIRY OF THE SELLER(S) AS TO THE CONDI-TION OF THE PROPERTY AND BASED ON A REASONABLY COMPETENT AND DILIGENT

VISUAL INSPECTION OF THE ACCESSIBLE AR-EAS OF THE PROPERTY IN CONJUNCTION WITH THAT INQUIRY, STATES THE FOLLOW-ING: _____

_____

_____

Agent (Broker

Representing Seller) _____ By _____ Date
_____   (Associate Licensee
                or Broker-Signature)

_____

_____

_____

_____

Agent (Broker

obtaining the Offer) _____ By _____ Date
_____   (Associate Licensee
                or Broker-Signature)

I/WE ACKNOWLEDGE RECEIPT OF A COPY OF THIS STATEMENT.

Seller _____ Date _____ Buyer
_____ Date _____

Seller _____ Date _____ Buyer
_____ Date _____

Agent (Broker

Representing Seller) _____ By _____ Date
_____   (Associate Licensee
                or Broker-Signature)

Agent (Broker

obtaining the Offer) _____ By _____ Date
_____   (Associate Licensee
                or Broker-Signature)

A REAL ESTATE BROKER IS QUALIFIED TO ADVISE ON REAL ESTATE. IF YOU DESIRE LEGAL ADVICE, CONSULT YOUR ATTORNEY.

You must also tell prospective buyers if your property is within a state-designated "special studies zone."[2] Special studies zones are areas along earthquake faults identified by state geologists. The designations are puzzling, at least to a layperson; for example, San Francisco is not within a special study zone.

To find out if your property is within a special studies zone, check with your local city or county planning department. It should have state maps that show the areas. Here is a form you can give the buyer:

SPECIAL STUDIES ZONE DISCLOSURE

The real property at _____,
_____ County, California, lies within a special studies zone designated by the California Department of Geology.

This disclosure is made under Public Resources Code § 2621.9.

_____   _____, 19_____
Seller

I acknowledge that I have received a copy of this disclosure form.

_____   _____, 19_____
Buyer

Like the more detailed Real Estate Transfer Disclosure Statement, you should give the special studies zone disclosure to anyone you think is a serious potential purchaser. After you give the disclosure form to the buyer, have him sign the acknowledgment at the bottom of the form, and keep a copy (or have him sign two copies, one for you to keep). A tear-out form is included in the Appendix.

---

[2]Public Resources Code § 2621.9.

CHAPTER 8

WHO CAN AFFORD TO BUY YOUR HOUSE?

Before you entertain offers to purchase your house, you should ask a basic question: "Who can afford to buy it at my asking price?" Your first answer may be to chuckle and say, "Not me!" Certainly, if you are like many homeowners, you would have trouble buying your own house at current prices if you were just starting out in the world.

But why worry about the fact that a lot of people can't afford your house? Isn't that the buyer's problem, not yours? Not necessarily. Your ability to sell your home is directly related to the ability of others to buy it. Two basic rules of thumb come into play here:

• The higher the price you ask, the smaller the percentage of the population who can afford to purchase it.

• As the percentage of people who can qualify to purchase your house goes down, the number of people who will look at it, but can't afford to buy it, will go up.

Prospective sellers often dream of a wealthy purchaser who will pay all cash down, period. The only thing wrong with this dream is that it's not a whole lot more likely to happen than winning the California Lottery "Big Spin." While, of course, there are a few buyers with a substantial nest egg, or generous relatives who will help them, these people are definitely in the minority. The typical homebuyer must borrow heavily in order to buy. Even then, many people can't qualify either because they don't make enough in the first place or because they have already over-utilized their credit to buy a car, furniture, appliances or other items. Or, put another way, the unhappy truth is that the majority of people who would like to buy your house can't afford to. This chapter outlines home financing basics—the terms and concepts you need to know—and how to find out if a prospective buyer can use one of the available financing options to buy your house.

A. HOME FINANCE BASICS

As you already own a house, you are surely familiar with the basic ways homes are financed in California. Just the same, a short review of house finance rules won't hurt. Some of this information is of more concern to the buyer than it is to you. It is included because it's my experience that the more unrealistic a potential buyer's chances are to buy your house, the more likely the person is to cloud his offer with all sorts of grandiose lingo. For example, if you have a $300,000 house and someone proposes financing it under the FHA or VA programs, you need to know from the start that they are whistling Dixie.

Deed of Trust: A deed of trust is the functional equivalent of a mortgage. This term is used almost exclusively in California, although many people continue to incorrectly call it a "mortgage." It works like this: the buyer/borrower signs a promissory note promising to pay the loan back to the lender. He also signs a deed of trust giving legal title to the property to a third party, the trustee (usually a title company). The trustee does nothing unless the borrower defaults on the loan. Then the trustee has the power to sell the property to pay off the loan to the lender.

Fixed-Rate Loans: Most people buying single-family homes for their own occupancy favor fixed-rate loans rather than the variable- or adjustable-rate mortgages pushed by lenders in recent years. With a fixed-rate loan, you normally make a down payment in the range of 20% of the appraised value of the house and then pay X dollars a month for 15 or 30 years.[1] When you make your last payment, you own the house. Interest rates vary slightly from one lender to the next, but the differences are typically small. The Sunday real estate sections of metropolitan newspapers often publish the rates.

---

[1] Recently some affluent buyers have come to prefer 5- or 10- year loans in order to reduce the total amount of interest paid. These shorter term loans, which, of course, have higher monthly payments, are available for slightly lower rates than the longer term ones.

People prefer this system because they like the certainty of knowing that their home payments (except for increases in property taxes and insurance premiums, if these are included in the payment) won't go up. In the real estate business, this type of loan is often called an "A loan" or "cream puff" loan.

Variable-Rate Loans: Variable-rate loans are an alternative to fixed-rate loans. These loan "products" (as the banking folks call them) are often identified by initials: ARM (adjustable-rate mortgage), VRM (variable-rate mortgage), VIR (variable interest rate), etc. Though these alphabet soup labels have slightly different meanings, this is normally the buyer's concern, not yours. The disadvantage to a buyer with a variable-rate loan is obviously that the interest rate on the loan can go up during the mortgage term if market interest rates go up. However, these days most variables cap the maximum amount that the interest rates can go up at some amount between 2% and 5% over the initial rate.

The chief difference from a seller's point of view is that the initial interest rate for variable loans is usually about 2% lower than a fixed-rate loan. This means it is easier for the buyer to qualify to buy your house if he gets a variable-rate loan with lower monthly payments. For instance, when someone is buying a $220,000 home, her monthly payment might be as much as $300 lower on a variable-rate loan than on a fixed-rate loan.

Points: The term "points" is simply shorthand for a loan origination fee charged by a financial institution. One point is 1% of the loan. Thus, if a bank charges a buyer two points for a $200,000 loan, this means the borrower must pay the bank $4,000 (2% of $200,000) to get the loan.

Low Down Payment Loans: In some situations, a lender loans more than 80% of the appraised value. If this is done, the loan terms are almost always less favorable to the buyers. Normally it means a higher loan origination fee ("points"), a higher interest rate, maybe a shorter term in which to pay off the loan (perhaps 15 or 20 years instead of 30), and probably a requirement that the buyer pay for mortgage insurance to indemnify the lender against loss in case of the buyer's default. Mortgage bankers are less likely than other lenders to impose these conditions.

Seller Financing: The standard loan, where the buyer puts up 20% of the purchase price, doesn't work for many buyers because, with today's high home prices, the buyer often doesn't have the 20% down payment. In this situation, the seller is often asked to help finance the purchase.[2] The seller may extend credit for part of the down payment (often 10% of the purchase price) with payment of this money secured by a second deed of trust in favor of the seller.[3] For your purposes, this means that you are loaning the buyer part of the purchase price. You don't actually loan him cash, like the bank, savings-and-loan, or mortgage brokerage company does. Instead, you extend the buyer a credit, against the purchase price of the home, in escrow calculations. The buyer executes a second promissory note and trust deed in your favor. The paperwork needed is prepared by the title or escrow company, but you and the buyer must work out the terms.

Many sellers are initially reluctant to do this. They want to get all their cash out of the house, period. However, this "I won't take a second" position can change if the seller realizes that it will be difficult to sell the house at a decent price without helping out with the financing.

One reason for a seller being reluctant to take a second is the fear that the buyer will fail to make the required payment. If the buyer doesn't make payments on either your loan or an obligation senior to it (the first mortgage or trust deed or property taxes), you will have to start making the payments on the first loan, so as to make it current, and then foreclose your junior (second) trust deed loan. This will cost you some money up front (though you will probably get it back), and about four months or so of your time and grief. It also means that you will get your house back and have to resell it. A title insurance company or attorney can assist you with initiating foreclosure, and will probably refer you to a specialized foreclosure company that will go through the steps for.

An alternative to risking "carrying back a second" is to sell the note and trust deed, as soon as reasonably possible, to another investor, which you can do as a private party (within the limits mentioned in Chapter 2). Usually, though, you'll go through a real estate loan broker for this, and the procedure is beyond the scope of this book. Suffice it to say that you will probably sell the note and trust deed for a discount of at least 20%, meaning that you will only receive about 80¢ on the dollar. Thus, if you sell a $10,000 "second," you'll net $8,000 in cash and not collect interest in the future on the principal amount, but you're

---

[2]There are no special legal requirements for doing this unless you are extending credit secured by real estate six or more times a year (if you are, contact the Federal Trade Commission for guidelines). In addition, if a broker arranges a loan for you, including a second that you are carrying, California law requires the broker to make certain disclosures to the buyer. If no broker is in the picture, you need not worry about this.

[3]Of course, the seller can provide financing for a greater percentage of the purchase price, even all of it. This typically occurs when interest rates are sky high and buyers can't get conventional financing. With today's interest rates, it is extremely unusual, unless the seller wants to sell to someone who doesn't qualify to get a loan. Except in family situations, getting involved in this sort of deal is usually foolish.

selling your risk. Obviously, because of the monetary loss from discounting the note, and the risk in keeping it, sellers who "carry paper" often compensate themselves for this by insisting on a higher selling price than they would have accepted if the buyer were not getting financing help from the seller.

What are some typical terms for a second deed of trust? As far as interest is concerned, seller-lenders want more than they could obtain on a safer first mortgage. Try comparing bank first mortgage rates with certificate of deposit rates, pick the higher of the two and raise it at least one full percentage point. This will usually allow you to compete favorably with mortgage brokers.

You probably want your money back fairly soon, like three to five years (lest your fixed-rate loan become economically obsolete), even if you've extended the payment calculation over a long period of time (e.g., 30 years) to keep the monthly payment affordable for the borrower-buyer. This necessitates a "balloon payment" of all unpaid principal at the end of the three to five year term.

Some loans call for no payment of principal until maturity ("interest only" loans), while other loans delay all payments of principal and interest until maturing ("straight loans"). I discourage both of these because they put a greater burden on the buyer, increasing the risk of default. A buyer also may accuse the seller, in litigation, of not making full and fair disclosure of the financing terms.

Assumable Loans: Many home loans used to be assumable. A buyer with good credit assumed the existing loan (or took title "subject to" the seller's loan), and paid cash to the seller to make up the difference between the loan amount and the purchase price. If the buyer didn't have enough cash to make up the difference, the seller often provided a second deed of trust for some of it. In recent years, assumable loans have become unpopular with financial institutions because people only want to assume loans that are below the current rate. Today, for the most part, only a minority of fairly old loans are assumable. If you believe you have an assumable loan, check with the financial institution. If it says otherwise, talk to a lawyer.

Bridge Loans: An increasingly popular option for homeowners who are simultaneously selling one house and looking for another is a short-term "bridge loan," or "gap loan," which allows them to go ahead with the purchase of a new home before selling the old one. Bridge loans are based on the equity in the current home, and are usually limited to 75% of the home's value less the value of any outstanding mortgage. That covers the down payment and closing costs on the new house. Interest rates are generally a couple of points above the prime rate, and the loan lasts only a month or so. Not all banks offer bridge loans. If they are available, it is usually from the lender that is providing the permanent financing on the new house.

Lender Appraisals: Before it agrees to finance the sale of your home, a financial institution will have it appraised independently. All loans it makes will be based on the appraisal. This means if you and the buyer agree on a price higher than the value of the financial institution's appraisal, it will base its loan on the appraised value, not the selling price. Thus, if you sell your house for $200,000, but the bank appraises it at $180,000 and agrees to loan 80%, it will loan $144,000, not $160,000.

Federal Housing Administration Loans: Under Title II of the Federal Housing Administration (FHA) program, it is possible for creditworthy borrowers to purchase homes through a federally-insured loan program, which indemnifies the lender against loss if the borrower defaults. As a consequence, financial institutions that are protected by FHA loan at a lower interest rate than other lenders (usually about a half to a whole interest point lower) and require a lower down payment (3% of the first $25,000 of appraised value and 5% of the balance of the appraised value).

However, FHA appraisals of a house's value tend to be conservative, and the borrower/buyer must pay any excess in price above the appraised value, in cash, in addition to the down payment. Additionally, since the borrower/buyer pays a lower than market interest rate, the financial institutions often demand that the seller pay points when the loan is given. Such points (each point is 1% of the loan amount) are usually anywhere from 2% to 4%, and sometimes as high as 8% of the loan amount. FHA loan limits vary by FHA region but are almost never sufficient to purchase a house in most of California.

FHA loans require a termite clearance and may require certification for some electrical work. They used to be fully assumable, but now buyers assuming the loans must be approved if less than two years have elapsed since the previous sale.

Veterans' Administration Loans: The Veterans' Administration (VA) makes low-interest loans to qualified veterans (depending on when they served in the armed forces and for how long; check with a local VA office for details) by guaranteeing a lender (bank, savings and loan or mortgage company) against default by the veteran buyer/borrower. VA loans with no down payment required may be made for up to $110,000 if the property meets the VA's standards for a Certificate of Reasonable Value. As with FHA loans, seller's discount points are involved, and these loans do not work in many areas because prices are too high. They cannot be combined with a conventional loan or secondary financing.

Cal-Vet Loans: California, through its Department of Veterans' Affairs, lends veterans money to buy homes, providing the veteran was born in California or was a California resident when he entered the service and served for an adequate period of time during specified years (rules can be checked with a local DVA office).

The DVA issues bonds and passes on to veteran borrowers the relatively low cost of this money. There are no points charged the seller. The maximum loan on a home is currently $75,000. A 5% down payment is required, assuming the property is worth more than $35,000. This means, for practical purposes, a borrower utilizing Cal-Vet can buy a home worth $78,947.37 by paying $3,947.37 down, plus a minimum in closing costs (kept low because DVA handles as much of the closing process as possible, once more passing savings along to the veteran buyer/borrower). It is possible to combine a Cal-Vet loan with other financing, such as a deed of trust carried by the seller or made by a third party, as long as the total loaned to the buyer doesn't exceed 90% of the property's value as conservatively appraised by Cal-Vet.

B. EVALUATING POTENTIAL BUYERS

As mentioned above, finding a person who wants to buy your house is usually a lot easier than is finding a person who can afford to do so. Okay, assume that you accept the fact that many people who would love to live in your house can't afford to. Logically, this should lead you to the conclusion that, in order not to waste time by accepting formal offers from incurable optimists who will never qualify to purchase your house, you should do considerable preliminary financial screening. But in a world where many people are more willing to talk about their sex lives than about their bank accounts, how do you ask a stranger about her financial position?

Start by understanding that you are in the business of selling your house and that business transactions routinely involve checking credit. Another way to say this is that no one in commercial life will seriously negotiate to sell anything to an unknown person or business without carefully checking their credit. This doesn't mean you need be abrasive or insensitive in your inquiries. It does mean that you should establish a fair, but firm, procedure to check the credit of all serious prospective purchasers, and stick to it.

1. Informal Inquiries

You can often get a glimpse of the prospect's financial position in an opening conversation by asking friendly questions about the type of work they do, how they like it, how long they have worked for their present employer, and whether they currently own a house. This is not a substitute for later documentation, but it is still useful. Remember, however, that labels and titles are often deceiving, to say nothing of people who simply make false statements. I've found that if you walk outside with prospective purchasers as they leave and check their car, you can often learn a lot. For example, if someone claims to head his own prosperous company but drives a ten-year-old red Chevette with one blue fender, you will want to proceed with caution.

When should the first gently probing conversation about finances take place? Not immediately. It makes no sense to eagerly quiz every person who pokes her nose in your door about the state of her bank balance. After all, most lookers have no intention of making an offer. However, if a looker begins oohing and aahing over your newly built deck and starts planning to change the wallpaper in the kitchen, it's time to get to know both her and her financial situation a little better. If she is really interested in your house, she will appreciate your interest.

2. Credit Checks

Assuming the answers to your informal questions are satisfactory, your next step is to actually qualify the buyer as being financially able to purchase your house. To do this, you need to learn the criteria financial institutions use to qualify a person to purchase a house in your price range, unless, of course, the buyer can demonstrate that her credit has already been approved up to a level sufficient to buy your house.

Note on Advance Credit Approval: Many financial institutions will approve a prospective buyer's credit in advance. The bank issues a written guarantee that it will finance the purchase of a house in a certain price range at a certain interest rate (or range) for a set period of time, and as part of doing this may also agree to issue a bridge loan if the buyer has an existing home that must be sold. If a person with such an authorization wants to buy your house, you can skip the rest of this chapter—after you check the authenticity of the authorization, of course. Indeed, this method of advance credit approval is so efficient that some people who sell their own houses require that a prospective buyer arrange their loan authorization in advance and won't sign unless he does so.

To get basic information about a potential buyer's credit worthiness, you will need to have the buyer fill out a form like the one below.

This brings us back to a point I made at the beginning of the chapter. You need to politely but firmly require that information about a purchaser's financial situation be made available to you at a reasonably early stage in the purchase transaction. The usual (and latest advisable) time to do this is when the buyer presents you with a formal offer. Before you accept the offer, check all financial information carefully and make a conservative assessment as to whether the purchaser is likely to qualify to get a loan. If you need more information, ask for it. If you conclude that the purchaser is very unlikely to qualify, it's usually best not to accept her offer. There is simply little to be gained from dealing with the all too prevalent type of "buyer" whose optimism has run away with his common sense. You don't want to waste time signing a contract to sell the house and perhaps even take your property off the market only to find out later that the buyer is, in fact, a non-buyer because he can't finance the deal. You will find a copy of the form in the Appendix.

CREDIT INFORMATION

Name: _____

Soc. Sec. No. _____

Home phone: _____

Work phone: _____

Address: _____

_____

[ ] own   [ ] rent for $_____/mo. from

Phone:_____

Previous address if less than 2 years at current address:

_____

_____

Name, address and phone of employer:

_____

_____

_____

Title: _____

How long with employer: _____

If less than 2 years, name, address and phone of previous employer:

_____

_____

_____

Title: _____

How long with employer: _____

If less than 2 years, name, address and phone of previous employer:

_____

_____

_____

Title: _____

How long with employer: _____

Current monthly gross income: $ _____

Creditors (include holders of credit card and charge accounts):

Name	Address	Account Number

Other credit references:

_____
_____
_____
_____

Assets:

1. Checking and savings accounts

    Bank   Address
                                                    $_____
    _____ $_____
    _____ $_____
    _____ $_____

2. Stocks and bonds
                                                    $_____
    _____ $_____
    _____ $_____
    _____ $_____

3. Real estate _____

    Market value: $_____   Mortgages/liens: $_____   Net equity: $_____

4. Vehicles (make, year and market value)
                                                    $_____
    _____ $_____
    _____

5. Business
                                                    $_____
    _____ $_____
    _____

6. Other
                                                    $_____
    _____ $_____

Total assets $_____

Liabilities:		Unpaid Balance	Monthly Payment
1.	Vehicle loans _____	$_____	$_____
2.	Real estate loans _____	$_____	$_____
3.	Spousal/child support _____	$_____	$_____
4.	Other _____	$_____	$_____

Total $ _____   Monthly total $ _____

   We authorize _____ to verify our deposits with all banks, savings
and loan associations, credit unions, and stockbrokers listed above. We further authorize
_____ to receive any and all information about our credit from credit-
reporting agencies and to verify employment with the employers listed above.

_____   _____ , 19 ___
_____   _____ , 19 ___

Checking credit information and references is not usually difficult. Credit reporting agencies are one good source of this information. Some, however (including California's biggest—TRW), give information only to companies, not individuals. If you have someone's written permission, you can probably find a credit agency that will release information to you. The Credit Information form set out above provides you with this consent. If you send the form provided in this chapter, complete with the prospective buyer's signature, to Tenant Verification Services, 215 Caledonia Street, Sausalito, CA 94965, with a check for $40, it will send you a full credit report on the buyer.

Also, this form gives you permission to verify employment information and the amount the potential purchaser has on deposit in banks, savings and loan associations, credit unions, stock brokerage houses, etc. The information you obtain from all these sources should tell you whether or not the people you are dealing with are on the level. These agencies and organizations will usually not provide this information orally; you need to provide them with a copy of the credit application form.

Note: If the purchaser shows up with a parent or friend who is going to put money into the deal or co-sign a loan application, it's important to check this person's credit too.

What if a relative or friend wants to give a buyer/borrower money towards a down payment? Gift funds cannot usually exceed 95% of the down payment. In other words, at least 5% of the down payment must be the borrower/buyer's own money. Banks enforce that rule by requiring that at least 70% of that amount have been in the buyer/borrower's own account for at least three months. Sudden increases of deposit are a red flag to lenders scrutinizing the qualifications of prospective borrowers.

You should also make sure there is a letter from the donor to the recipient explaining that the gift is just that, and need not be paid back. Otherwise, it is probably going to be construed by lenders as a debt and thus make qualifications more difficult.

An alternative to checking this information yourself is to ask potential buyers to do at least some of the work for you. When they provide you with the credit application, ask them to have the various employers, banks, brokers, etc. provide you with written verification of the facts stated therein. Depending on the circumstances, this may be enough, or if you are in doubt as to the authenticity of any of these documents, you can check further.

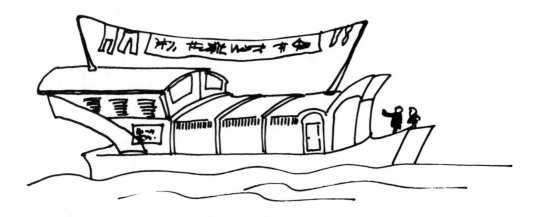

C How To Finance a Typical Home Purchase

Now that you know the gross income and significant debts of the prospective buyer, you need to figure out what the monthly payment on a loan for your house would be. If the monthly payments (including principal, interest, and monthly amounts for taxes and insurance) are more than about 28-32% of the buyer's monthly income, he probably won't qualify for a loan.

The figure varies depending on the lender's philosophy and whether money is in plentiful or short supply. Financial institutions also want to be sure that a potential borrower's other debts are not too high. Typically, a lender wants to see that a borrower's total payments, including the house payment, are no more than 36% of his gross income, although some lenders will go as high as 45% on "B minus" or "C" loans with unattractive terms for buyers.

Now, to figure much more accurately how much income a buyer must have to afford your house, let's imagine a typical sale of a house priced at $152,000. In the chart below, I analyze the financing in five different circumstances:

• **Column 1:** the buyer puts up a 20% down payment and gets a fixed-rate, 30-year deed of trust for the other 80% of the purchase price;

• **Column 2:** the buyer puts up 10% of the purchase price and gets a fixed-rate, 30-year deed of trust for the other 90% of the purchase price;

• **Column 3:** the buyer puts up a 20% down payment and gets a variable-rate, 30-year deed of trust for the other 80% of the purchase price.

• **Column 4:** the buyer puts up a 10% down payment, borrows 80% of the amount needed from a financial institution on a 30-year fixed-rate deed of trust, and the seller carries back a second deed of trust for the remaining 10%.

CAN THE BUYER AFFORD YOUR HOUSE?

Home Price (constant in all cases): $152,000

30-Year Loan For:	80% from institutional lender (fixed)	90% from institutional lender (fixed)	80% from institutional lender (variable)	80% from institution; 10% carried by owner (both fixed rates)	90% carried by owner alone; no institutional financing (fixed rate)
Amount	$121,600	$136,800	$121,600	$121,600 plus $15,200	$136,800
Interest Rate	9%	10%	8%	10% 13%	12.5%
Points (1 point is 1% of loan; assume 2 points)	$2,432	$2,736	$2,432	$2,432 none	none
Estimated Fees	$200	$290	$200	$200 none	none
Property Tax (est. per month)	$123	$123	$123	$123	$123
Fire Insurance (est. per month)	$67	$67	$67	$67	$67
Monthly Payment (principal and interest)	$978	$1,201	$892	$1,067 plus $169* = $1,236	$1,460*
Total PITI (est)	$1,176	$1,388	$1,080	$1,426	$1,650
Divide this by:	.36	.33-.45	.36	debt to income ratio required by institutional lender (no seller)	
Monthly Income	$3,239	$4,207 - $3,085	$3,000	$3,485 plus	whatever the seller feels makes it possible for the buyer to repay him
x 12 = Annual Income Necessary	$38,872	$50,402 - $37,020 (a range depending on each institution)	$36,000	$41,816 plus	whatever the seller feels makes it possible for the buyer to repay him

*Owner-carried loans typically allow a 30-year amortization to keep payments low, but the balance unpaid as of a certain date (3, 5 or 10 years) is typically due then in a "balloon payment"—up to 98-99% of the principal.

Remember, the above are illustrations only, and are no substitute for information from a bank, savings and loan association or mortgage broker in any particular case.

• **Column 5:** the buyer puts up a 10% down payment and the seller extends credit for the other 90% of the purchase price.

Common Sense Note: Of course, there are many other possible combinations of interest rates, types of deeds of trust, loan lengths, and house prices. The ones we present here are among the most common.

For these examples, I use an interest rate of:

• 9% for the fixed-rate institutional first loan for 80% of value;

• 12.5% for the owner-carried first loan for 90% of value;

• 8% for the variable-rate institutional loan;

• 10% for the institutional fixed-rate loan for 90% of the purchase price.

These interest rates are fairly typical as this book goes to press. Obviously, they may be different by the time you read these words.

The bottom line of the chart shows the gross income needed for the buyer to qualify, given the particular type of loan. It is based on the requirement, mentioned above, that the buyer's total monthly cost to purchase your house not exceed 28%-32% of her income.

After looking at the examples in the chart, it's obvious that to apply this approach to your house, so that you will know exactly how much income a prospective purchaser needs to qualify to buy your house, you have some work to do.

Step 1: Start with the asking price for your house.

Step 2: Decide what interest rate you think a buyer will have to pay based on current interest rates.

Step 3: Look at the amortization chart below and determine the monthly payment needed to amortize (pay off) that rate over whatever number of years you think is reasonable. As mentioned above, 30 years is common.

Step 4: Multiply the amount necessary to amortize $1,000 by the number of thousands the buyer will have to borrow. This is usually 80% of the sales price.

Example 1: Your house is for sale for $200,000, and the current interest rate is 9.75% for a 30-year fixed-rate deed of trust. The monthly payment necessary to pay off a $1,000 loan over 30 years at this interest rate is $8.60. The monthly payment necessary to pay off $160,000 (80% of $200,000, the sales price) is $1,374.65 (using an amortizing calculator), rounded up to $1,375 using the chart.

Example 2: If the interest rate is 11.25%, the monthly payment on a $1,000 loan is $9.72. This means the payment needed to amortize a $160,000 loan (the sales price less 20% down payment) over the same time period is $1,555.20.

AMORTIZATION CHART

NECESSARY TO FULLY AMORTIZE A LOAN OF $1,000

TERM OF YEARS	INTEREST RATE 7½% PER ANNUM		INTEREST RATE 8% PER ANNUM		INTEREST RATE 8½% PER ANNUM		INTEREST RATE 9% PER ANNUM		INTEREST RATE 9¼% PER ANNUM		INTEREST RATE 9½% PER ANNUM		INTEREST RATE 10% PER ANNUM		TERM OF YEARS
	PER MO.	PER QTR.	PER MO.	PER QTR.	PER MO.	PER QTR.	PER MO.	PER QTR.	PER MO.	PER QTR.	PER MO.	PER QTR.	PER MO.	PER QTR.	
5	20.04	60.43	20.28	61.16	20.52	61.90	20.76	62.65	20.88	63.02	21.01	63.40	21.25	64.15	5
8	13.89	41.85	14.14	42.62	14.40	43.39	14.66	44.18	14.79	44.57	14.92	44.97	15.18	45.77	8
10	11.88	35.76	12.14	36.56	12.40	37.37	12.67	38.18	12.81	38.59	12.94	39.01	13.22	39.84	10
12	10.56	31.78	10.83	32.61	11.11	33.44	11.39	34.29	11.53	34.71	11.67	35.14	11.96	36.01	12
15	9.28	27.91	9.56	28.77	9.85	29.65	10.15	30.54	10.30	30.99	10.45	31.44	10.75	32.36	15
16	8.96	26.97	9.25	27.84	9.55	28.73	9.85	29.64	10.00	30.10	10.15	30.56	10.46	31.49	16
17	8.69	26.15	8.99	27.04	9.29	27.94	9.59	28.86	9.75	29.32	9.90	29.79	10.22	30.74	17
18	8.45	25.43	8.75	26.33	9.06	27.25	9.37	28.18	9.53	28.65	9.68	29.13	10.00	30.09	18
19	8.25	24.80	8.55	25.71	8.86	26.64	9.17	27.59	9.33	28.07	9.49	28.55	9.82	29.52	19
20	8.06	24.24	8.37	25.17	8.68	26.11	9.00	27.07	9.16	27.55	9.33	28.04	9.66	29.03	20
21	7.90	23.74	8.21	24.68	8.53	25.64	8.85	26.61	9.01	27.10	9.18	27.60	9.51	28.60	21
22	7.75	23.30	8.07	24.25	8.39	25.22	8.72	26.20	8.88	26.70	9.05	27.20	9.39	28.22	22
23	7.62	22.90	7.94	23.86	8.27	24.84	8.60	25.84	8.77	26.34	8.93	26.85	9.28	27.88	23
24	7.50	22.54	7.83	23.52	8.16	24.51	8.49	25.52	8.66	26.03	8.83	26.54	9.18	27.58	24
25	7.39	22.22	7.72	23.21	8.06	24.21	8.40	25.23	8.57	25.75	8.74	26.27	9.09	27.32	25
26	7.30	21.93	7.63	22.93	7.97	23.94	8.31	24.97	8.49	25.49	8.66	26.02	9.01	27.08	26
27	7.21	21.67	7.55	22.68	7.89	23.70	8.24	24.74	8.41	25.27	8.59	25.80	8.95	26.87	27
28	7.13	21.43	7.47	22.45	7.82	23.48	8.17	24.53	8.35	25.07	8.52	25.60	8.88	26.68	28
29	7.06	21.21	7.40	22.24	7.75	23.29	8.11	24.35	8.29	24.88	8.47	25.42	8.83	26.52	29
30	7.00	21.02	7.34	22.05	7.69	23.11	8.05	24.18	8.23	24.72	8.41	25.27	8.78	26.37	30
35	6.75	20.26	7.11	21.34	7.47	22.44	7.84	23.55	8.03	24.11	8.22	24.68	8.60	25.82	35
40	6.59	19.77	6.96	20.88	7.34	22.02	7.72	23.16	7.91	23.74	8.11	24.32	8.50	25.50	40

TERM OF YEARS	INTEREST RATE 10¼% PER ANNUM		INTEREST RATE 10½% PER ANNUM		INTEREST RATE 11% PER ANNUM		INTEREST RATE 11¼% PER ANNUM		INTEREST RATE 11½% PER ANNUM		INTEREST RATE 12% PER ANNUM		INTEREST RATE 12¼% PER ANNUM		TERM OF YEARS
	PER MO.	PER QTR.	PER MO.	PER QTR.	PER MO.	PER QTR.	PER MO.	PER QTR.	PER MO.	PER QTR.	PER MO.	PER QTR.	PER MO.	PER QTR.	
5	21.38	64.53	21.50	64.91	21.75	65.68	21.87	66.06	22.00	66.45	22.25	67.22	22.38	67.61	5
8	15.31	46.18	15.45	46.58	15.71	47.40	15.85	47.81	15.98	48.22	16.26	49.05	16.40	49.47	8
10	13.36	40.26	13.50	40.68	13.78	41.54	13.92	41.97	14.06	42.40	14.35	43.27	14.50	43.71	10
12	12.10	36.45	12.25	36.89	12.54	37.78	12.69	38.22	12.84	38.67	13.14	39.58	13.29	40.04	12
15	10.90	32.82	11.06	33.29	11.37	34.23	11.53	34.70	11.69	35.18	12.01	36.14	12.17	36.62	15
16	10.62	31.96	10.78	32.43	11.10	33.39	11.26	33.87	11.42	34.35	11.74	35.33	11.91	35.83	16
17	10.38	31.22	10.54	31.70	10.86	32.67	11.02	33.16	11.19	33.65	11.52	34.65	11.68	35.15	17
18	10.16	30.57	10.33	31.06	10.66	32.05	10.82	32.55	10.99	33.05	11.32	34.06	11.49	34.57	18
19	9.98	30.02	10.15	30.51	10.48	31.51	10.65	32.02	10.82	32.53	11.16	33.55	11.33	34.07	19
20	9.82	29.53	9.99	30.03	10.33	31.05	10.50	31.56	10.67	32.08	11.02	33.12	11.19	33.64	20
21	9.68	29.10	9.85	29.61	10.19	30.64	10.37	31.16	10.54	31.68	10.89	32.74	11.07	33.27	21
22	9.56	28.73	9.73	29.25	10.08	30.29	10.25	30.81	10.43	31.34	10.78	32.41	10.96	32.95	22
23	9.45	28.40	9.62	28.92	9.98	29.98	10.15	30.51	10.33	31.04	10.69	32.12	10.87	32.67	23
24	9.35	28.11	9.53	28.63	9.89	29.70	10.06	30.24	10.25	30.78	10.61	31.87	10.79	32.42	24
25	9.27	27.85	9.45	28.38	9.81	29.46	9.99	30.00	10.17	30.55	10.54	31.65	10.72	32.21	25
26	9.19	27.62	9.37	28.16	9.74	29.25	9.92	29.79	10.10	30.35	10.47	31.46	10.66	32.02	26
27	9.13	27.41	9.31	27.96	9.67	29.06	9.86	29.61	10.05	30.17	10.42	31.29	10.61	31.86	27
28	9.07	27.23	9.25	27.78	9.62	28.89	9.81	29.45	9.99	30.01	10.37	31.14	10.56	31.71	28
29	9.01	27.07	9.20	27.62	9.57	28.74	9.76	29.30	9.95	29.87	10.33	31.01	10.52	31.58	29
30	8.97	26.92	9.15	27.48	9.53	28.61	9.72	29.18	9.91	29.75	10.29	30.89	10.48	31.47	30
35	8.79	26.39	8.99	26.97	9.37	28.14	9.57	28.72	9.77	29.31	10.16	30.49	10.36	31.09	35
40	8.69	26.09	8.89	26.68	9.29	27.87	9.49	28.47	9.69	29.07	10.09	30.27	10.29	30.88	40

TERM OF YEARS	INTEREST RATE 12½% PER ANNUM		INTEREST RATE 13% PER ANNUM		INTEREST RATE 13¼% PER ANNUM		INTEREST RATE 13½% PER ANNUM		INTEREST RATE 14% PER ANNUM		INTEREST RATE 14¼% PER ANNUM		INTEREST RATE 14½% PER ANNUM		TERM OF YEARS
	PER MO.	PER QTR.	PER MO.	PER QTR.	PER MO.	PER QTR.	PER MO.	PER QTR.	PER MO.	PER QTR.	PER MO.	PER QTR.	PER MO.	PER QTR.	
5	22.50	68.00	22.76	68.78	22.89	69.18	23.01	69.57	23.27	70.37	23.40	70.76	23.53	71.16	5
8	16.53	49.89	16.81	50.73	16.95	51.16	17.09	51.59	17.38	52.45	17.52	52.88	17.66	53.31	8
10	14.64	44.15	14.94	45.03	15.08	45.48	15.23	45.93	15.53	46.83	15.68	47.29	15.83	47.74	10
12	13.44	40.50	13.75	41.43	13.91	41.90	14.06	42.37	14.38	43.31	14.53	43.79	14.69	44.27	12
15	12.33	37.11	12.66	38.09	12.82	38.59	12.99	39.09	13.32	40.09	13.49	40.60	13.66	41.11	15
16	12.07	36.32	12.40	37.32	12.57	37.83	12.74	38.34	13.08	39.36	13.25	39.87	13.43	40.39	16
17	11.85	35.65	12.19	36.67	12.36	37.18	12.53	37.70	12.88	38.74	13.05	39.26	13.23	39.79	17
18	11.67	35.08	12.01	36.12	12.18	36.64	12.36	37.16	12.71	38.21	12.89	38.75	13.06	39.28	18
19	11.50	34.59	11.85	35.64	12.03	36.17	12.21	36.70	12.56	37.77	12.74	38.31	12.92	38.85	19
20	11.37	34.17	11.72	35.23	11.90	35.77	12.08	36.31	12.44	37.39	12.62	37.94	12.80	38.48	20
21	11.25	33.80	11.61	34.88	11.79	35.42	11.97	35.97	12.33	37.07	12.52	37.62	12.70	38.17	21
22	11.14	33.49	11.51	34.58	11.69	35.13	11.87	35.68	12.24	36.79	12.43	37.35	12.62	37.91	22
23	11.05	33.21	11.42	34.31	11.61	34.87	11.79	35.43	12.17	36.55	12.35	37.11	12.54	37.68	23
24	10.98	32.97	11.35	34.09	11.53	34.65	11.72	35.21	12.10	36.34	12.29	36.91	12.48	37.48	24
25	10.91	32.76	11.28	33.89	11.47	34.45	11.66	35.02	12.04	36.16	12.23	36.74	12.43	37.32	25
26	10.85	32.58	11.23	33.72	11.42	34.29	11.61	34.86	11.99	36.01	12.19	36.59	12.38	37.17	26
27	10.80	32.42	11.18	33.57	11.37	34.14	11.56	34.72	11.95	35.88	12.14	36.46	12.34	37.05	27
28	10.75	32.28	11.14	33.43	11.33	34.01	11.52	34.60	11.91	35.76	12.11	36.35	12.30	36.94	28
29	10.71	32.16	11.10	33.32	11.29	33.90	11.49	34.49	11.88	35.66	12.08	36.25	12.28	36.85	29
30	10.68	32.05	11.07	33.22	11.26	33.81	11.46	34.40	11.85	35.58	12.05	36.17	12.25	36.77	30
35	10.56	31.68	10.96	32.88	11.16	33.48	11.36	34.08	11.76	35.29	11.96	35.90	12.17	36.50	35
40	10.49	31.48	10.90	32.70	11.10	33.31	11.31	33.92	11.72	35.15	11.92	35.76	12.13	36.38	40

TERM OF YEARS	INTEREST RATE 15% PER ANNUM		INTEREST RATE 15¼% PER ANNUM		INTEREST RATE 15½% PER ANNUM		INTEREST RATE 16% PER ANNUM		INTEREST RATE 16¼% PER ANNUM		INTEREST RATE 16½% PER ANNUM		INTEREST RATE 17% PER ANNUM		TERM OF YEARS
	PER MO.	PER QTR.	PER MO.	PER QTR.	PER MO.	PER QTR.	PER MO.	PER QTR.	PER MO.	PER QTR.	PER MO.	PER QTR.	PER MO.	PER QTR.	
5	23.79	71.97	23.93	72.37	24.06	72.77	24.32	73.59	24.46	73.99	24.59	74.40	24.86	75.22	5
8	17.95	54.19	18.10	54.63	18.24	55.07	18.53	55.95	18.68	56.40	18.83	56.85	19.13	57.75	8
10	16.14	48.66	16.29	49.13	16.45	49.59	16.76	50.53	16.91	51.00	17.07	51.47	17.38	52.42	10
12	15.01	45.23	15.18	45.72	15.34	46.20	15.66	47.19	15.83	47.68	15.99	48.18	16.32	49.17	12
15	14.00	42.13	14.17	42.65	14.34	43.16	14.69	44.21	14.87	44.73	15.04	45.26	15.40	46.32	15
16	13.77	41.43	13.95	41.96	14.12	42.48	14.48	43.54	14.65	44.08	14.83	44.61	15.19	45.69	16
17	13.58	40.85	13.76	41.38	13.94	41.91	14.30	42.99	14.48	43.53	14.66	44.08	15.02	45.17	17
18	13.42	40.35	13.60	40.89	13.78	41.44	14.15	42.53	14.33	43.08	14.51	43.63	14.88	44.74	18
19	13.29	39.94	13.47	40.49	13.65	41.04	14.02	42.14	14.21	42.70	14.39	43.26	14.77	44.38	19
20	13.17	39.59	13.36	40.14	13.54	40.70	13.92	41.82	14.11	42.38	14.29	42.95	14.67	44.08	20
21	13.08	39.29	13.26	39.85	13.45	40.41	13.83	41.55	14.02	42.11	14.21	42.69	14.59	43.83	21
22	12.99	39.03	13.18	39.60	13.37	40.17	13.75	41.31	13.95	41.89	14.14	42.47	14.53	43.67	22
23	12.92	38.82	13.12	39.39	13.31	39.96	13.69	41.12	13.89	41.70	14.08	42.28	14.47	43.45	23
24	12.86	38.63	13.06	39.21	13.25	39.79	13.64	40.95	13.83	41.54	14.03	42.12	14.42	43.30	24
25	12.81	38.47	13.01	39.06	13.20	39.64	13.59	40.81	13.79	41.40	13.99	41.99	14.38	43.18	25
26	12.77	38.34	12.97	38.92	13.16	39.51	13.56	40.69	13.75	41.29	13.95	41.88	14.35	43.07	26
27	12.73	38.22	12.93	38.81	13.13	39.40	13.52	40.59	13.72	41.19	13.92	41.79	14.32	42.98	27
28	12.70	38.12	12.90	38.72	13.10	39.31	13.50	40.51	13.70	41.11	13.90	41.71	14.30	42.91	28
29	12.67	38.04	12.87	38.63	13.07	39.23	13.47	40.43	13.67	41.03	13.87	41.64	14.28	42.85	29
30	12.65	37.96	12.85	38.56	13.05	39.16	13.45	40.37	13.65	40.97	13.86	41.58	14.26	42.79	30
35	12.57	37.72	12.78	38.33	12.98	38.95	13.39	40.17	13.59	40.78	13.80	41.40	14.21	42.63	35
40	12.54	37.61	12.74	38.23	12.95	38.84	13.36	40.08	13.57	40.70	13.77	41.32	14.19	42.56	40

TERM OF YEARS	INTEREST RATE 17½% PER ANNUM		INTEREST RATE 18% PER ANNUM		INTEREST RATE 18½% PER ANNUM		INTEREST RATE 19% PER ANNUM		INTEREST RATE 19½% PER ANNUM		INTEREST RATE 20% PER ANNUM		INTEREST RATE 20½% PER ANNUM		TERM OF YEARS
	PER MO.	PER QTR.	PER MO.	PER QTR.	PER MO.	PER QTR.	PER MO.	PER QTR.	PER MO.	PER QTR.	PER MO.	PER QTR.	PER MO.	PER QTR.	
5	25.13	76.05	25.40	76.88	25.67	77.72	25.95	78.56	26.22	79.40	26.50	80.25	26.78	81.10	5
8	19.43	58.65	19.73	59.57	20.03	60.49	20.34	61.41	20.65	62.35	20.96	63.29	21.27	64.23	8
10	17.70	53.38	18.02	54.35	18.35	55.32	18.67	56.30	19.00	57.29	19.33	58.28	19.66	59.28	10
12	16.66	50.18	17.00	51.19	17.34	52.22	17.68	53.24	18.02	54.28	18.37	55.32	18.72	56.37	12
15	15.75	47.38	16.11	48.46	16.47	49.54	16.83	50.63	17.20	51.73	17.57	52.83	17.94	53.94	15
16	15.55	46.77	15.92	47.87	16.28	48.97	16.65	50.07	17.03	51.19	17.40	52.31	17.78	53.44	16
17	15.39	46.27	15.76	47.38	16.13	48.50	16.51	49.62	16.88	50.75	17.26	51.88	17.65	53.03	17
18	15.26	45.86	15.63	46.98	16.01	48.11	16.39	49.25	16.77	50.39	17.15	51.54	17.54	52.70	18
19	15.15	45.51	15.53	46.65	15.91	47.79	16.29	48.94	16.68	50.10	17.07	51.26	17.46	52.43	19
20	15.05	45.23	15.44	46.38	15.82	47.53	16.21	48.69	16.60	49.86	16.99	51.03	17.39	52.21	20
21	14.98	44.99	15.37	46.15	15.76	47.32	16.15	48.49	16.54	49.67	16.93	50.85	17.33	52.04	21
22	14.91	44.79	15.31	45.96	15.70	47.14	16.09	48.32	16.49	49.51	16.89	50.70	17.29	51.89	22
23	14.86	44.62	15.26	45.80	15.65	46.99	16.05	48.18	16.45	49.37	16.85	50.57	17.25	51.78	23
24	14.82	44.48	15.21	45.67	15.61	46.87	16.01	48.06	16.41	49.27	16.82	50.47	17.22	51.68	24
25	14.78	44.37	15.18	45.56	15.58	46.76	15.98	47.97	16.39	49.18	16.79	50.39	17.20	51.60	25
26	14.75	44.27	15.15	45.47	15.55	46.68	15.96	47.89	16.36	49.10	16.76	50.32	17.18	51.54	26
27	14.72	44.19	15.13	45.40	15.53	46.61	15.94	47.82	16.34	49.04	16.75	50.26	17.16	51.49	27
28	14.70	44.12	15.11	45.33	15.51	46.55	15.92	47.77	16.33	48.99	16.74	50.22	17.15	51.45	28
29	14.68	44.06	15.09	45.28	15.50	46.50	15.91	47.72	16.31	48.95	16.72	50.18	17.14	51.41	29
30	14.67	44.01	15.08	45.23	15.48	46.46	15.89	47.69	16.30	48.92	16.72	50.15	17.13	51.38	30
35	14.62	43.86	15.03	45.10	15.45	46.34	15.86	47.58	16.27	48.82	16.69	50.06	17.10	51.30	30
40	14.60	43.80	15.02	45.04	15.43	46.29	15.85	47.53	16.26	48.78	16.68	50.03	17.09	51.27	30

TERM OF YEARS	INTEREST RATE 21% PER ANNUM		INTEREST RATE 21½% PER ANNUM		INTEREST RATE 22% PER ANNUM		INTEREST RATE 22½% PER ANNUM		INTEREST RATE 23% PER ANNUM		INTEREST RATE 23½% PER ANNUM		INTEREST RATE 24% PER ANNUM		TERM OF YEARS
	PER MO.	PER QTR.	PER MO.	PER QTR.	PER MO.	PER QTR.	PER MO.	PER QTR.	PER MO.	PER QTR.	PER MO.	PER QTR.	PER MO.	PER QTR.	
5	27.06	81.96	27.34	82.82	27.62	83.68	27.91	84.55	28.20	85.43	28.48	86.31	28.77	87.19	5
8	21.59	65.18	21.90	66.14	22.22	67.10	22.54	68.07	22.87	69.04	23.19	70.02	23.52	71.01	8
10	20.00	60.29	20.34	61.31	20.67	62.33	21.02	63.35	21.36	64.38	21.71	65.42	22.05	66.47	10
12	19.07	57.43	19.43	58.49	19.78	59.56	20.14	60.64	20.50	61.72	20.87	62.81	21.23	63.90	12
15	18.31	55.06	18.69	56.18	19.06	57.31	19.44	58.45	19.82	59.59	20.20	60.73	20.59	61.88	15
16	18.15	54.57	18.53	55.71	18.92	56.85	19.30	58.00	19.69	59.16	20.07	60.32	20.46	61.48	16
17	18.03	54.17	18.41	55.33	18.80	56.49	19.19	57.65	19.58	58.82	19.97	59.99	20.36	61.17	17
18	17.93	53.86	18.32	55.02	18.71	56.19	19.10	57.37	19.49	58.55	19.89	59.73	20.29	60.92	18
19	17.85	53.60	18.24	54.78	18.63	55.96	19.03	57.15	19.43	58.34	19.83	59.53	20.23	60.73	19
20	17.78	53.40	18.18	54.58	18.58	55.77	18.97	56.97	19.38	58.17	19.78	59.37	20.18	60.58	20
21	17.73	53.23	18.13	54.42	18.53	55.62	18.93	56.83	19.33	58.03	19.74	59.24	20.14	60.46	21
22	17.69	53.09	18.09	54.30	18.49	55.50	18.90	56.71	19.30	57.93	19.71	59.14	20.11	60.36	22
23	17.65	52.98	18.06	54.19	18.46	55.41	18.87	56.62	19.27	57.84	19.68	59.06	20.09	60.29	23
24	17.62	52.89	18.03	54.11	18.44	55.33	18.84	56.55	19.25	57.77	19.66	59.00	20.07	60.23	24
25	17.60	52.82	18.01	54.04	18.42	55.27	18.83	56.49	19.24	57.72	19.65	58.95	20.06	60.18	25
26	17.58	52.76	17.99	53.99	18.40	55.22	18.81	56.45	19.22	57.68	19.63	58.91	20.05	60.15	26
27	17.57	52.71	17.98	53.94	18.39	55.17	18.80	56.41	19.21	57.64	19.62	58.88	20.04	60.12	27
28	17.56	52.68	17.97	53.91	18.38	55.14	18.79	56.38	19.20	57.61	19.62	58.85	20.03	60.09	28
29	17.55	52.64	17.96	53.88	18.37	55.12	18.78	56.35	19.20	57.59	19.61	58.83	20.03	60.07	29
30	17.54	52.62	17.95	53.86	18.36	55.09	18.78	56.33	19.19	57.58	19.61	58.82	20.01	60.06	30
35	17.52	52.55	17.93	53.79	18.35	55.04	18.76	56.28	19.18	57.53	19.59	58.77	20.01	60.02	35
40	17.51	52.52	17.93	53.77	18.34	55.02	18.76	56.26	19.17	57.51	19.59	58.76	20.01	60.01	40

Note: If you hate making even simple calculations, you can purchase a calculator to do it for you. Amortizing calculators vary as to bells, whistles and prices. One top-of-the-line model is the HP-12C, produced by Hewlett Packard Company, which sells for about $120. For less than a quarter of that, you can purchase the Texas Instruments Student Business Analyst (TI-BA-35), which will do a loan amortization just as well. You can probably pick up a TI-BA-35 at a discount store for about $20.

When you arrive at the monthly payment needed to pay off a loan on your house, add to it a reasonable monthly amount to cover taxes and insurance. You can use the amounts you pay for your homeowner's insurance as a rough guide, although remember the buyer will have to pay somewhat more if you expect to sell the house for more than its currently appraised value. You can usually get quotes in advance from fire insurance agents, and there's a good chance that the fire insurance premium for the new owner won't vary too much from your own if you've kept your coverage current with inflation.

When it comes to real estate taxes, remember that under California's Proposition 13, the new owner will begin paying tax on the new assessed value (market price) pro-rated as of the date of transfer of title, according to the following formula:

Market Value	**x1%**	**= Annual Tax**
Actual Price (as of date of sale, less $7,000 homeowner's exemption if new owner lives on the property and furnishes this information to the County)	(or other rate in county, to allow for voter approved bonds— for instance, in San Francisco County recent rates have been 1.11-1.17% of assessed value)	(divide by 12 to find the monthly tax equivalent, even though tax is not actually paid on a monthly basis)

Now, to arrive at the income level a typical purchaser needs to buy your house, you have to do just a little more arithmetic. As I said earlier in this chapter, a financial institution normally requires that a buyer be able to pay the PITI (loan interest, taxes and insurance payments) and all other debts with about 36% of his gross income. To arrive at this number, divide the PITI by .36 (36%). This will tell you the monthly gross income needed, assuming there are no other monthly debts and assuming the lender's qualification ratio is, indeed, 36%.

Other debts lenders consider significant are what they call "long term" debts, i.e., debts involving payments that last longer than ten months. This includes most revolving charge accounts at department stores, spousal and child support payment obligations, car purchase or lease payments, etc. Some lenders are willing to loan to borrowers whose total debts and PITI, combined, are somewhat more than 36% of monthly gross income, as I mentioned above, providing the borrower is willing to pay a little more. For instance, a lender might insist on a higher interest rate, or more points, or a shorter amortization period for the loan—or even a 30-year amortization—but with the balance all due and payable in shorter time, like 15 years. For the simplificity of illustration in this chapter, I assume that a PITI of 36% is the total debt obligation of the borrower. However, if the prospective purchaser also has $500 a month in long-term debt payments, it would be necessary to add this $500 to the PITI and then divide that amount by .36. The point should be obvious. The more debts the prospective purchaser has, the more monthly gross income she needs to qualify for a loan.

CHAPTER 9

THE HOUSE SALE CONTRACT

This chapter takes you on a brief but extremely important detour from the step-by-step path to selling your house followed by the rest of the book. Its purpose is to discuss in detail all the elements of the real estate contract you'll be entering into. Here I set out a contract and explain each clause. I ask you to take the time to study this material carefully because I believe it is essential that you know what the fine print in a real estate contract means before you get involved in negotiating your own. In Chapter 10, I go back to the step-by-step process of receiving the offers of potential buyers, negotiating, and then, by accepting an offer, entering into the kind of contract that is discussed in this chapter.

A. How Contracts Are Formed

A contract to purchase real estate must be in writing to be enforceable. A written contract comes into existence when:

• a buyer makes a written offer to purchase and the seller accepts it in writing in the time provided, unless the buyer withdraws the offer prior to acceptance; or

• a seller makes a written counter-offer to a buyer's offer to purchase and the buyer accepts that in writing in the time allowed (and before it is withdrawn).

It is important to understand that a seller's advertisement to sell a house at a certain price is not a formal offer. As I discuss in more detail in the next chapter, the seller has no legal obligation to sell at the price and on the terms she advertises in a newspaper, on a sign, as part of a multiple listing service, or anywhere else.

To form a binding contract to sell your house, there is no need for offer and acceptance to be combined in one document. Indeed, in many situations, most of the fine print terms of the contract are in the buyer's original written offer, with the seller's acceptance consisting of a short written statement on a separate piece of paper.

Example: Homer advertises his house for $200,000 in the newspaper. Millie, using the detailed written offer form set out in this chapter, offers $190,000. Homer accepts Millie's offer by writing: "I accept the offer of Millie to purchase my house, dated February 8, 1987." Homer and Millie have a binding contract.

Reminder: Both buyer and seller must be sane adults (or "emancipated" minors[1]) in order to create a binding contract. If either is married, the signature of his spouse is needed (see Chapter 2).

B. THE REAL ESTATE CONTRACT

Now it's time to focus on your house sale contract in detail. The best way to do this is to read the sample offer set out immediately below and the accompanying explanation of its terms (you will find a tear-out copy of this offer in the Appendix). Remember, an offer (or counter-offer) automatically becomes a binding contract when it is accepted in writing (and has not been previously revoked) during the time period for which it is extended. For the rest of this chapter, I assume that a buyer has used the offer form contained in this book (or one of several commercially published in California that are similar), and that you, the seller, want to accept it. We refer to theaccepted offer as a contract.

---

[1]Civil Code Sec. 60 et seq.

OFFER TO PURCHASE REAL PROPERTY

Property address:
324 LAFAYETTE AVE., SAN FRANCISCO, CA.
SCOTT GARDENER AND RACHEL GARDENER, Buyer(s),
herein offer to _KAREN SHULTZ_, Seller(s)
to purchase the property described above, on the terms set out below.

1. Purchase Price and Down Payment

ONE HUNDRED TWENTY THOUSAND DOLLARS to be paid as follows:

Down payment of $_24,000.00_, in cash, to be paid into escrow on or before close of escrow.

Deposits as specified in Section 2 below.

Balance of purchase price to be paid on or before close of escrow.

2. Deposit

A deposit of $_1,000.00_, in the form of a _CASHIER'S_ check made out to _ABC TITLE CO._, is submitted with this offer. The check will be held by the Seller uncashed until and unless this offer is accepted, and will be returned to the Buyer if this offer is not accepted. If this offer is accepted, the check will be deposited with the escrow holder.

This deposit will be increased to a total of $_6,000.00_ upon removal of all contingencies in this contract or not later than _FEBRUARY 20_, 1987, whichever is earlier.

3. Liquidated Damages

If Buyer defaults on this contract, Seller shall be released from Seller's obligations under this contract and, by signing their initials here, Buyer _SG   RG_ **and Seller _____ agree that Seller shall keep all deposits, up to an amount equal to three percent (3%) of the purchase price stated above.**

4. Dispute Resolution

Disputes arising from this contract shall be settled:

[X] by binding arbitration under the rules of the American Arbitration Association.
[ ] according to the laws of California.

5. Attorney's Fees

If litigation or arbitration arises from this contract, the prevailing party shall be reimbursed by the other party for reasonable attorney's fees and court or arbitration costs.

Page 1

6. Contingencies

This offer is conditioned upon the following:

☒ Submittal to Seller of Buyer's written approval of the following inspection reports, indicating Buyer's acceptance of the physical condition of the property, by ___FEB. 10___, 19*87*. Buyer shall have the following inspections of the property made, at Buyer's expense.

    ☒ Inspection by a licensed Pest Control Operator
    ☒ Inspection by a licensed General Contractor as to the physical condition of the property in general, including, but not necessarily limited to, heating and plumbing, electrical systems, solar energy systems, roof and condition of appliances included in this transaction
    [ ] Inspection by a licensed Plumbing Contractor
    [ ] Inspection by a licensed Roofing Contractor
    [ ] Inspection by a licensed Energy Conservation Inspector in accordance with local ordinances
    [ ] Inspection by a geologist registered with the State of California
    [ ] Other _____

☒ Buyer's obtaining of financing as specified in Section 13 below, by _FEB. 15_, 19*87*.

[ ] Written consent of the present lender(s), within _____ days of acceptance of this offer, to Buyer's assumption of any existing loans on the property.

[ ] Receipt of, and approval by Buyer of preliminary title report within _____ days of acceptance of this offer.

☒ At close of escrow, title to the property is to be clear of all liens and encumbrances of record except those listed in the preliminary title report.

[ ] Sale of Buyer's current residence at _____ in _____, _____ County, State of _____ not later than _____, 19__.

If Buyer, after making a good-faith effort, cannot remove in writing the above contingencies by the dates specified, this contract shall become void, and all deposits shall be returned to Buyer.

7. Escrow

Title insurance company selected by Buyer and Seller is:
_____ABC TITLE CO._____

Escrow company selected by Buyer and Seller is:
_____.

Buyer and Seller agree to execute escrow instructions by _MARCH 1_, 19*87*. Buyer and Seller agree that deed shall be recorded in favor of Buyer and all net proceeds of sale distributed to Seller no later than _MARCH 10_, 19*87*.

8. Prorations

Seller shall be responsible for payment of Seller's prorated share of real estate taxes accrued until recordation of the deed.

Buyer agrees to assume non-callable assessment bond liens (i.e., those which cannot be paid off early by the Seller) as follows: _____ *NONE* _____.

9. Possession

Seller shall deliver physical possession of property to Buyer

       [X] at close of escrow.
       [] no later than _____ days after the close of escrow.

If Seller continues to occupy the property after close of escrow, Seller shall pay to Buyer $*28.00* _____ for each such day.

10. Fixtures

All fixtures, including built-in appliances, electrical, plumbing, light and hearing fixtures, garage door openers, attached carpets and other floor coverings, and window shades or blinds, are included in the sale except:

_____ *DINING ROOM CHANDELIER* _____

_____.

11. Personal Property

The following items of personal property are included in this transaction:

_____ *STOVE AND REFRIGERATOR IN KITCHEN* _____

_____.

12. Risk of Damage to Property

If, before Buyer has received title to the property or possession of the property, the premises of the property are substantially damaged by fire, flood, earthquake or other cause, Buyer shall be relieved of any obligation to buy the property and shall have all deposits returned to him. When Buyer receives title to or possession of the property, Buyer assumes sole responsibility for the physical condition of the property.

Seller is responsible for maintaining fire insurance on the property until the date of recordation of the deed.

13. Buyer's Financing

Buyer shall, by the date specified in the financing contingency of Clause 6, provide Seller with written evidence of having obtained financing as described below:

First Loan:

$*96,000.00*_____ Amount of loan amortized over not less than ___*30*___ years.

$*850.00*_____ Maximum amount of monthly loan payment including principal, interest and, if applicable, private mortgage insurance (PMI), but not including taxes or insurance on the property (e.g., fire insurance), during the first year of the loan agreement.

      [X] Conventional (non-subsidized)
      [ ] Owner financing
      [ ] VA   [ ] FHA   [ ] Cal-Vet
      [ ] Other: _____

      [X] *TWELVE*_____ % fixed rate **or**

      [X] *TEN*_____ % beginning rate on an adjustable rate loan, with the highest possible rate not to exceed __*THIRTEEN*_____ % and rate to be adjusted not more frequently than ___*ONCE PER YEAR*_____ .

Loan origination fee (points) of not more than ___*THREE*___ % of the loan amount and application. Appraisal fees to total not more than $*350.00*_____ , with no balloon payment unless stated below: ___*NONE*_____ .

Second Loan:

$_____ Amount of loan amortized over not less than _____ years.

$_____ Maximum amount of monthly loan payment including principal, interest and, if applicable, private mortgage insurance (PMI), but not including taxes or insurance on the property (e.g., fire insurance), during the first year of the loan agreement.

      [ ] Conventional (non-subsidized)
      [ ] Owner financing
      [ ] Other: _____

      [ ]_____ % fixed rate **or**

      [ ]_____ % beginning rate on an adjustable rate loan, with the highest possible rate not to exceed _____ % and rate to be adjusted not more frequently than _____ .

Loan origination fee (points) of not more than _____ % of the loan amount and application. Appraisal fees to total not more than $_____ , with no balloon payment unless stated below: _____ .

Third Loan:

$_____ Amount of loan amortized over not less than _____ years.

$_____ Maximum amount of monthly loan payment including principal, interest and, if applicable, private mortgage insurance (PMI), but not including taxes or insurance on the property (e.g., fire insurance), during the first year of the loan agreement.

[ ] Conventional (non-subsidized)
[ ] Owner financing
[ ] Other: _____

[ ] _____ % fixed rate **or**

[ ] _____ % beginning rate on an adjustable rate loan, with the highest possible rate not to exceed _____ % and rate to be adjusted not more frequently than _____.

Loan origination fee (points) of not more than _____ % of the loan amount and application. Appraisal fees to total not more than $_____, with no balloon payment unless stated below: _____.

Subsidized Loans:

If any of the above loans involves a state or federal government agency, the Buyer shall provide to the Seller, within ten (10) business days of acceptance of this offer, copies of any documents pertinent to Buyer's eligibility for the loan(s), e.g.:

[ ] DD-1 for Cal-Vet
[ ] Certificate of Eligibility for VA
[ ] Other:_____

14. Expenses of Sale

Expenses of sale shall be paid for as follows:

Buyer	Seller	Both equally	
[ ]	[ ]	[X]	Escrow fees
[X]	[ ]	[ ]	Title search
[X]	[ ]	[ ]	CLTA policy for Buyer
[X]	[ ]	[ ]	ALTA extended policy for lender(s)
[ ]	[X]	[ ]	Documentary transfer tax
			Recording and Notary fees
[X]	[ ]	[ ]	Grant deed
[ ]	[X]	[ ]	Reconveyance of existing trust deed
[X]	[ ]	[ ]	Trust deed(s)

15. Seller's Disclosures

Buyer acknowledges receipt from Seller of

ꭗ Seller's Real Estate Transfer Disclosure Statement (Cal. Civ. Code § 1102) dated ___DEC. 30___ , 19_86_.

[] Other inspection reports obtained by Seller, as follows:

Type   Preparer   Date

_____

_____

_____

_____

_____

[] Documents set out in Civil Code § 1368 relating to condominiums and other common interest developments.

[] Documents containing all conditions, covenants, and restrictions that affect the property.

16. Time is of the Essence

Time is of the essence in this transaction.

17. Duration of Offer

This offer is submitted to the Seller by the Buyer on ___JANUARY 10___ , 19_87_ at ___5:00___ _P._.M., Pacific Time, and will be considered revoked if not accepted by seller in writing by ___5:00___ _P._.M. on ___JANUARY 13___ , 19_87_, or if Buyer communicates in writing to Seller, prior to notification of acceptance of this offer by Seller, Buyer's revocation of this offer.

18. Commission to Brokers

Seller shall pay only those broker's commissions for which Seller has separately contracted in writing with a broker licensed by the California Commissioner of Real Estate.

If Buyer or Seller wishes advice concerning the legal or tax aspects of this transaction, Buyer or Seller shall separately contract and pay for it.

19. Credit Information

Buyer shall deliver to Seller, within ___TWO___ days of submittal of this offer, information showing Buyer's financial condition on a form provided by Seller. Seller shall keep the statement confidential. Buyer will also authorize disclosure to Seller of credit information about Buyer from credit card and charge account holders, banks, savings and loan associations, credit unions and brokerages where Buyer has accounts, and from credit-reporting agencies.

20. Entire Agreement

This document represents the entire agreement between Buyer and Seller. Any modifications or amendments to this contract shall be made in writing, signed and dated by both parties.

21. Foreign Investors

If Seller is a foreign person as defined in the Foreign Investment in Real Property Act, Buyer shall, absent a specific exemption, have withheld in escrow ten percent (10 %) of the gross sale price of the property. Buyer and Seller shall execute and provide the escrow holder specified in Clause 7 above with all documentation required by the Act.

22. Rent Control

The property [X] is [ ] is not located in a city or county subject to local rent control. A rent control ordinance may restrict the rent that can be charged for this property.

23. Transfer Requirements

Local and state law may require certain disclosures, inspections, modifications or repairs before transfer of the property, including (but not limited to):

   Disclosure that property is located in a Special Flood Hazard Area as set forth on a Federal Emergency Management Agency "Flood Insurance Rate Map" or "Flood Hazard Boundary Map."

   Smoke detector(s) installed and operational.

   Local energy efficiency ordinance requirements met.

   Disclosure that property is in a special studies (earthquake) area.

   Payment of local anti-speculation taxes.

   Other:_____N/A_____
   _____
   _____

Seller shall take responsibility for complying with all such applicable requirements except:
_____NONE_____
_____

24. Seller's Right to Accept Backup Offers

Seller may enter into subsequent contracts with other persons for sale of the property. Any such contracts shall be contingent on the termination of the contract between Buyer and Seller. Seller shall notify all other offerors of the existence (though not necessarily the terms) of this offer.

Page 7

25. Seller's Right to Demand Removal of Contingencies

If, any time at least two weeks from the date Buyer and Seller enter into a contract for purchase of the property, Seller gives Buyer a written demand to remove all contingencies in Clause 6 of this contract concerning inspection reports and/or the Buyer's ability to arrange financing and/or get approval for assumption of loans, and/or the Buyer's ability to sell an existing residence, Buyer shall have ninety-six (96) hours from receipt of the demand if personally delivered (or five days from the date of mailing, if the demand is mailed by certified mail) in which to remove all these contingencies. If Buyer cannot do so, then this contract shall be terminated immediately, Buyer and Seller shall sign a mutual release, and all deposits shall be returned to Buyer.

26. Other Terms and Conditions

NONE

27. Notice to Backup Offeror(s)   [To be completed only if Buyer is a backup offeror]

Buyer is aware that Seller has entered into contracts for the sale of the property with:

N/A

and that Seller's acceptance of Buyer's offer is contingent upon the contracts with the above persons no longer being in force, either by default on the part of the above offeror(s) or because the above offeror(s) cannot remove contingencies as provided for in their contract(s).

28. Buyer's Signature

Buyer has read and understands Clauses 1-27 of this contract, which constitute the entire offer Buyer hereby makes to Seller.

Buyer(s) signature(s)

Scott Gardener   Date: Jan. 10 , 1987

Rachel Gardener   Time: 5:00 P. M.

29. Acceptance By Seller(s)

Seller(s) accept(s) this offer as stated.
Seller(s)' signature(s):

_____   Date:_____, 19___

_____   Time:_____ M.

Here now is an explanation of each important provision of the contract, along with some practical suggestions for filling in the blanks. As discussed in Chapter 10 in more detail, each of these provisions can be negotiated by you and the buyer.

Preliminary Information: The first items on the offer are blanks for the names of the buyers and sellers and the address of the property. The full names of all the parties (all co-owners of the property and their spouses) should be used. A street address is sufficient for the property address at this stage of the transaction. If for some reason the property can't be identified by a street address, just describe it unambiguously ("the Norris Ranch on County Highway 305, two miles south of Geyserville") or attach a legal description to the contract and refer to that in the appropriate blank as follows: "See Attachment A, Legal Description."[2]

Note: Don't forget to exchange home and work phone numbers.

1. Purchase Price and Down Payment

Here the buyer both enters the entire purchase price he is offering and specifies the amount of the down payment. As I discuss in Chapter 8 in the section on seller financing, if the buyer is not willing to come up with 20% down, warning flags should be flying, unless you are willing to carry back a second deed of trust. It can be difficult to arrange a commercial loan for more than 80% of the purchase price. In Clause 13 of this contract, the buyer is asked to specify exactly how financing will be arranged.

---

[2]The legal description is the description of the property on the deed.

2. Deposit

In exchange for signing a contract with a buyer and tying up the property, the seller typically expects some money up front in the form of a deposit or "earnest money." As discussed in Chapter 10, Section D, this is commonly in the range of $1,000 to begin with, or $2,000 or more if the house is in the luxury class. In addition, most real estate sale contracts, including the one set out in this chapter, require that the buyer increase the deposit by a certain date or when the various contractual contingencies are met (e.g., the loan is approved, the buyer OK's the pest control report, etc.). Usually the final amount of the deposit, just before the sale goes through, is in the range of 5% to 10% of the purchase price.

Note: Make sure the final date for removal of contingencies is not more than a month from acceptance of the offer unless there is a potentially troublesome contingency such as the need to sell an existing residence.

3. Liquidated Damages for Breach of Contract

What happens if a buyer backs out on a deal? Can the seller keep the deposit? It depends on both the terms of the written contract and the circumstances. Under the terms of the contract in this book (which is fairly standard), if one or more of the contingencies written into the contract is unfulfilled (e.g., the buyer fails to qualify for a loan, the pest control inspection is not satisfactory to the buyer), the seller must return the entire deposit. However, if the buyer defaults—that is, just backs out of the deal for no good reason or fails to make a good faith effort to remove the contingencies (e.g., doesn't even apply for a loan), the deposit need not be returned. The amount of the deposit that the seller may keep if the buyer defaults is called "liquidated damages." By adopting this provision, it means that buyer and seller agree that in case of buyer's default, instead of going to court and arguing about how the seller was damaged by the default, the buyer and seller decide beforehand what the seller's damages will be. However, California law restricts the amount of the deposit the seller can keep, even if the buyer backs out of the deal without adequate reason, to 3% of the agreed-upon sales price of the house.[3] By law, the liquidated damages provision must be in at least 10-point bold type and separately signed or initialed by both parties. This makes clear that they have an

---

[3]Civil Code Sec. 1675 states that liquidated damages that exceed 3% of the purchase price of residential property with one to four units (one of which the buyer intends to occupy as his personal residence) are generally invalid unless the seller establishes that a larger amount is reasonable.

option to not agree to liquidated damages, in which case a dispute would be headed for the courtroom.

It's important to realize, however, that in practice, sellers rarely get to keep a buyer's deposit, even if the buyer backs out of the deal. Why? Because a contract to purchase a house almost always contains one or more contingency clauses (e.g., the sale is contingent upon the buyer getting financing). These are usually written fairly broadly to give the buyer considerable discretion to pull out of the deal if she isn't completely satisfied. For example, if the purchase is contingent upon the buyer approving the results of various physical inspections, all the buyer has to do to get out of the deal without penalty is not approve. Similarly, if a sale is contingent upon a purchaser selling her existing house within a certain period of time, she can effectively queer the deal with you simply by dragging her feet. Although buyers are legally required to use "good faith" in attempting to fulfill the contractual contingencies, the practical problems of proving bad faith make it difficult to enforce this requirement in most circumstances. In addition, title companies generally require written approval of both parties, or a court order, before they'll release the deposit money from escrow. What all this amounts to is that while a deposit check is some indication of a buyer's seriousness about wanting to buy your house, you are very unlikely to get to keep it if the buyer wants to back out of the deal.

4. Dispute Resolution

This clause lets you pick whether you want to settle any disputes that may arise by arbitration or according to the laws of California (in the courts). I usually recommend choosing the arbitration alternative. Arbitration is a private way to solve disagreements—you must pay for it. In the long run, however, it is almost always considerably cheaper and faster than the court system. An arbitrator, in many ways, is like a judge without a jury. You and the other party can agree on your own arbitrator(s) or go to an organization that provides them, such as the American Arbitration Association (AAA). The contract provides that the arbitration is governed under AAA rules, which set out detailed procedures and make the arbitrator's decision final. Neither party can normally obtain review of the decision in a court.

5. Attorney's Fees

The contract we provide makes the losing party in litigation or arbitration responsible for both sides' attorney fees and court costs. This is standard.

6. Contingencies

Real estate contracts almost always contain contingencies. For example, the buyer's acceptance is commonly contingent on a satisfactory structural pest control inspection and the buyer arranging financing. What this amounts to is this: if a contract contains one or more contingencies, there is absolutely no certainty that your house is sold when you sign a contract with a buyer. Indeed, if there are a number of contingencies written into the deal, you simply do not have a deal that fully binds both parties, but rather an expression of the buyer's intention. If that intention changes, the buyer can normally find a number of reasons not to go through with the deal.

Common contractual contingencies include:

√ **Physical Inspections:** The house will pass certain types of physical inspections (the common ones are listed in the contract in this chapter). The most important inspection under California law[4] deals with structural pest control (termites, fungal conditions, beetles, etc.), but it is also normal and wise from both the buyer's and the seller's point of view to make sale of the house contingent upon satisfactory (to the buyer) inspections of wiring, plumbing, and the roof. The contract set out in this chapter allows the buyer to indicate which inspections she wants and makes completion of the sale contingent on the reports being satisfactory to the buyer. Normally, 20 working days is a reasonable time to allow for the buyer to arrange for inspections and get reports. However, if you have already had the house inspected and know that it is in excellent condition, you may want to shorten this time. Inspections can often be accomplished in a week or two, if need be.

Note: The seller should never agree in advance to pay for needed repairs discovered by inspection reports. If the buyer tries to require this in her offer, the seller should eliminate this requirement in his counter-offer, or agree to be obligated to make repairs up to a certain dollar amount only.

√ **Financing:** Virtually all contracts contain a contingency that financing be available to the buyer on reasonable terms. If you agree to this contingency, you can reduce the possibility of later grief by doing four things.

1. Reread Chapter 8 and make sure you understand how much cash and income the buyer needs to purchase your house.

2. Get credit information from the buyer (on a form like the one in the Appendix) and check it. Don't accept offers from people who clearly don't qualify.

3. Limit the time in which the buyer must arrange financing. Make sure that this time is reasonably short.

4. Include a 96-hour wipeout clause in your contract (clause 25). This provision allows the seller to get out of the deal after two weeks on 96 hours notice to the buyer to satisfy all contingencies if the seller gets another satisfactory offer. It reduces the possibility that the seller will have to wait around for months while the buyer tries to get financing, only to learn that she can't.

√ **Selling an Existing Home:** If the buyer owns a home already, then she often needs to sell it to buy yours, unless, of course, she has been able to arrange a bridge loan with a bank (see Chapter 8) or you are dealing with someone with enough money to own two homes at the same time. Obviously, before you agree

---

[4]Secs. 8516, 8518, 8519 and 8614 of the Business and Professions Code, and Sec. 1099 of the Civil Code refer to Structural Pest Control Inspections and Reports. Suffice it to say that such a report is generally required in the transfer of residential property except when the right to such a report is waived by the buyer and the buyer has not been induced by the seller or any agent to make such a waiver. Even then, the waiver may become a moot point, since most lenders require such a report. For all practical purposes, this means you had better plan on it.

to a contingency which states that the buyer must sell her existing home before closing on yours, you want to consider whether the buyer is likely to be able to sell her present home. For instance, is she talking about a realistic sales price? (Comparable sales data, such as you obtained in appraising your own home, can help you answer this question. See Chapter 5.) Since you are selling your own home, you should have a pretty good idea of whether your buyers are acting reasonably to sell their house.

Note on 96-Hour Wipeout Clause: Including a 96-hour wipeout clause (Clause 25 of the contract) in the contract can go a long way towards allowing you to relax if the buyer makes his offer contingent upon selling his house. As long as you have this clause in the contract, you can look for another buyer if the original deal looks like it may be stalled because the first buyer's house hasn't sold. If you find a second buyer, you can, after allowing two weeks from the date of contract signing, give the first person 96 hours' written notice to satisfy the financing contingency. If he can't, the contract is over and you can go ahead and sell to another purchaser.

Warning: To repeat, never sign a contract with a buyer unless you are pretty sure she can afford to buy your house. If you have doubts, ask the buyer to go to a financial institution and arrange advance loan authorization in an amount necessary to buy your house. If the buyer needs a loan from a relative or someone else to close the deal, make sure that person has the money and is committed in writing to make the loan.

√ **Title:** All contracts also contain a contingency that the deal will not go through unless title to the house is in suitable condition to be conveyed. This means there are no legal claims against the title to the property by previous lenders or owners unknown to the present buyer. As discussed in more detail in Chapter 11, this title contingency is normally satisfied when a title company checks the title and issues a title report. The title report takes care of disclosing most of the encumbrances that can "cloud title." It is by no means impossible to conclude a transaction when unexpected encumbrances are discovered, even if they cannot all be eliminated. However, you may need the help of a lawyer.

If any of the buyer's or seller's contractual contingencies can't be met in the time specified in the contract, after a good faith attempt to do so, there is no deal. From the time a written sales contract is signed, it sometimes takes as long as several months to satisfy all contingencies. Unfortunately, in many instances one or more contingencies is never met (e.g., the buyer is unable to sell her existing house, so can't arrange financing). The unhappy result is that the sale falls through and the house goes back on the market.

7. Escrow

You and/or the buyer will need to select a title company to handle your escrow. In some areas of California, you may need to choose an escrow company as well (see Chapter 11).

This clause also specifies dates for executing final escrow instructions (this is usually done shortly before closing) and completing the sale (called "closing escrow" in the real estate business). Final escrow instructions basically authorize the escrow company to give the seller the buyer's money and give the buyer a deed to the property. You and the buyer need to allow enough time for everything that has to happen (e.g., financing, inspections, etc.) before the contract calls for the escrow to close. Unless the buyer already has her financing completely lined up, this should be at least 45-60 days from the date the contract is signed. If the buyer has money in hand, then the time necessary to close can be much shorter. Normally, in this situation, only 20 to 30 days (or sometimes less) need be allowed to complete physical inspections of the condition of the property.

8. Prorations

This clause allocates responsibility for the payment of the expenses that go along with property ownership, including fire insurance and property taxes. Responsibility to pay these amounts is divided based on the percentage of the billing or assessment period for which buyer and seller own the property. For example, if property taxes are $1,000 for a fiscal year beginning July 1, and the buyer takes possession on the next April 1, the buyer's prorated share would be $250 for one quarter of the year and the seller's share would be $750 for three quarters of the year.

This clause also provides that buyers assume what are called "non-callable" bond liens.[5] These are assessment bonds that finance improvements such as curbs, street lights, or gutters and are used in some (but by no means all) California localities. Often the bond lien is paid off when a home is sold, but in some instances the bonds cannot be paid off early—that is, they are "non-callable." The buyer assumes the bond lien, and the amount of the lien is usually a credit to the buyer against the selling price. So if there were a $3,000 non-callable bond lien, the price of the home would typically be lowered by that amount.

---

[5]If you don't know whether or not your house has any such liens, they'll show up on the preliminary title report.

9. Possession of the Property

Section 9 of the contract concerns when you will physically move out and the buyer can put out her own welcome mat. All sorts of factors play a part here, including the needs and desires of the people who presently occupy (or are building) the place you are moving to. Sometimes your moving date will be established in the contract as the same day as the close of escrow. More often it is after the escrow closes and the house legally belongs to the buyer. For example, the contract might provide that you can move out anytime within 60 days after the close of escrow. In this instance, under the contract you are responsible to pay the buyer rent from the day escrow closes until the date you actually get out.

Rent is computed on a daily basis, based on the new owner's cost of owning the property. To arrive at the daily rental amount, take the new owner's mortgage payment (principal and interest), add to it the monthly cost of the buyer's property tax and fire insurance, and divide by 30. Of course, not all months have 30 days, but in real estate proration, the "broker's year" is commonly used; this year has 12 months of 30 days each, or a total of 360 days.

Note: In general, it's most unwise to allow the buyer to occupy the property in any way—even just "moving in a few things"—before escrow closes.

10. Fixtures

Fixtures are things permanently attached to real estate, like built-in appliances or bookshelves, carpeting attached to the floor, and outside landscaping. Fixtures are transferred with the real estate unless you and the buyer agree otherwise in the contract. You will need to negotiate and modify this clause if you wish to dig up the apple tree in the back yard or rip out a built-in stove and take it with you. Be sure to specify in the contract any things you wish to exclude. Unusual exclusions or inclusions should also be mentioned up front in your advertising flyer or open house statement.

11. Personal Property

Everything that isn't real property or permanently attached to it (fixtures) is personal property. This property doesn't pass with the real property unless you say so. If you're including appliances (unless they are built-in) or other personal property, such as rugs, beds, etc., list the items here.

12. Risk of Damage to Property

In accordance with California law, this paragraph states that the buyer takes the risk of destruction of the property only after he gets either possession of the property or title to the property. Thus, for example, if the house is destroyed by fire before the buyer moves in or takes title, it's the seller's problem. The buyer can either back out of the sale (and get his deposit back) or go ahead with the purchase and require the seller to restore the property to its original condition. This is why the contract also states that the seller will maintain insurance on the property through the closing.

13. The Buyer's Financing

Obviously the buyer must satisfy you that she can pay for the property in a timely manner before you accept her offer. In Clause 6 of this contract, there is a place to indicate whether the sale is contingent on the buyer arranging financing. But whether or not there is a financing contingency, you need to know exactly how the buyer proposes to pay for the property. For the buyer's protection as well as yours, the terms of financing and payment should be specified in as much detail as possible. As part of doing this, the buyer should specify the maximum rate of interest and monthly payments she can make to a financial institution as well as the minimum term of years over which the loan is to be repaid (amortized). You can then plug these numbers into a financial analysis like the one in Chapter 8 (you will also need the buyer's credit information) to get a pretty good idea if the buyer can really afford your house. You want this financing clause to be written as pessimistically (from the buyer's point of view) as possible. The reason for doing this should be obvious. If the buyer is able to obtain more favorable terms, the deal will obviously go through. However, you want to be protected just in case financing turns out to be a little tougher to arrange than expected.

Example: If current 30-year fixed rate loans are at an interest rate of 9.5% and the loan origination fee (points) is 2.5%, it's a good idea to insist that the contract provision covering financing require the deal to go through if the buyer can arrange financing at a rate of "not more than 10%," and has to pay a loan origination fee (points) of no more than 3%.

This clause also requires the buyer to show you that he is eligible for any special loan programs (Cal-Vet or VA) he is applying for. If the buyer is seriously in the market, he'll have the documents.

14. Expenses of Sale

This clause allocates the major expenses of sale between the buyer and seller. Clause 6 states that the buyer pays for physical inspections, and Clause 8 takes care of prorated expenses such as fire insurance. The following chart lists other common expenses in selling a house and indicates whether buyer or seller typically agrees to pay for each. It's not unusual, however, to negotiate different payment responsibilities.

WHO PAYS FOR WHAT?

ITEM	WHAT CONTRACTS USUALLY CALL FOR	WHO BENEFITS	REMARKS AND RECOMMENDATIONS
Pest control inspection	Buyer to pick inspector and pay for inspection (see Clause 6)	Buyer benefits from inspection, seller from disclosure satisfactory to buyer	To make sure inspection satisfies buyer, buyer should select and pay inspector
General contractor inspection	"	"	"
Roofer's inspection	"	"	"
Plumber's inspection	"	"	"
Electrical inspection	"	"	"
Asbestos inspection	"	"	"
Energy conservation inspection	Seller to arrange for and pay for inspection under local ordinances where required	Seller primarily, to satisfy ordinances; buyer secondarily, as to disclosure	Seller should pay
Title report; title insurance	Buyer customarily pays in northern California; seller in southern California (see Chapter 11)	Buyer primarily	Buyer should pay
Escrow fees	Buyer customarily pays in northern California; seller in southern California (see Chapter 11)	Both parties	Both may divide it
Recording and notary fees for documents in transaction	By custom buyer pays for: Grant deed Trust deed(s)	Buyer	This is logical; the fees are nominal anyway
	By custom seller pays for: Reconveyance in payoff of existing trust deed loans on property	Seller	
Documentary transfer tax	Seller usually pays, but buyer must pay in probate sales	Seller primarily (fulfills legal obligation)	Why not try to get the buyer to pay? It's a negotiable item in any case, but you can use it as one more bargaining chip.
Real estate tax Fire insurance Bond liens (unless able to be paid off)	Buyer and seller usually prorate/divide as of close of escrow, when the deed is recorded (see Clause 8)	Both parties	Unless there's a good reason to do otherwise, prorate it

15. Seller's Disclosures

In Chapter 7, I discuss the very real legal and practical necessity of the seller's full disclosure of all known and suspected defects in the property, along with any inspection reports discussing the physical condition of the property made in at least the last two years. This clause provides a place for the buyer to acknowledge receipt of the statutory Real Estate Transfer Disclosure Form as well as any other reports you list and provide. When the buyer signs the contract, she acknowledges that she has, in fact, received all the pertinent reports. If trouble develops in later years and the buyer conveniently forgets that one or more inspection reports warned of this particular possibility, you will be very glad you have the buyer's written acknowledgment of receipt.

Note on Condominiums, Co-ops, Other Common Interest Developments, and Subdivisions: As mentioned earlier, special rules govern sales of these types of property, and you will need to check boxes in Clause 15 stating that you have complied with them.

If you live in a co-op or condo, you must provide the buyer with the following documents, all of which you can get from your homeowners' association:[6]

1. A copy of the "governing documents" of the development. These include bylaws of the association and the "Covenants, Conditions and Restrictions" (CC&R's) that bind each owner.

2. If residency is limited by age (e.g., only persons over 55 allowed), a statement that the restriction is enforceable only to the extent allowed by Civil Code Sec. 51.3 (the Unruh Civil Rights Act).

3. A copy of the association's most recent financial report.

4. A written statement from an authorized representative of the association as to the amount of any unpaid assessments that may be made against the property.

The association is required to respond to a written request for these materials within 10 days. It may charge you a reasonable fee for their preparation.

If you live in a subdivision that has a homeowners' association, you must give the buyer a copy of the CC&R's that limit use of the property. This is required by the statutory disclosure form set out in the Appendix and discussed in Chapter 7. The preliminary title report usually turns these up, but some title insurance companies don't give the buyer the full text of the CC&R's unless pressed. The buyer should definitely get the CC&R's in full. The restrictions are often very detailed and comprehensive, covering everything from what kind of pets are allowed to what color you can paint your garage. You don't want to have to deal with an unpleasantly surprised buyer later.

---

[6] Civil Code Sec. 1368.

If your sale involves a condominium, check the following in Clause 15 (Seller's Disclosure) of the contract:

[x] Documents set out in Civil Code Section 1368 relating to condominiums.

If your sale involves property in a subdivision having covenants, conditions and restrictions, check the following in Clause 15:

[x] Documents containing all conditions, covenants, and restrictions that affect the property.

16. Time Is of the Essence

This is a standard clause that emphasizes the importance of the closing dates you specified earlier in the contract. It means that missed deadlines by either party are considered a major violation of the contract.

Don't, however, time contract deadlines with a stopwatch. Recent legal decisions have come down against excessively strict construction of the expression "time is of the essence." If a buyer, say, fails to fulfill a financing contingency within the time allowed, but does so a few days later—probably because things are backed up at the bank or savings-and-loan—has the buyer actually fulfilled the contingency within a reasonable time? In today's legal atmosphere, the answer is likely to be affirmative. It would be the seller's task to demonstrate that he has suffered or will suffer damages as a result of the buyer's failure to fulfill the contingency within the strictly allotted time.

17. Duration of the Offer

Here the buyer gives you a deadline for accepting the offer. See Chapter 10, Section E for a discussion of the rules of accepting and revoking offers.

18. Commission to Brokers

This clause is designed to avoid misunderstandings about payments to brokers. For example, if the buyer makes her offer through a broker, she may mistakenly assume you will pay the broker's fee or split it. This paragraph says you won't pay any broker unless you have arranged it separately in writing.

19. Credit Information

This obligates the buyer to furnish you with detailed financial information in a credit questionnaire—even though another will probably be required by an institutional lender—so you can evaluate the likelihood of his obtaining the financing he needs to buy your house. It also gives you needed authority to check on buyer's statements concerning income, assets and liabilities.

Ideally, you will have gotten this financial information before the buyer submitted his offer (see Chapter 8). If you haven't, give the buyer a few days (three should be plenty) to fill out the form

20. Entire Agreement

This clause, which states that this contract is the whole agreement between the parties (neither can rely on other statements not included in the contract) and that all modifications to the contract must be in writing, is primarily a reminder to both parties that oral agreements are simply not enforceable when it comes to real estate contracts. The discussion under Clause 26, below, shows you how to modify the contract, if necessary

21. Foreign Investors

To comply with a federal law called FIRPTA (Foreign Investment in Real Property Tax Act, Internal Revenue Code Sec. 1445), the seller must fill in a form (which you should receive from the escrow or title company, or can get from your regional office of the IRS) stipulating whether or not you are a foreign investor. Uncle Sam wants to know where the money comes from and goes in real estate transactions. If in fact you are a "foreign person" under the terms of the Act, the buyer must withhold in escrow 10% of the gross sale price of the house and comply with the reporting provisions of the Act.

22. Rent Control

A number of California cities have local rent control ordinances. These can have a negative effect on the value of houses in the controlled area, especially those that are likely to be rented in the future. Because any house can be rented, it is a good idea to make sure the buyer is informed about the existence of any local rent control ordinance. If you are in doubt whether your house is covered by rent control, call your city or county planning office and find out.

23. Transfer Requirements

Some California cities and counties, as well as the state, impose their own local rules on real estate transfers. Common ones include requirements that there be a smoke detector in the house and that certain steps be taken to make the house energy efficient. Other requirements have to do with notifying the buyer of certain important facts, such as the location of the house in a legally designated coastal or earthquake zone. I list most types of requirements on the chart below. As mentioned in Chapter 5, it's a good idea to find out exactly what the rules are beforehand. A local title company, broker or your city should be able to tell you. The contract assumes that you are responsible for taking care of these requirements. You may, however, wish to negotiate with the buyer about who pays for them. If you reach a different conclusion, indicate that on the contract.

LOCAL REQUIREMENTS

LAW	JURISDICTION	APPLICATION	WHAT TO DO
Smoke detector requirement	Various municipalities	Requires owner to install smoke detectors in certain places before conveying title	Check with your escrow or title insurance company to see if the requirement affects your home.
Energy conservation ordinance	Various municipalities	Requires inspection for compliance with energy conservation criteria as specified by law	Again, check with the escrow or title insurance company to see if this applies to your home; also your power company may provide helpful information
Alquist-Priolo Special Studies Act (earthquake hazard areas)	Areas specified as special study zones for seismic or geological hazards	Disclose to buyer if your property is in a special studies zone (a disclosure form is contained in the Appendix)	Once more, your title insurance or escrow company, in protecting itself, should disclose to you whether your property is affected
Coastal Act	Many coastal areas of California	Governs future development of land, but usually not sale of a house	Contact the California Coastal Commission for information and assistance
3R Report (residential report requirement)	Daly City, San Francisco and some other areas	Requires seller to pay (approx. $11) for report from City to buyer of zoning, building permits, etc., on property	Contact 3R department of municipality
Anti-speculation taxes	Several cities	Requires the seller to pay a tax to the city (usually 1% of sale value) if he has not owned the house for a certain number of years (often 5-7)	Contact your city or county tax office

24. Seller's Right to Accept Backup Offers
and
25. Seller's Right to Demand Removal of Contingencies: The 96-Hour Wipe-Out Clause

It is common for contingencies in real estate contracts never to be satisfied (e.g., the buyer does not get financing, or the house is found to be structurally unsound). Because of this, Clause 24 authorizes the seller to accept other offers to purchase, providing, of course, that each subsequent offer that is accepted is in "backup" or secondary position to the one(s) accepted before it. If the deal falls through, the second offer automatically moves up. If this one also falls through, the third offeror gets her chance, and so on.

In some cases, you won't want to wait until the deal actually falls through to take advantage of backup offers. When it looks like a buyer isn't going to be able to go through with the purchase, the "96-hour wipeout clause" allows you to demand, anytime at least two weeks after you accept an offer, that the buyer remove specified contingencies (e.g., financing and inspection approval) within 96 hours.[7] If she can't, you are free to go ahead with the first backup offer you accepted. I recommend that sellers insist that this clause be included if the buyer's offer is obviously weak in terms of financing (e.g., the buyer must get a 90% loan or sell an existing home) or the buyer is asking for an exceptionally long time in which to approve inspections or satisfy other contingencies.The two-week initial waiting period assures the buyer that you're not going to turn around and immediately try to back out of the contract. If the buyer balks about accepting this clause, you may want to negotiate a longer period for the buyer to remove contingencies after you involve the "wipeout" clause. How to actually remove contingencies is discussed in Chapter 11.

---

[7]Some real estate people use a 72-hour wipe-out clause. Frankly, I don't think this is fair, as it allows a seller to give a buyer 72 hours' notice to remove all contingencies on a Friday afternoon, which means the buyer really only has one business day, Monday, to accomplish this task. By including a 96-hour wipe-out clause in the contract, you give the buyer a fairer chance.

Example: Jane accepted Toby's offer to purchase her house for $210,000, although, secretly, she would have been delighted to get $195,000. She had asked $215,000, hoping to take advantage of an upward hop in the market, and was delighted to find that the hop turned out to be more like a jump. The problem was that Jane wasn't 100% sure of Toby's ability to secure a loan, even though the financial information he provided looked pretty decent. One problem was that Toby was hoping to obtain a bank loan for 90% of the purchase price, with only a 10% down payment.

Jane insisted on a 96-hour wipeout clause in her contract with Toby. This allowed her to realistically deal with backup offers while keeping Toby's deal on the front burner. Of course, Jane disclosed the fact of the contract with Toby to backup offerors. Two weeks later, a second offer came in for $215,000. This buyer was willing to make a 20% down payment and had the necessary cash in hand. Using the form and directions in Chapter 11, Jane gave Toby 96 hours to wipe out the contingency that he be able to arrange the financing his offer described. As it turned out, Toby's bank told him that, despite his good credit, it would not make a loan on the terms he could afford with only 10% down. Unable to wipe out this contingency, and aware that he wouldn't be able to complete the transaction, Toby was out of the deal quickly. He signed a form releasing Jane from obligation under the contract, got his deposit back, and Jane was able to sell to the other buyer without delay. A release form is included in Chapter 11.

26. Other Terms and Conditions

This is a space to list any contract terms or conditions not already set forth in the contract. If you don't have enough room, attach the following form to the contract (a copy is included in the Appendix):

ADDITION TO REAL PROPERTY PURCHASE CONTRACT

The material set out below is hereby made a part of the contract dated
_____ ,19 _____ between _____
_____ , Buyers and _____
_____ , Sellers to purchase real property
located at _____
_____ .

Read, understood, and agreed to by:

_____   _____
Signature of Buyer   Date

_____   _____
Signature of Seller   Date

---

27. Notice to Backup Offerors

Obviously, you fill this section in only if you have already accepted one or more offers to buy the property and the offeror is a backup offeror. Here is where you let backup offerors know where they stand in line to buy your house. You should set out the names of the other offerors, but you don't need to disclose any of the terms of the other offers.

28. Buyer's Signature

By signing this clause, the buyer(s) agrees to make this offer which will become a binding contract if accepted by the seller(s). If the buyer is married, their spouse must also sign.

29. Seller's Acceptance

Signing the Seller's Acceptance means you accept the buyer's offer as it stands. If you want to change any of the terms, you will need to make a counter-offer on a separate form, as discussed in Chapter 10, Section B. If you are married, both spouses must sign.

CHAPTER 10

THE BIDS COME IN

‎--------------------------------------

Now you're ready for the big moment when someone (or hopefully several someones) makes an offer to buy your house. In this chapter I give the information necessary to respond sensibly. But before I do, a few words for those of you who are still waiting at the gate, watching the customers slowly circle like 747's over LAX or SFO on a busy afternoon.

A. WAITING FOR OFFERS

It's common to start receiving offers a week or two after the first open house." If you receive none during this period, don't despair. However, even at this early stage it does make sense to review your marketing efforts with the idea of increasing them if reasonably possible (see Chapters 6 and 7).

If you still have no offers after a full month or so, your situation is obviously getting more serious. One possibility is to remove your house from the market for a while and try again later. If real estate prices are in a temporary slump and you can afford to wait, this may well be the best response. However, if other houses in your area are selling well (or, even if they aren't, but you simply have to sell as soon as possible), an obvious alternative is to reduce your asking price. It's important not to allow yourself to get so pessimistic at this point that you reduce it more than necessary. Indeed, I recommend that you decide how much to lower your price only after you again study what comparable houses are selling for in your area. To do this, repeat the steps necessary to arrive at a realistic appraisal of the value of your house set out in Chapter 5.

Note on Brokers: If your house remains on the market for some time, real estate brokers are likely to conclude that you are probably getting sick of trying to sell it yourself. A number may contact you and try to get the listing. A few may be extremely aggressive and tell you what a fool you are to represent yourself. If you are honestly fed up with handling your own sale, you may want to give them a hearing (and reread Chapter 4, which covers the types of listing contracts available). However, since the basic reason you wanted to sell your own house in the first place—to save the broker's commission —hasn't changed, you're probably best off to grit your teeth and stick it out a while longer. If this means you have to maneuver the few persistent brokers who won't take "no" for an answer out the door, so be it.[1] Always keep in mind that if you price your house fairly, a buyer will materialize before long.

B. The Legal Status of a Listing to Sell

Assume now that your house goes on the market and you have several offers within a short period of time, all at or near your asking price. Do you have to accept the first offer that meets or beats your price and other terms? No. As I stated in Chapter 9, listing or advertising your home for sale is not a contract with the general public that you will sell it to anyone who offers you your price. You have a legal right to remove your home from the market whenever you wish, even at a moment's notice. The only legal hang-ups involved in doing so are limited to:

√ **Broker's Rights:** As discussed in Chapter 4, if you list your home for sale with a broker under an Exclusive Authorization or Exclusive Agency contract, and the broker brings you an offer that meets your exact listing price and terms, you owe a commission, providing this offer is procured during the term of this listing contract. This is true whether you go through with the sale or not.

√√ **Discrimination:** If you refuse to sell to buyer "A" but then promptly sell to buyer "B" at a similar or less good price and terms, buyer "A" may well cry foul

---

[1]A few large brokerage offices train their agents to use especially aggressive means when they call people selling their own houses. If you are overwhelmed by these calls, you may have to be as assertive as your callers are.

if he is a member of a group which has a history of being discriminated against. If there is any evidence to support the idea that you made your decision based on the person's race, color, religion, sex, marital status, disability, etc., you are in legal hot water.

C. Only a Written Offer to Buy Real Property Is Binding

As I stressed in Chapter 9, an oral offer to purchase real property is legally worthless if the buyer wants out of the deal. In other words, people don't have to "put their money where their mouths are" unless they have also put their promises in writing.

A written offer should be detailed, covering all important issues, including the price the buyer will pay and time allowed for the property owner to accept the offer. If the offer is contingent upon the buyer qualifying for financing, or your home passing certain inspections (pest control, roof, plumbing, etc.) or anything else, the contingencies should be clearly stated along with the time allowed to remove them. In addition, if the offer is contingent upon your taking back a second deed of trust or otherwise participating in the financing, this, too, should be stated.

Note: It's always preferable to type offer and counter-offer forms. If you don't, be sure to print legibly when you fill in the blanks.

If the buyer is working with a broker, or is reasonably sophisticated about business concerns, he will probably present you with a detailed written offer. Unfortunately, many prospective buyers will not know how to present you with a written offer which covers all necessary issues. If this occurs, you should be prepared to give them the offer form set out in the Appendix to this book and discussed in Chapter 9. Obviously, this particular offer form is not required. A prospective purchaser may present you with one of several other commercially available forms, or simply write out an offer on a blank sheet.

One way to be sure that all issues important to you are covered is to compare the buyer's offer with the form set out in Chapter 9. For example, if the buyer's offer is contingent on selling an existing house or arranging financing, does it contain a 96-hour wipe-out clause? And does it give you a reasonable amount of time in which to say "yes" or "no?" If it doesn't include all the terms you want, simply make a counter-offer (see Sec. 6 below) that includes them. To help you do this, the Appendix includes a tear-out counter-offer form.

Example: The buyer presents you with a typed piece of paper offering to purchase your house for $200,000 with 20% down contingent on a satisfactory structural pest control report. This is fine with you, but realizing that many other provisions should be included in the final contract, you fill out the detailed counter-offer form in the Appendix, plugging in the buyer's proposals in the appropriate places. The buyer reads your counter-offer and asks for a few minor changes. You make these on the counter-offer form and initial and date them. The buyer also initials and dates the changes and then accepts in writing by signing the counter-offer form in the appropriate place, and the deal is done.

Warning: If you are dealing with an inexperienced purchaser or someone with a language problem, who obviously can't complete a written offer on his own, ask him to have his offer prepared by someone more knowledgeable. One good alternative is for the buyer to hire a real estate broker or lawyer at a reasonable hourly rate. Do not prepare or help prepare an offer for someone who can't do it himself. If trouble develops later, he will almost surely claim that you took unfair advantage of him.

D. The Offer Conference

In the lingo of the real estate world, the seller receives the buyer's offer at an "offer presentation" or "offer conference." Whether you use a fancy term or not, here are some tips on how best to conduct yourself when a prospective buyer contacts you and wants to make an offer.

Make an appointment with the prospective purchaser for the presentation of his offer. If more than one buyer contacts you close to the same time, you may wish to schedule the appointments simultaneously or shortly after one another.

Although it's not legally required, I recommend entertaining offers in the order in which the prospective purchasers have contacted you.

At this stage you are very likely to again get calls from brokers who say they want to make offers on behalf of buyers, but only if you will "cooperate." As I discuss in Chapter 4, in real estate terminology, "cooperating" means that you agree to pay the broker who produces a buyer a commission, usually 2.5% to 3.5% of the sales price. If you do not wish to do this, politely decline to meet with brokers. An alternative to completely rejecting the idea of cooperating is to state that you will cooperate and pay a commission only if offers to purchase are above a certain amount.

Make it clear to the people who call that you expect the offer to be in writing and accompanied by a deposit check made out to an escrow or title company you and the buyer agree to. As discussed in Chapter 9, it's typical to receive at least $1,000 as a deposit (though no deposit is required by law). We recommend that you only accept a certified or cashier's check. Never accept cash.

If you are working with a broker or a lawyer hired by the hour, you may want this person to help conduct the offer conference. I realize this involves paying for several hours of professional time, but as this is a key stage of your sale, it may be worth it. Aside from having a knowledgeable friend at your side, it allows you to distance yourself a little from negotiations over price and terms. In other words, your representative can be the tough guy and then you can step in and compromise when the time is right.

Prepare for a quiet, businesslike meeting. You will want to utilize a study or den if you have one. Failing that, use the dining room table or a coffee table in the living room, making sure the area is quiet, private and free of clutter.

When a prospective purchaser arrives, introduce any third parties present and make their roles clear. If you are paying a lawyer or broker by the hour to help with paperwork or advice, say so.

Ask the person making the offer to present her written offer and deposit check to you. Here is a sample of a receipt you should give the seller (a tear-out copy is in the Appendix).

Deposit Receipt

_____, Seller(s) of the property

located at _____

_____ in _____, California, hereby

acknowledge receipt from _____, Offeror(s) of the sum

of $_____ in the form of a cashier's check payable to _(escrow or title

insurance company)_ .

This check will be held by the Seller uncashed until and unless Offeror's offer is accepted, and will be returned to the Offeror if this offer is not accepted.

Signed   _____

              _____

Date   _____, 19_____

As the receipt (and the tear-out offer in the Appendix) states, you should hold the cashier's check uncashed until you decide to accept or reject the offer. If you reject the offer, return the check. If you accept the offer, deposit the check with an escrow holder (title insurance company, escrow company or bank escrow department) acceptable to you both. Sometimes the buyer will have nominated such an escrow holder in his offer (this is covered in Clause 7 of the offer in this book). If so, go along with this choice unless you have strong reason to disagree with it. If no nomination of an escrow holder is made by the buyer, you will probably want to suggest one (see Chapter 11 for information on how to choose one).

Normally, once you receive the offer, you will want to do the following:

• If the written offer is not adequately detailed, suggest that the prospective purchasers substitute the form in the Appendix to this book, getting independent help if necessary, or plan to make your own counter-offer using the counter-offer form in the Appendix.

• Pay particular attention to any time limit the buyer provides for you to respond in writing. If the offer demands a decision "upon presentation" or in a time period you find unreasonably short (say, less than two or three days), request a written amendment to the offer on the spot, so as to allow you more time. This can be done by changing and initialing the time provision. Remember, it's your house and you are entitled to call the shots.

• Request that the buyer provide you with a financial statement. A form is in the Appendix. Examine it, following the instructions in Chapter 8, to see if the buyer is likely to be able to afford to purchase your house.

• Carefully study the offer, including all contingencies, with the idea of arriving at a preliminary opinion as to whether it is likely to go through if you accept.

• Ask necessary questions and give the buyer the opportunity to explain any points that are not clear.

• Make sure that the offeror has a copy of the Real Estate Transfer Disclosure Statement form set out in Chapter 7 (a copy is in the Appendix), along with all inspection reports that have been issued concerning the condition of the house in at least the last two years. Remember that if the disclosure statement isn't given until after the offer is made, the buyer has three days to back out of the deal.

Typically, at this stage, you will want more information and clarification of particular aspects of the offer, not debate or an on-the-spot decision, unless you are absolutely convinced that the buyer is financially qualified to make the purchase and is offering you a price and terms you simply cannot refuse, or, alternatively, that the offer is so low (or the offeror so off the wall) that you want to reject it without further consideration. In other words, it's usually best to thank the offerors courteously and tell them you will consider their offers and get back to them. If they press you for a decision, simply stand up, usher them to the door politely, and insist on time to think.

Note on multiple offers: If you receive more than one offer, you have no obligation to disclose the terms to other offerors. Even if the offerors do not object, disclosure may work against your interest, since the offerors get a sense of the market in a manner which could wind up lowering your price. Of course, in others it may be your best negotiating strategy.

You may want to counter all the offers in an identical fashion or tailor your responses to each offer. Just keep in mind that it's illegal to discriminate on arbitrary grounds (sex, race, etc.) and give only certain people a fair chance to meet your price and terms.

Remember that whoever accepts your counter first makes a binding contract with you. That's why including the exact date and time on all offers, counter-offers, and acceptances is so important.

E. THE LEGAL STATUS OF AN OFFER TO PURCHASE

It's important for you to know that an offer may be revoked (literally "called back") in writing by the offeror any time before you communicate your acceptance. For this reason, sellers are usually quick to accept very favorable offers. In addition, almost all offers come with a time limit during which the offer must be accepted in writing, or it automatically ends. For instance, "This offer is extended until 5:00 p.m., P.D.T., Saturday, July 12...." If the seller tries to accept after that date and time, the offeror may simply shrug his shoulders and say "Sorry, but you acted too late." Even if an offer contains a time limit, it can be revoked by the offeror prior to that time.

If you do decide to accept, do it in writing. You may create a valid contract if you accept an offer over the phone,[2] but who wants to fight about it later? All owners, all buyers, and all their spouses should sign the contract.

There is no legal need for buyer and seller to sign the same piece of paper. The buyer can make an offer and the seller can accept in writing by a separate letter or document. However, the usual procedure is to have both signatures on one document. Have the seller sign the bottom of the buyer's offer, stating that he accepts it. If for any reason you do need a separate acceptance form, use the one set out below. A tear-out copy is in the Appendix.

---

[2]It's the kind of thing that gives law students fits: the law says a contract for the sale of real estate must be in writing, but does that mean you can't accept a written offer orally? Apparently the answer is that technically you can, but no lender will work with you unless both offer and acceptance are in writing.

ACCEPTANCE OF PURCHASE OFFER

_____, the owner(s) of the
property at _____
_____in the city of _____,
county of _____, California, hereby accept the offer
to purchase the property made on __ _(offer date)_ _, 19__, by
_____ _(names of all offerors)_ _____.

Signed   _____

              _____, Sellers

Date   _____, 19_____

Example 1: Helen offered her home for sale at $235,000. After her second
open house, she received an offer from Bill on a form virtually identical to the
one provided in this book, for $229,500, which allowed her four days to accept.
She hoped another offer would come in because a lot of people had expressed
interest at the open house. She decided to wait three days before responding.
At the end of the three days, she called Bill to tell him that she was bringing
over her written acceptance. Before she could do so, Bill said, "I'm so glad you
called, Helen; I was just about to call you to tell you that I'm revoking my offer,
since I've found another home to buy while you were mulling over my offer."
Bill's revocation is legal, although he should ideally follow it up in writing.
Fortunately for Helen, she got another offer, the following week, for $230,000.
This time she promptly accepted in writing.

Example 2: Jacob held an open house and asked $275,000 for his house. A
number of prospective purchasers appeared and seemed interested. One of them,
Nancy, immediately made an offer of $269,000. Jacob decided to sell to Nancy if
she would accept his counter-offer of $273,000 and gave her three days to do so.
While Nancy thought about whether to accept Jacob's counter-offer, Jacob
received a second offer from Bill for $276,000. Since Nancy hadn't yet accepted

Jacob's counter-offer, Jacob gave Nancy a written revocation and accepted Bill's higher offer. Nancy lost out.

Note on Option Contracts: It is possible, but quite unusual, for seller and prospective buyer to make an enforceable agreement—a separate contract—that states that a particular offer (or counter-offer) will remain open for (can't be revoked during) a certain period of time. This type of agreement is called an "option contract." The person who gets the option to buy (or more rarely, sell) the house usually must agree to pay something in exchange for the option. I discuss—and recommend against —option contracts in Chapter 1.

F. IF AN OFFER DOES NOT MEET YOUR EXPECTATIONS

Since you are selling your own house, only you can accept an offer. You can and should reject offers that you believe aren't adequate, or which are made by people whom you don't believe are financially qualified to purchase your house. This doesn't mean you should stop talking to the potential buyer, however. If an original offer is anywhere near your asking price, you may wish to make a counter-offer, changing the price or other terms. Most potential buyers fully expect you to do this, bidding a little low precisely so that they can see what you will come back with. In this context, remember that many buyers may assume that you have overpriced the house slightly to leave room for bargaining and will be almost as surprised as a serape vendor in a Mexican market if you aren't willing to do so. In fact, if your negotiating strategy is to name a price, but not bargain at all, you should go out of your way to make this clear at the offer conference.

Example: Sally puts her house on the market for $210,000. Within two weeks, she has two offers for $195,000—not full price but not too bad. This suggests to me that the buyers probably realize that Sally's house is worth $210,000, or close to it, but are trying to bargain to get it for a little less. What are Sally's negotiation options?

1. Sally can say "no" and stick to her price.

2. Sally can say "no" but lower her price to some amount between $195,000 and $210,000.

3. Sally can say, "I'm sorry, but because a number of people are interested in the house, the price is no longer $210,000—I'm raising it to $220,000." Don't laugh at the third option; it can work beautifully. The potential buyers, of course, are likely to be shocked. This gives Sally a chance to say that she will honor the original price if they really want to commit to buy it immediately. A variant of this strategy would be for Sally to announce from the beginning that she will raise her price on a certain date if her terms aren't met by then. For instance, she could advertise, "Price is only $210,000 for quick sale. After Sunday, April 15, at 5 p.m., it's $220,000." Of course, even if Sally does this, she can still legally decide to take the property off the market or lower or raise the price even before the date stated.

I am often asked how long it's wise to wait for more offers to come in after an initial open house at which lot of people walk through your house and someone immediately offers to purchase it. Suppose you have an open house on Sunday afternoon and 100 people come. At 7 p.m. Sunday, you receive a phone call from a prospective purchaser who wants to come by. He does, and offers you your asking price. Do you accept it? The answer, of course, is that it depends on lots of factors particular to your sale. Perhaps the most important of these is whether you feel your asking price was high or low. Obviously, if you've asked for a very high price and get it, you will probably want to accept. Otherwise you are probably best advised to slow things down a little and wait for other offers. Remember, the best feedback you can get on your asking price comes now, from potential buyers.

Example 1: Harry offered his home for sale for $225,000, thinking he would be delighted to accept $215,000. After his first open house, Harry was surprised to receive an offer from Eddie and Ethel for $100 more than his full asking price. The offer was on a form virtually identical to the one provided in this book, and included a contingency that Eddie and Ethel be able to sell their existing home as part of arranging financing and that Harry's home be inspected with a resulting report satisfactory to Eddie and Ethel. Harry wasn't sure what to do, so he called a broker friend. Here is the advice he got, which, incidentally, I think is pretty good: "If you believe you priced the property accurately, accept the offer, subject to all its conditions and provisions, but make sure the buyer's offer, or your counter-offer, contains a 96-hour wipe-out clause. This way, if your deal with Eddie and Ethel is stalled and you receive another offer, you can ask Eddie and Ethel to remove their contingencies within 96 hours. On the other hand, if you believe that you may have underpriced the property, you might want to wait a week or even raise the price to Eddie and Ethel in a counter-offer."

Example 2: Ellen offered her home for sale at $250,000, although she would have accepted $240,000. After her first open house, she received no offers and decided she'd simply try again. After the next open house, the following week-end, when the weather was better and the 49ers weren't playing the Rams on TV, more lookers showed up and she received three offers at or near her full asking price—one for $249,500, another for $247,900, and a third for $245,000.

I DID IT MYSELF

I was surprised at my first open house to hear almost everyone commenting that my house was underpriced. Raising the price by $15,000 for the next open house, I heard the same thing. Given my experience with other business negotiations, I expected everyone to mutter complaints about the price and was delighted, instead, to get very helpful, honest and accurate feedback. This was, for me, one of the most important benefits of showing my house myself.

Negotiation Note: When it comes to meeting and negotiating with potential purchasers, you may feel intimidated or unsure if you have no negotiation experience. There may even be a danger that a savvy buyer will talk you into agreeing to a contract that is not in your best interest. Obviously, you don't want to give away as much money by negotiating poorly as you save by selling your own house. If you have any doubt as to your negotiating skill or the best strategy to follow, arrange to get help. As noted in Chapter 4, you can hire an experienced broker to help you with this crucial stage of the house selling process at a reasonable hourly rate.

G. How to Make a Counter-Offer

If you receive an offer (or several), which doesn't satisfy you, it usually makes sense to counter it (or them) in writing, making it clear how long the potential buyer has to accept. This normally ranges from as little as a few hours to as long as a few days, depending on the situation and your needs. Because counter-offers are often extended for a very short time, it is especially important that all counter-offer documents show not only the date, but the exact local time (Pacific Daylight Time or Pacific Standard Time) of presentation and expiration.

Important: As stated earlier in this chapter, when you make a written counter-offer, you are not legally bound to hold it open for the time allowed for the buyer's response. You can revoke your counter-offer in writing at any time before the buyer accepts it (see the counter-offer revocation form in Section H). This means that if you get a better offer in the meantime, you can withdraw your counter-offer and accept that better offer as long as your counter-offer hasn't been accepted. However, if the buyer accepts and communicates acceptance in writing during the time allowed by your counter-offer and before you revoke it, a binding legal contract is established. This is true even though you and the buyer never sit down and sign the same document. See Section C above.

Several of the important issues on which you might want to base a counter-offer are:

• **Price:** The offeror has offered a price that is too low. You may or may not want to shave something off of or add to your original price.

Example: Recently a seller I worked with priced her home at $125,000. When a number of offers came in for more than this amount, she realized that she had asked too little and countered all offers at $145,000. One of her counter-offers was accepted.

• **Financing:** If the offer contains financing terms that you believe are impractical, or if the buyer proposes to get a loan from a program such as the VA, for which you believe he doesn't qualify, change the unacceptable provisions in your counter-offer. Also, the offeror may propose that you carry a second deed of trust yourself. If you have no intention of doing so, give him a counter-offer eliminating this provision.

• **Occupancy:** If the offer doesn't propose enough time for you to move out, change it in your counter-offer.

• **Contingency of Buyers Selling Their House:** Often an offeror will propose to buy your house contingent on first selling the one she already owns. Ask yourself if the buyer has a realistic chance of selling her present home during the time period allowed. If you don't think she does, refuse to accept this term. This may kill the deal, of course. But if a buyer really wants your house, she may be able to get short-term financial help from family or friends, or a bridge loan from a bank (see Chapter 8, Section A). Again, including a 96-hour wipe-out clause in the contract makes it much more palatable to accept an offer that may never go through, because you can go ahead with backup offers if the original offerors can't eliminate any contingencies within 96 hours of your written notice.

• **Inspections:** Some of the buyer's inspection proposals (see Chapters 9 and 11 for more on inspections) may allow too much time. If so, propose changes.

Now it's time to make your written counter-offer. Assuming the basic terms of the deal are specified in writing in the original offer, all you need to do is specify the items you wish to change. Do this by using the short-form counter-offer included in the Appendix. Here is a filled-out sample.

SHORT FORM COUNTER-OFFER

__HELEN AND ROBERT MCCLOSKEY__, Seller(s) of the real property at __291 CORNELL AVE.__, __SAN JOSE__, California, accept(s) the offer to purchase the property dated __JUNE 9__,19 __87__ made by __SANDRA MARLOWE__,with the following exceptions:

1. *Price to be $170,000.*
2. *Financing contingency to be removed by July 1, 1987.*

Helen McCloskey   June 10, 1987, 3 p.M.
Robert McCloskey   6-10, 1987, 3 p.M.

However, if as noted in Section F of this chapter, the offer you receive is simply not detailed enough to form the basis of a good contract, use the long form counter-offer in the Appendix. This is basically the same as the offer form discussed in detail in Chapter 9.

The written counter-offer should be presented at a conference much like the original meeting. You can make minor changes to the counter-offer (or offer) right on the form. Both parties should initial and date the changes (see Section C, above).

H. COUNTER-OFFER REVOCATION

As stated above, you can revoke a counter-offer in writing at any time before the buyer accepts it.[3] Obviously, one reason why you may want to withdraw your counter-offer (and return the buyer's deposit check) is if another potential buyer materializes with a better offer. Here is a counter-offer revocation form. You will find a tear-out copy in the Appendix.

COUNTER-OFFER REVOCATION

_____

_____, the seller(s) of the property at

_____ in

_____, California, hereby revoke the counter-offer made to

_____ *(name(s) of all buyer(s) on original offer)* _____ on

_____, 19_____, and hereby authorize escrow holder(s) to return to buyer(s) any deposit funds tendered by buyer(s).

Signed   _____

                _____, Seller(s)

                on _____, 19_____, ___. M.

Deposit
Received By   _____

                _____, Buyer(s)

                on _____, 19_____, ___. M.

---

[3]The rules about the effectiveness of oral revocations are the same as those about oral acceptances discussed above in Section D. Put everything in writing!

I.   Counter-Counter Offers

Commonly, there are counter-counter offers, counter-counter-counter offers and yes, Virginia, sometimes even counter-counter-counter-counter offers! It simply depends on how many rounds of real estate ping-pong the buyer and seller are willing to play until both are so exhausted they can't bat the deal back and forth one more time. My own experience suggests that two or even three counters, from each party to the other, is not unusual (my personal record is nine rounds). All of this dickering should be in writing. Again, however, you don't have to rewrite the whole offer from scratch each time. You can accept most of the terms already on the table (contained in the offer or early counter-offers) and simply indicate those you wish to change.

J.   When You Accept an Offer

When the buyer's offer (or the seller's counter-offer) has been accepted in writing, a contract is formed. Your next steps are as follows:

• Make several photocopies of all documents and make sure the buyer has copies of everything. (The buyer's lender will require a copy of the contract from the buyer, but this is not your direct responsibility);

• Keep the originals in a safe place and make sure you have copies stored someplace else in case the originals disappear;

• Give a copy to any broker, attorney, or tax accountant you have hired to assist you;

• Give the title insurance company or escrow holder the information it asks for from the contract; it will not normally want a copy;

• Deposit the buyer's cashier's check with an escrow holder agreed upon (see Chapter 11).

K. Accept Backup Offers

There is no law saying you can't accept several backup offers so long as you disclose to each offeror what's going on. Tell the person making the first offer you accept that you will accept other favorable offers in a "backup" position (Clause 24 of the offer in Chapter 9 makes your right to do this clear). When you do accept a backup offer, make sure you complete the section of the formal written offer set out in Chapter 9, Section B that tells the backup offeror you've already accepted an offer. If the backup offeror's offer does not contain this provision, add it to your written acceptance or counter-offer and ask the buyer to initial it and sign the form at the bottom.

CHAPTER 11

AFTER THE CONTRACT IS SIGNED: CONTINGENCIES, TITLE INSURANCE, AND ESCROW

When you have a signed contract with a buyer, your next step is to get started on several technical tasks involved in completing your house sale. You and the buyer must establish an escrow account, and the buyer must arrange for title insurance. The buyer should also be working toward closing the deal by removing the contingencies set out in the contract. (In Section D below, you will find a chart listing responsibilities of both buyer and seller.)

How long does escrow take? There's no one answer. If you're waiting for a buyer to sell his existing house, it could take a long time. If you don't have such unpredictable contingencies and foresee no serious problems with financing or inspections, you can expect to close the deal in one to four months.

Note: The information necessary to open and successfully close escrow is detailed, picky and often overlapping in the sense that a number of things must be done almost simultaneously. Before you take any concrete action, please read this entire chapter carefully to be sure that you understand both the big picture and all the details.

A. Opening Escrow

As part of finalizing the sale of your house, you and the buyer need a neutral third-party stakeholder to hold and exchange deeds and money, pay off existing loans, record deeds, etc. To do this, you must "open an escrow."[1]

The first thing to understand is that, by custom, opening an escrow is done slightly differently in Northern and Southern California. This is strictly a matter of custom and not law.

Northern California: An escrow is normally opened with a title company immediately after the purchase contract is signed by both buyer and seller. Title insurance companies not only provide necessary insurance (see Section C below), but normally handle the financial arrangements of paying off the seller's existing deed of trust and preparing a new one for the buyer, as well as preparing the deed and handling most of the final details of the sale of your house.

Southern California: An escrow is usually opened and escrow instructions filed by both seller and buyer with an escrow company. Title insurance is obtained separately from a title insurance company. The escrow company exchanges the seller's deed for the buyer's money after deducting the amount necessary to pay off all the seller's financial obligations to lenders (the seller's deed of trust), past due taxes and any other liens, etc.

Note: Although it is somewhat unusual, escrows can be legally handled by an attorney representing one of the parties, one party's real estate broker who has a trust account approved for this purpose by the Commissioner of Real Estate, or the escrow department of a bank.

I DID IT MYSELF

When I thought about selling my own house, the thing that intimidated me the most was getting all the paperwork through escrow. I had nightmares about all the ways I could screw it up. As it turned out, there were almost no problems. The title company was easy to deal with. The person I sold to had her credit preapproved, so there were no financing contingencies to remove. My house was in good shape (I had owned it three years and done all the necessary work at the time of purchase), so the structural pest control inspection indicated only a few hundred dollars worth of necessary work, which the buyer agreed to split. The upshot was that the whole escrow process took about 30 days—and wouldn't have taken that long, except the buyer's bank was behind in pro-cessing loans and held things up a few days in getting its check to the title company.

---

[1] Back east, the escrow function is commonly handled by lawyers. What in California is called "closing escrow" is termed "settlement" there.

1. How to Select a Good Escrow Holder

How do you know which title company (in Northern California) or escrow company (in Southern California) to select? After all, you want to be sure that you do business with an organization that is prepared to extend a helping hand to the self-help home seller, not someone who thinks it's beneath his dignity to work with a nonprofessional. If you know someone in your area who has sold her own home, ask her for a recommendation. In addition, a person in the real estate business sympathetic to self-help efforts may be able to make a sound suggestion. Failing this, here are some suggestions. I am personally partial to one company in the San Francisco area which has afforded me excellent service —Founders Title Company. I also have been pleased with the work done by Northern Counties Title Insurance Company and First American Title Insurance Company.

In Southern California, a few of the many reputable companies include the Escrow Department of City National Bank, and both the Nettie Becker and Vera Pollack escrow companies. In addition, Southland Title Insurance Company has traditionally provided reliable insurance and title report services.

In all areas of California, there are some escrow and title companies that simply will not deal with people who are selling their own houses. Others have an attitude which is so negative that by the time you finish dealing with them you will surely wish that they had simply declined your business in the first place. In the years to come, as the number of people selling their own houses increases, this prejudice will disappear. In the meantime, rather than getting mad, it's probably better to think of yourself as a pioneer and realize that while pioneering is mostly fun, there is sure to be the occasional swamp to avoid.

One reason some companies don't want to work with you directly is that they feel they must waste a lot of time explaining terms and concepts which they are sure you don't know. The main ones are defined in the "Escrow Terms Translated Into English" section below. As with the gobbledygook of most professions, the concepts behind the strange lingo are quite simple.

Escrow Terms Translated Into English

• **Prelim, or simply, pre:** The preliminary title report on which, ultimately, your policies of title insurance will be substantially based at close of escrow. See Section C below.

• **Legal description, or simply, legal:** The description of the land being sold in the transaction, regardless of improvements (i.e., buildings). There are different types of "legals," which need not really concern you here, such as Lot and Block numbers and metes and bounds (a complicated exercise in map-reading). The legal description appears on the deed to the property.

Demand (also called "beneficiary statement"): Letter from a lender asking to be paid off. This comes up in the context of a house sale when the holder of your loan is notified by the escrow holder that you are in the process of selling the house. The lender then sends the escrow holder a demand. If the time allowed to close escrow in your contract is reasonably short, you want to request a demand as soon as possible upon opening escrow, so the calculations and arrangements may be completed for closing your deal on the projected closing date. However, if you have a long loan commitment time, if you ask for the demand too soon, it may expire before you close. If you redo the demand, the bank will probably charge you an extra fee. If you owe money to a private party, you may want to try to negotiate a prepayment discount before the escrow holder notifies them that they have the right to full payment.

Good faith or Reg. Z disclosure: The lender's disclosure to the buyer/borrower of all material terms of the loan he is applying for.

Loan commitment: A written statement from a lender promising to lend the buyer a certain amount of money on certain terms.

Funding the loan: After the bank issues a loan commitment, it still must actually fund the loan—that is, get the money to the escrow holder. This is sometimes delayed by backups at the bank.

2. When to Select an Escrow Holder

Although you do not actually open an escrow until you accept an offer to purchase your house, it is wise to do some preliminary investigation in advance, so that you have at least a tentative idea as to whom you will use. After all, if you and the buyer sign a contract on Sunday afternoon, you want to know whom the deposit check should be made out to.

3. Working with the Escrow Holder

It's important to realize that some companies take more initiative than others. In some cases, you have to instruct the company in writing to do every little thing, while in others, the company is more helpful. Your first job should be to clearly understand what the company needs from you and when it needs it. The best way to get this information is to make an appointment with the person in charge of the office you are dealing with and ask. Use the information in this chapter as your guide to asking questions. Check in regularly—call once a week or so.

4. Ordering Title Insurance

It is the buyer's responsibility to order title insurance through the title company. The company will first issue a preliminary report, and then, just before closing, the final title report and the title insurance policy. I discuss title insurance in detail in Section C below.

5. What Will Escrow Services Cost?

Generally, the total cost of title insurance, preliminary title report, final title report, recordation, notarization and escrow services should not exceed 1.5% of the purchase price of the property (see the chart below).[2] I include in this estimate the fees of the escrow and title companies as well as premiums for two title insurance policies, one for the buyer (CLTA policy) and one for the

---

[2] As noted above, in Northern California it is typical to pay all fees to a title insurance company, while in Southern California, the fee is divided between a title insurance and escrow company.

lender in the amount of the loan (ALTA policy). Again, title insurance is discussed in Section C below, so please read this entire section before making any decisions. The insurance premium rates are competitive, so there is little room for negotiation in this area. However, fees for escrow services do vary to some degree. My feeling is that you are wiser to shop for service, not for differences in fees, since levels of service, especially to the non-professional, vary considerably, but fees are pretty much the same.

Finally, you should realize that since the escrow process benefits both buyer and seller, the buyer may want to participate in the selection of the escrow holder.

TYPICAL TITLE INSURANCE AND ESCROW FEES

Sale Price of House	Fees
$100,000	$1,441.25
$150,000	$1,841.75
$200,000	$2,213.25
$250,000	$2,552.75
$300,000	$2,899.25

6. Who Pays for Escrow Services?

There is no law as to who pays escrow costs; it's a matter of custom and negotiation. My usual suggestion is that the seller and buyer split the fee for escrow services, but that the buyer pay for the title insurance premium since that insurance primarily benefits the buyer. See chart as to who pays for what in Chapter 9, Section B.

Local custom, however, plays an important part here. In Southern California the seller traditionally pays for title insurance. Why have the seller pay for a service that benefits the buyer? Who knows, but since it has usually been done that way, you may have a hard time convincing the buyer to pay.

In some Northern California counties, it is customary for the buyer and seller to split the title insurance costs. Sometimes this is done 50-50 and in other locations it is more typical for the buyer to pay only 25%. No matter what the local custom, you and the buyer are free to split this fee in any way you agree.

B. Removing Contingencies

Depending on the exact provisions of the contract you and the buyer sign, there will probably be several contingencies that must be removed before your sale becomes final. Satisfaction of all contingencies included in the contract (clause 6 of the offer in this book) must be acknowledged by the buyer in writing.

1. Inspection Contingencies

Before inspection contingencies can be removed, it's obvious that inspections must be made. It's up to the buyer to hire inspectors (the telephone book Yellow Pages contains a list, if the buyer doesn't have a preference). It's up to the seller to cooperate by arranging for the inspectors to get into the house. There is no compelling reason for you to accompany inspectors on their rounds, but if you wish to, there should be no objection. Inspectors should have copies of your own disclosure statement and all other inspection reports done in the last few years.

Sometimes problems are discovered as a result of inspections. For example, there may be termite damage, or wiring or a roof may need to be replaced. If the problems, whatever they are, will be expensive to fix, the buyer may refuse to go ahead with the deal unless you are willing to pay to correct the problems, or at least some of them. This is her right.

At this point it is normal for buyer and seller to negotiate over who pays for what repairs. It is common that a seller agrees to pay for most or all repairs, but all sorts of other financial arrangements are possible. If you think you have gotten a great price for the house, agreeing to pay for all or most of the repairs may be no problem. However, if you think that you may have underpriced the house in the first place, you will not want to agree to pay for a lot of fix-up work. You would be better off to let the buyer walk away from the deal and then put the house back on the market at a higher price. In short, it will be necessary for you to adopt a negotiating strategy based on the realities of the situation you face.

In many situations, negotiating to remove contingencies can be emotionally difficult. Understandably, neither buyer nor seller wants to expend large sums of money at a point where each probably feels she has already compromised enough. In a sense this is really the crunch point where buyer and seller agree to turn their joint expression of intention to transfer ownership of the house (as evidenced by the original offer and acceptance) into a binding contract or back away from the deal. As part of doing one or the other, either you or the buyer may benefit from the advice of someone with experience in putting together real estate deals, especially if serious problems are discovered by the inspection reports. Don't hesitate to consult an experienced broker or real estate lawyer to help with negotiations or help you custom-tailor paperwork if the removal of contingencies is conditioned upon either or both parties agreeing to do several more or less complicated things.

At this stage, the amount the seller is willing to reduce the price to take into account necessary repairs is called an "escrow credit." In other words the buyer gets a credit against the price of the house for the amount of the repairs. In some instances the buyer's financial institution will require that the money "credited" by the seller actually be used to make the repairs before escrow closes.

However, if the buyer assumes the responsibility of paying for some or all repairs, one or two things will probably happen. One, she will take title to the house in its substandard condition and have to make repairs later Or, two, the buyer's lender will insist that the repairs be made before the sale closes, in which case the buyer will have to come up with the necessary additional cash. The more work that needs to be done, the more likely it is that a financial institution will require that it be done prior to closing. If repairs are major, this can be an impossible burden for a buyer whose finances are already stretched to come up with the down payment.

Example: Mary agreed to sell her home to Albert for $221,000, after having asked $225,000. Mary knew her house was old and hadn't had a pest control inspection in ages, if ever. She told Albert this, and he made his offer contingent upon having a satisfactory pest control inspection. The inspection turned up problems to the tune of $10,000. Albert wrote Mary a memo stating that he would not remove the contingency unless Mary agreed to credit him in escrow with the amount of work recommended by the inspector. Mary refused to do this, feeling that she had given Albert a good deal on the price of the house and he should pay for the problems. After negotiation, Albert and Mary agreed in writing (using the contingency release form set out below) to split the difference. In other words, Mary gave Albert a $5,000 escrow credit. This meant that, even with the sales price staying at $221,000, Albert, in effect, paid Mary

$216,000. Since the financial institution that gave Albert a loan did not require that he do the repairs prior to the close of escrow, he was free to do them at a convenient future date.

A contingency release form is set out below. You should have the buyer date and sign the inspection report and write "Approved as read" on them. Attach the signed report to the release form and keep a copy.

CONTINGENCY RELEASE

_____, Buyer(s) of the property at _____
_____, California, hereby remove the following contingencies from the purchase contract dated _____, 19___.

If this release is based on accepting any inspection report, a copy of the report signed by the Buyer(s), is attached.

Buyer(s) release Seller(s) from liability for any physical defects disclosed by the attached report(s).

_____   _____

_____   _____
Buyer(s)   Seller(s)
_____, 19____   _____, 19_____

If you have agreed to pay for any repairs, add the following language to the release and sign the release along with the buyer:

> providing that by _____ __.M. on _____, 19___,
> the seller agrees in writing to extend to the buyer in escrow a credit
> in the amount of $_____ against the purchase price and
> other debits to be paid by buyer.

Note: We include two copies of the Contingency Release form in the Appendix because it is wise to complete the paperwork to remove each contingency as soon as possible. In other words, if the Structural Pest Control Report and General Contractor's Report are made within a couple of weeks after the real estate sale contract is signed, but financing hasn't yet been approved, the buyer should still remove these first two contingencies. One reason for this is that the time limits in which to remove contingencies having to do with the physical condition of the property are usually shorter than those having to do with financing or the sale of an existing house. As with the contract, make copies of the contingency release for the buyer and keep this form safe and accessible. Your attorney, if you have one, will want to see the release.

2. Financing Contingencies

To remove a financing contingency, the buyer must provide you with written evidence that he has obtained financing that will allow him to go through with the purchase of your house. Usually this is in the form of a written "loan commitment" from a bank (see Section A). It can also be a check for the amount of the purchase price not yet paid. The buyer should also sign a contingency release form like the one in the Appendix.

3. Extending Time Limits

Buyers frequently need more time to satisfy one or more contingencies included in the contract, as might be the case if the buyer is having trouble selling her house. If the time necessary to accomplish some required act runs out and the act has not been done, it is necessary for both parties to agree to extend the time; otherwise the contract is over.

Example: Julie agrees to buy Steve's house for $200,000 contingent upon her arranging financing for 80% of the purchase price with a fixed-rate mortgage at 9-1/2% or lower within 60 days. Julie's loan application gets stuck at the bottom of the pile at the bank, and no action is taken by the 59th day. The bank states that they will get to her application within a week. Julie and Steve agree in writing, using the contract modification form in Chapter 9, Section B, to extend the time necessary to fulfill this contingency for 10 days.

ADDITION TO REAL PROPERTY PURCHASE CONTRACT

The material set out below is hereby made a part of the contract dated
_____,19 _____ between _____
_____, Buyer(s) and _____
_____ , Seller(s) to purchase real property
located at _____
_____.

Read, understood, and agreed to by:

_____   _____
Signature of Buyer   Date

_____   _____
Signature of Seller   Date

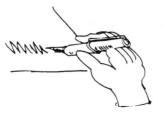

4. Demanding Removal of Contingencies: 96-Hour Wipe-outs

As discussed in Chapter 9, the contract in this book gives you the right to demand (two weeks after the offer is accepted) that the buyer remove all contingencies within 96 hours. If the buyer can't comply, you can terminate the contract and activate a backup offer if you have accepted one. Here is a form you should use to make the demand:

SELLER'S DEMAND FOR REMOVAL OF CONTINGENCIES

Under the terms of the contract dated _____ , 19 ____ between

_____ , Seller(s), and

_____ , Buyer(s), for

purchase of the real property at_____ , California,

Seller(s) hereby demand(s) that Buyer(s) remove the following contingencies specified in Clause

6 of the contract:

☐ ninety-six (96) hours from receipt of this demand (personally delivered) or

☐ five days from mailing of this demand by certified mail.

If Buyer(s) does not remove these contingencies within the time specified, the contract shall

become void, and all deposits shall be promptly returned to Buyer(s) upon Buyer(s)' execution of

a release, releasing Buyer(s) and Seller(s) from all obligation under the contract.

_____   _____ , 19 ____
Seller

Personally delivered: _____ , 19 ____, _____ _ M.

Mailed by certified mail: _____ , 19 ____

5. If a Contingency Cannot Be Met

If the deal fails because a contingency cannot be met, there is neither default nor dispute, and the buyer and seller sign a release cancelling the contract and authorizing the return of the buyer's deposit. .

Here is a release form you and the buyer should sign to release each other from the contract. A tear-out copy is included in the Appendix.

C. TITLE REPORT AND TITLE INSURANCE

Title insurance guarantees the institution that provides the buyer with financing security of good legal title to the property. The title insurance company insures the lender against the possibility that there are undisclosed legal challenges or liens against the property, such as an unrecorded deed, a forged deed, or an unrecorded easement. If such a claim comes up and is covered by the title insurance policy, the title insurance company will pay it off. The result is that the buyer will still own the property and the particular claim will be extinguished, or the buyer (or lender) is paid off if the claim is honored.

REAL ESTATE PURCHASE CONTRACT RELEASE

_____ , Seller(s), and

_____ , Buyer(s), hereby

execute this mutual release, releasing all our legal rights with respect to the contract dated

_____ for sale of the real property at _____

_____ , and declaring the contract void and of no effect.

Each of us expressly releases the others, their heirs, insurers and legal representatives,

from all claims known or unknown to us that have arisen or may arise from the contract.

In executing this release we intend to bind our spouses, heirs, legal representatives,

assigns, and anyone else claiming under us, in addition to ourselves. None of us has assigned to

another party a claim arising from the contract.

Buyer(s) acknowledge(s) that Seller(s) has returned to Buyer(s) or directed the escrow

holder to return all deposits made by Buyer(s) in connection with the contract.

Signatures: Date:

_____   _____
Seller

_____   _____
Seller

_____   _____
Buyer

_____   _____
Buyer

A policy of title insurance is required as part of every house sale that is financed by a bank or other financial institution. If you are financing the sale yourself, it's up to you and the buyer whether to pay for insurance. I strongly recommend title insurance. Because title insurance benefits the buyer, she will probably want to purchase it.

For all situations where the buyer is taking out a loan from a financial institution, both a California Land Title Association (CLTA) policy and an American Land Title Association (ALTA) policy are required. The CLTA policy covers items in the public record (e.g., mortgage or trust deed liens, judgment liens from court actions). In addition to insuring against encumbrances that appear on the public record, an ALTA policy also insures against many defects in title that do not appear on the public record, such as would be discovered by a survey (encroachments, squatters in possession, etc.)[3] Before either title insurance policy will be issued, the title company will want to be sure that the title to your property is in good shape. It does this by first examining it and then issuing a preliminary title report (often called a "pre" or "prelim" in real estate lingo). This should be done soon after your deposit receipt contract with the buyer is signed (whether or not a lender is involved) so that the buyer, seller and lender have time to decide what to do if problems are turned up. If there are serious problems, you will almost surely need the help of a lawyer.

When your deal is ready to "close" (just before the deed from you to your buyer is recorded), the title insurance company will make a last-minute check of the public record to see if any changes have taken place in the condition of title since the preliminary title report was issued. If not, then the "prelim" stands in effect as a final title report and forms the basis for the policy of title insurance. If changes have taken place, they will be investigated and the results reported to the parties in a supplemental title report. The buyer and lender will then decide whether to proceed or to call the deal off (under the contract provision that requires the seller to provide clear title to the property). Usually, no changes in the condition of title occur between the issuance of the "prelim" and recordation of the deed closing the transaction.

---

[3]The coverage of these two types of policies is also somewhat different. The CLTA policy insures title up to the amount of the purchase price and benefits the buyer. The ALTA policy generally insures title up to the amount of the loan and benefits the lender. The buyer can, however order an ALTA policy to protect himself up to the full price of the property.

D. Closing Escrow

Escrow cannot close until the deed is recorded in favor of the buyer, and the escrow holder issues a check for the seller and another to pay off existing loans on the property. All of the preliminary paperwork necessary to get this to happen should be completed not less than four working days before the buyer expects to actually take title. This allows for delays in transmittal of loan documents between lender(s) and the escrow holder. It is normal for the buyer and seller to go to the escrow company's office, though not necessarily at the same time, to handle this paperwork.

The last form you need to sign instructs the escrow holder to record the new deed. These "final escrow instructions" are on a standard form the escrow company will give you to approve and sign.

Here now is what the buyer and seller need be responsible for:

THE ESCROW PROCESS

BUYER NEEDS TO:	SELLER NEEDS TO:
Southern California only: Open escrow by filing and signing escrow instructions, along with seller, although these will be amended later. (In Northern California, escrow instructions are signed later.)	Open escrow by depositing buyer's deposit check upon acceptance of purchase offer or counter-offer.
Apply for loan(s). If loans are assumable, get written consent of lenders to have their loans assumed. The escrow holder prepares the loan assumption documents.	Obtain receipt for buyer's deposit check from escrow holder and give copy to buyer (obtained directly by buyer if buyer and seller visit title or escrow company together).
Order preliminary title report.	Cooperate with buyer's attempt to arrange inspections of property.
Arrange for inspection of property by pest control operator, general contractor and any others called for in contract (e.g., roofer). Obtain the reports within time allowed by contract and give copies to seller.	Make sure buyer has signed copy of Real Estate Transfer Disclosure Statement and any other disclosure statement(s).
Inspections (if called for in contract)	Cooperate with buyer's loan institution to allow appraiser to visit property. This is necessary for lender to approve loan.

Inspections (if called for in contract)

Pest control	Energy
General	Asbestos
Roofing	Geology
Electrical	Other _____
Plumbing	

BUYER NEEDS TO:	SELLER NEEDS TO:
Approve inspection reports and remove contingencies. If price or credit needs to be renegotiated because inspection turns up problems, make written addendum to contract.	Make sure buyer has signed copies of inspection reports "approved as read" and executed contingency release form. If problems are discovered, it may be necessary to renegotiate price.
Increase deposit in escrow according to clause 2 of contract.	Make sure local ordinances are complied with: energy conservation, smoke detectors, disclosure of rent control ordinance(s), etc. Title or escrow company can often help to spell these out, as can county clerk or city real estate, public works or planning department.
Provide written evidence to seller of commitment by lender for loan. Once this is provided, the escrow holder will contact the lender directly to get the loan documents and the money.	Be sure escrow company contacts lenders for demands so existing loan(s) may be paid off.
Give written notice of approval of title report. (If the title report turns up problems, see a lawyer.)	Approve and sign final escrow instruction form, with anticipated closing date.
Provide "binder" (provided by insurance agent) showing your fire insurance coverage for house.	Sign Grant Deed provided by escrow company, transferring title of the house to buyer; this will be recorded (in the county recorder's office) by the escrow holder when it is certain that the buyer's money is "in."
Approve and sign final escrow instruction form, with anticipated closing date.	Sign bill of sale for any personal property transferred to buyer as part of this transaction.
Sign truth-in-lending disclosure statements, promissory notes, deeds of trust, and, if applicable, loan assumption documents supplied by lender(s).	Give keys (and garage door opener, etc.) to escrow holder with instructions as to when to release them to buyer.*
Write "closing check," including down payment and agreed on portion of closing costs and final deposit in escrow.	*This is done at the close of escrow if the seller has agreed to move out at that time. If seller is staying on after the close of escrow and renting from buyer, keys are turned over on the date seller agrees to get out.

First American Title Company of San Francisco

MAIN OFFICE: 300 PINE STREET (94104) · P.O. BOX 3078, RINCON ANNEX · (415) 989-1300
SAN FRANCISCO, CALIFORNIA 94119

PLEASE REPLY TO: 531 Second Street, San Francisco CA 94102   (415) 931-6834

XX SELLER'S   ☐ LENDER'S   **ESCROW INSTRUCTIONS**

Order Number N-150900-MN   Date October 8, 1986

To: FIRST AMERICAN TITLE COMPANY

I/We hand you herewith

1)   Grant deed to subject property;
2)   Bill of Sale;

which you are authorized to deliver and/or record when you have received for my account the following:

1)   Funds as set forth below;

and when you can issue your standard coverage form policy of title insurance with a liability of $ 184,000.00

on the property described as   1535 Bradley Street
                                     San Francisco CA 94117

showing title vested in   GREGORY RANDOLPH and FREIDA RANDOLPH, husband and wife

---NOT APPLICABLE---

Subject to:

1. Printed exceptions and conditions in said policy.
2. ☐ all   ☐ 2nd half   General and special taxes for fiscal year 19   19
3. Assessments and/or bonds not delinquent.
4. Exceptions numbered   as shown in your preliminary title report dated   , 19
   issued in connection with the above order number.

ALL AMOUNTS SHOWN HEREIN ARE ESTIMATES AND ARE NOT TO BE CONSTRUED AS FINAL FIGURES.

Upon consummation of this escrow, you are authorized to disburse in accordance with the following statement. Prorate as of
October 10, , 19 86 on the basis of a 30 day month. Taxes based on the latest available tax figures.
OR RECORDATION

	Debits	Credits
Sales Price		184,000.00
Deposit Retained (paid outside of escrow)		
Encumbrance of Record		
Loan Trust Fund		
Loan Discount Fee		
Deed of Trust ☐ 1st ☐ 2nd ☐ 3rd		
☐ Pay Taxes		
☐ Personal Property Tax		
☐ Pay Assessments or Bonds		
X Prorate Taxes Fr. 7/1/86 To 10/10/86 on $347.67-6 mons.	191.22	
☐ Prorate Fire Ins. Fr. To on $		
☐ Prorate Int. @ % Fr. To on $		
Hold in escrow for drain-pipe repairs -release upon	300.00	
authorization of both brokers		
Pay Commission GEORGE DEVINE REALTY and License No.		
ESTATE INTERNATIONAL	11,040.00	
3R Report - George Devine Realty	11.00	
Pay energy conservation -	400.00	
Pay Demand of COAST SAVINGS - Principal	37,463.42	
Interest from 10/15/86		
Reconveyance & Statement Fees	100.00	
Hold in escrow for receipt of actual payoff demand	2,500.00	
PAY DEMAND OF: Saul Greenstein, as Trustee - Principal	19,639.19	
Prepayment Penalty	1,066.74	
Recon. $65.00	65.00	
OOOOOOOOOX Interest 9/25/86 to receipt	160.44	
Notary Fee $10.00	10.00	
Title Prem. Std. $ ALTA $		
Escrow $		
Documentary Transfer Tax $ 920.00	920.00	
Recording $ 10.00	10.00	
Balance to Seller ☐ Mail ☐ Will Call FIRST AMERICAN TITLE N150926	110,122.99	
Totals	184,000.00	184,000.00

These instructions are effective until   , 19   and thereafter unless revoked by written demand and authorization
satisfactory to you. Incorporated herein and made a part hereof by reference are the "General Provisions" and any additional instructions
appearing on the reverse side of this page.

Received: , 19   X

First American Title Company   PETER P. MILLER   X

                    Address   CAROL L. MILLER

By_____ Phone No. _____

CHAPTER 12

WHAT IF SOMETHING GOES WRONG?

░░

Hopefully, nothing will go wrong with your house sale, but realistically, there is always some chance that it will. I have already discussed the possibility that one or more contingencies will not be removed by the buyer (even though she makes a good faith effort to do so) and that the deal will fall through as a result. Here I briefly discuss other possible problem areas.

A. POTENTIAL PROBLEMS

• **Somebody dies.** Technically speaking, a ratified purchase contract for real property is enforceable even if one of the parties dies. This is because a person's estate is responsible for meeting his lawful obligations. Just the same, you can bet your bottom dollar the title insurance and/or escrow companies involved will put on the brakes and call their attorneys if one of the principals dies. You should do exactly the same. Chances are the estate will wish to get out of the deal and will be willing to pay you something for a release.

• **Somebody welshes on the deal.** Breach of contract, technically, means "failure to perform without legal excuse." What a court might consider a "legal excuse," justifying termination of the contract, depends on the circumstances. That subject is beyond the scope of this book. But if you back out of the deal simply because you get another offer which you feel is more likely to go through (or if the buyer has taken a number of significant actions in reliance on the existence of the contract, such as selling his existing house), the buyer can probably successfully sue you and make you comply with the terms of the contract.[1]

Example: John sold his home to Jack for $250,000, or so Jack thought. John felt, after a while, that Jack had driven too hard a bargain. Jack was well aware that he'd made a good deal for himself. After all, he had looked all over for a home with these features at this price. Jack sold his old home, allowing himself a month to stay there free until he could move into his new house. Before escrow could close— although all conditions had been met regarding inspections, financing, etc.—John received another offer of $270,000, which he wanted to accept. He offered, of course, to return all the money Jack had deposited, but Jack refused, claiming that if he did so, John would breach an enforceable contract and Jack—by putting up a substantial deposit, removing the contingencies in a timely manner and arranging financing—had complied with his part of the deal. John's lawyer advised him that if he accepted the second offer, he could wind up in a lawsuit, and the court would probably order him to sell to Jack, as well as to pay Jack's court costs and attorneys fees. John groused about the loss of the additional $20,000, but wisely decided to honor his contract with Jack.

If the buyer refuses to go through with the deal without a good reason (such as an unsatisfactory pest control report or the failure to sell an existing house, if those contingencies are written into the contract), the seller is entitled to recover actual damages. This amount is often difficult to figure exactly, because the seller has a duty to try to sell the house to another purchaser and by so doing, limit ("mitigate," in legalese), or even eliminate, her loss. As a result, in practice, when a buyer backs out of a purchase transaction without a good reason, damages are usually established contractually at 3% of the sale price or the amount of the deposit put in escrow, whichever is less. This issue is dealt with specifically in Clause 3 of the offer to purchase real property, in Chapter 9.

It is fairly rare that the seller actually sues the defaulting buyer for money over and above the amount of the deposit. First of all, most contracts (including the one in this book) limit damages to 3% of the deposit. But even if there is no contractual limit, the amount of damages the seller has suffered doesn't usually warrant it. After all, the seller can presumably sell the house to someone else and may even get more. Also, probably the principal reason that buyers default is financial difficulty. If this is your situation, you may be faced with the prospect of suing someone who's broke. Remember when your grandmother used to

---

[1]Of course, if you invoke a wipe-out clause such as clause 25 in the offer in this book and if the buyer does not remove the contingencies, you are free to sell to someone else.

say "You can't get blood from a turnip"? She was right. A court judgment against someone who suddenly can't afford to ride the bus isn't going to do you a lot of good.

Example: Alison was ecstatic when she accepted Susan's offer of $185,000 for her home, along with a deposit check for $1,000. She'd never thought she could get that much for it. And the best part was that it really looked like the sale would go through, as Alison felt that the contingencies having to do with inspections and financing could be fulfilled easily, as the home was in perfect condition, and Susan's financial statement showed her ability to qualify for the needed loan with no trouble. A week later, when the pest control inspector was supposed to arrive, Susan called Alison to say that she (Susan) had found another home she liked just as much for $170,000 and was cancelling her contract with Alison. Alison was irate and told Susan this constituted a default. Not so, insisted Susan, since the required inspections had yet to be made and approved, and there would probably be something wrong with the house anyway. Alison told Susan she could not disapprove of the inspection reports until they were ordered, paid for and made, and only then if they turned up real problems. Since the reports (including a roofing report, contractor's walk-through and plumber's inspection, as called for in the contract) would likely cost Susan almost $1,000, Alison suggested that Susan agree that she (Alison) could keep the $1,000 deposit as consideration for ending the contract. Although this annoyed Susan, she finally agreed when she realized that if the inspection reports didn't turn up any problems, she might be out both the cost of the reports and the deposit.

• **The property is destroyed by fire, earthquake, flood, etc.** As explained in Clause 12 of the purchase contract in Chapter 9, this matter is normally handled as follows: If the buyer has either physical possession or legal title, he is responsible for the physical condition of the property and for insuring it. If the buyer has neither of these, the seller remains the responsible party. The point is simple. To protect yourself, be sure your homeowner's policy is in force until the close of escrow.

B. THE ROLE OF THE ESCROW HOLDER IN A DISPUTE

If a dispute arises between buyer and seller during the escrow period, the escrow holder is not the appropriate party to make any decisions about what to do with title papers, deposit monies, etc. The escrow holder, after all, is only a neutral stakeholder. Normally, if a dispute arises, the escrow holder will do nothing until the buyer and seller resolve it. However, if the dispute drags on long enough, the escrow company may get uncomfortable, being stuck in the middle, and initiate a court action (usually called an "interpleader") to get the dispute resolved. This normally involves asking the court to take custody of the deposited funds and to render a judgment as to their disposition.

Important: Let me reiterate that the information provided in this chapter is designed only as a brief overview of what may happen in some of the instances when a house sale deal begins to unravel. In general, if buyer and seller have a binding contract, and something other than a simple buyer default (with liquidated damages paid to seller) occurs, you should probably be on your way to a lawyer's office. Hopefully, the attorney can help you resolve the matter, with no need to go to court.

GLOSSARY

Adjustable rate loan: A loan under which the interest rate charged may change depending on market interest rates. **Also called variable rate loan.**

Adverse possession: The process by which someone may acquire ownership of real estate by living on it for at least five years and meeting other legal requirements.

ALTA (American Land Title Association) Title Insurance Policy: A title insurance policy that covers more risks than the standard (CLTA) policy. Usually the buyer orders an ALTA policy for the lenders and a CTLA policy for himself.

Amortization: The payment of a debt, by installments over a period of time.

Arbitration: A method of resolving disputes by submitting the problem to an arbitrator and agreeing to abide by his decision.

Assumable loan: A real estate loan that may be taken over (assumed) by a new owner.

Assumption fee: The fee charged by a lender when a new owner takes over an existing loan.

Attorney in fact: Someone who has authority to act for another. See **power of attorney**.

Balloon payment: A payment of most of a loan (often 98% or more) that comes due at the end of a short loan term (3-5 years is common).

Basis: The figure from which profit on the sale of property is computed for income tax purposes. For example, if your basis in your house is $50,000, and you sell it for $75,000, you make a profit of $25,000. The basis is usually what you paid for the property or its value when you inherited it, subject to certain adjustments for improvements and other factors.

Beneficiary: A person who inherits under a will or receives property put in trust. When a deed of trust is executed, the beneficiary is the lender of the underlying loan.

Binder: A document, issued by an insurance company, that states that the company will insure certain premises.

Boot: Money or something else of value thrown in when real estate is exchanged.

Broker: A real estate broker is licensed by the state to represent someone else in the sale of real estate.

Cal-Vet Loans: Real estate loans for qualifying veterans, obtained through a program of the California Department of Veterans Affairs.

Capital improvements: Permanent improvements made to real estate.

CLTA (California Land Title Association) Title Insurance Policy: The standard form for title insurance policies in California.

Commission: The percentage of the sale price of a house that is paid to the real estate broker(s) who handled the sale.

Community property: Very generally, all property acquired by a couple during marriage and before permanent separation, except for gifts to and inheritances by one spouse only. The nature of the property (community or separate) can be changed by written agreement between the spouses. See **separate property.**

Comparable sales: Sales of houses comparable to the one you want to sell. The selling price of such houses is useful when pricing a similar home. Also called "comparables."

Condominium: An individually owned unit in a multi-unit building.

Conservator: Someone appointed by a court to manage the affairs of a mentally incompetent person.

Contingency: A condition of sale. A buyer often offers to buy real esate contingent on his obtaining financing, or selling his existing house, or receiving a satisfactory pest control inspection of the property.

Co-signer: Someone who signs a promissory note to guarantee payment by the primary signer/borrower.

Covenant: A promise, made in a deed or separate document, that restricts the use that can be made of land.

Covenants, Conditions and Restrictions (CC&R's): Restrictions that govern the use of property. They are usually enforced by a homeowners' association, and must be passed on the new owners of the property. If your property is subject to CC&R's, you must disclose this to the buyer before title is transferred.

Deed: A document that transfers ownership of real property.

Demand: A request from a lender that a loan be paid off. Also called "beneficiary statement."

Deposit: The "earnest money" given the seller by a buyer when he makes an offer to buy a house.

Dissolution: The legal term for divorce.

Documentary transfer tax: A tax imposed by cites and counties on sales of real estate, usually 55¢ per $500 of the sales price. The tax must be paid before the deed can be recorded.

Earnest money: A deposit, made to show the buyer's good faith, that accompanies an offer to buy real property.

Easement: A legal right to use another's land, usually for a limited purpose. For example, you can grant someone an easement to use a corner of your property as a shortcut to their property. An easement is a legal interest in land, and the written grant of an easement should be recorded.

Emancipated minor: A minor who has the rights of an adult because he has been married, is in the military, or has been declared emancipated by a court.

Encumbrance: An interest in real property owned by another, such as a lien, mortgage, trust deed, or other claim.

Equity: A property owner's interest in the property, over and above the amount of liens and other encumbrances.

Escrow: The process during which a buyer and seller of real estate deposit documents and funds with a third party (the escrow holder, which is usually an escrow or title company) with instructions for making the transfer. To close escrow, the company transfers the buyer's money to the seller and transfers the deed to the property to the buyer.

Exclusive Authorization and Right to Sell: The standard broker's contract. The seller agrees to pay a commission to the broker if the broker produces a full-price offer for purchase of the house.

Federal National Mortgage Association (FNMA): A corporation that buys FHA and VA mortgages from banks and other institutional lenders. Usually called "Fannie Mae."

Fee simple: Complete ownership of real property.

Fixed-rate loan: A real estate loan where the interest rate charged stays constant over the term of the loan.

Fixture: Something that is permanently attached to real property and is considered part of the real property. For example, bookshelves built into a house are fixtures; free-standing bookshelves are considered furniture, not part of the real property.

Foreclosure: The forced sale of real property, ordered by a court or under a trustee's power of sale, to pay off a loan that the owner of the property has defaulted on.

Government National Mortgage Association (GNMA): A federal agency that buys mortgages from institutional lenders. Usually called "Ginnie Mae."

Gross income: Total income, before expenses are subtracted.

Installment sale: A sale in which the sale price is paid over several years. Installment sales may have tax advantages.

Interest-only loan: A loan that the borrower repays by first making payments only of interest and then paying the principal back in one large balloon payment.

Joint tenancy: A way co-owners may hold title to property so that when one co-owner dies, her interest in the property passes directly to the surviving co-owners without probate and regardless of any will provision to the contrary. Compare **tenancy in common.**

Legal description: A description, in a deed, of the location of land, sufficiently detailed to enable a surveyor to identify the property.

Lien: A claim on property for payment of a debt. For example, a tax lien is a lien placed on property when the owner has not paid taxes. A mechanic's lien is imposed by someone who makes improvements on the house (a carpenter, for example). If the carpenter isn't paid, he can enforce his claim by foreclosing on the property. See Civil Code § 3110.

Liquidated damages: An amount, specififed in a contract for the sale of real estate, that the buyer agrees he will pay the seller if the buyer defaults on the contract.

Loan commitment: A written statement from a bank or savings and loan that binds the bank, for a certain period of time, to loan money to a purchaser.

Market value: The price property is worth on the open market.

Marketable title: Title to property that is free of encumbrances so that a reasonable buyer would accept it.

Minor: In California, anyone less than 18 years old.

Option: The right to buy property at a certain price (and other terms) for a certain period of time. The holder of the option pays something for the right.

Personal property: All possessions that aren't considered real estate (see **Real property**).

Points: A percentage of the amount of a VA or FHA loan, charged to the seller by the lender when the loan is made. One point is one percent of the loan amount. Points are comparable to the loan origination fee charged the borrower of a conventional loan.

Power of attorney: Authority, given by one person to another, to sign documents and make decisions for the first person.

Private mortgage insurance: Insurance for lenders that guarantees payment of a mortgage.

Promissory note: A written promise to pay money.

Property taxes: Local taxes imposed annually on real estate.

Quitclaim deed: A deed that transfers any interest the person signing it may have in particular property but does not guarantee anything about the extent of that interest.

Real Estate Transfer Disclosure Statement: A detailed disclosure form, which a seller is required by law to fill out and give to the buyer before title is transferred. The form covers the condition of the property.

Real property (real estate): Land and things permanently affixed to land, such as buildings.

Realtor: A real estate broker who belongs to the National Association of Realtors.

Recording: The process of filing a copy of a deed with the County Recorder for the county in which the land is located. Recording creates a public record of all changes in ownership of all property in the state.

Right of survivorship: The right of a surviving joint tenant to take ownership of a deceased joint tenant's share of the property.

Roll over: The term for a tax break given to homeowners who sell one house and invest the proceeds of the sale in another house within 24 months. The gain from the sale of the first house is "rolled over" into the new home.

Sale-Leaseback: An arrangement by which a homeowner sells her house but continues living there under a lease from the new owner.

Salesperson: A real estate salesperson is someone who is licensed by the state to work in real estate sales but must be employed and supervised by a licensed broker.

Security interest: A claim against property, given by a debtor to ensure payment of a debt. For example, if you borrow money, you may execute a deed of trust on your house, giving the lender the right to have the house sold to pay the debt if you don't pay back the loan. The lender has a security interest in your house.

Separate property: Property that is not community property; that is, property that is acquired by an unmarried person or acquired by gift or inheritance by a married person.

Special assessment: An assessment of real estate made for a specific project, such as installation of street lights or a sewer system.

Special studies zones: Areas of possible earthquake hazards, delineated by state geologists. Sellers must tell buyers if the property is located within a special studies zone.

Tenancy by the entirety: A way for married couples to hold title to property. It is no longer used in California, although some statutes refer to it.

Tenancy in common: A way for co-owners to hold title that allows them maximum freedom to dispose of their interests by sale, gift, or will. Upon a co-owner's death, his share goes to his beneficiaries (if there is a will) or heirs, not to the other co-owners. Compare **joint tenancy**.

Title: Evidence of ownership of real property.

Title company: A company that conducts title searches, issues title insurance and, often, handles escrow proceedings.

Title insurance : Insurance that guarantees a buyer or lender against loss from defects in the title of the real property being bought.

Title search: A search of the public records in the County Recorder's office, usually made by a title insurance company, to see if the current owner of real property actually has good title to the land and that no challenges have been raised.

Trust deed: In California, the most common instrument for financing real estate purchases (many other states use mortgages). The trust deed transfers title to land to a trustee, who holds the title as security for a loan. When the loan is paid off, title is transferred to the borrower. The trustee has no powers unless the borrower defaults on the loan; then the trustee can sell the property and pay the lender back from the proceeds.

Trustee: One who manages trust property for a beneficiary. When a deed of trust is used, the trustee has no powers unless the borrower defaults on the underlying loan. If that happens the trustee can foreclose on the trust deed and have the property sold to pay off the loan.

Truth in lending requirements: Federal laws that require lenders to disclose certain loan information to prospective borrowers. Also called "Regulation Z" requirements.

Usury: The practice of charging an illegally high rate of interest.

Variable rate loan: Same as **adjustable rate loan.**

APPENDIX

Recording requested by

and when recorded mail this deed
and tax statements to:

For recorder's use

QUITCLAIM DEED

☐ This transfer is exempt from the documentary transfer tax.

☐ The documentary transfer tax is $_____ and is computed on
    ☐ the full value of the interest or property conveyed.
    ☐ the full value less the value of liens or encumbrances remaining thereon at the
       time of sale.

The property is located in   ☐ an unincorporated area.
                       ☐ the city of _____.

For a valuable consideration, receipt of which is hereby acknowledged,

hereby quitclaim(s) to

the following real property in the City of _____,
County of _____, California:

Date: _____   _____
                                _____
                                _____
                                _____

State of California
County of   } ss.

On _____, 19____, _____, known
to me or proved by satisfactory evidence to be the person(s) whose name(s) is/are subscribed
above, personally appeared before me, a Notary Public for California, and acknowledged that
_____ executed this deed.

        [SEAL]   _____
                                  Signature of Notary

AGREEMENT WITH BROKER

_____, the seller(s) of the real
property located at _____in
the City of_____, County of _____,
California, hereby engage _____, a licensed real estate broker
in the State of California, to advise them as to the mechanics involved in selling their own house,
with the intention that the broker shall act as needed as an advisor as to typical sales procedures,
the preparation of routine forms, comparable sales prices, information on available financing, and
suggestions as to competent professionals, such as attorneys, accountants, pest control
inspectors, general contractors, etc. as needed.

　　Broker shall not receive a commission but shall be compensated at $_____ per
hour, not to exceed a total amount of $_____ , based on the broker's estimate that
the advice required shall not call for more than _____ hours of the broker's labor.
Broker shall be paid as follows: _____
_____.

If the seller and broker agree that more of the broker's time is needed, an additional written
contract will be prepared.

　　It is understood that sellers are handling their own sale and are solely responsible for all
decisions made and paperwork prepared. In addition, it is expressly agreed that broker will not
provide any legal direction or tax or estate planning advice, and shall make no representation
concerning the physical condition of the property or the legal condition of title to any party. Broker
expressly recommends that sellers seek the appropriate professional advice offered by attorneys,
tax accountants, pest control inspectors and/or general contractors as needed.

　　Agreed this _____ day of _____, 19__, by:

_____

_____
Seller(s)

_____
Broker

By _____

REAL ESTATE TRANSFER DISCLOSURE STATEMENT

THIS DISCLOSURE STATEMENT CONCERNS THE REAL PROPERTY SITUATED IN THE CITY OF _____, COUNTY OF _____, STATE OF CALIFORNIA, DESCRIBED AS _____. THIS STATEMENT IS A DISCLOSURE OF THE CONDITION OF THE ABOVE DESCRIBED PROPERTY IN COMPLIANCE WITH SECTION 1102 OF THE CIVIL CODE AS OF _____, 19___. IT IS NOT A WARRANTY OF ANY KIND BY THE SELLER(S) OR ANY AGENT(S) REPRESENTING ANY PRINCIPAL(S) IN THIS TRANSACTION, AND IS NOT A SUBSTITUTE FOR ANY INSPECTIONS OR WARRANTIES THE PRINCIPAL(S) MAY WISH TO OBTAIN.

I

COORDINATION WITH OTHER DISCLOSURE FORMS

This Real Estate Transfer Disclosure Statement is made pursuant to Section 1102 of the Civil Code. Other statutes require disclosures, depending upon the details of the particular real estate transaction (for example: special study zone and purchase-money liens on residential property).

Substituted Disclosures: The following disclosures have or will be made in connection with this real estate transfer, and are intended to satisfy the disclosure obligations on this form, where the subject matter is the same: _____

_____
_____
_____

(list all substituted disclosure forms to be used in connection with this transaction)

II

SELLERS INFORMATION

The Seller discloses the following information with the knowledge that even though this is not a warranty, prospective Buyers may rely on this information in deciding whether and on what terms to purchase the subject property. Seller hereby authorizes any agent(s) representing any principal(s) in this transaction to provide a copy of this statement to any person or entity in connection with any actual or anticipated sale of the property.

THE FOLLOWING ARE REPRESENTATIONS MADE BY THE SELLER(S) AND ARE NOT THE REPRESENTATIONS OF THE AGENT(S), IF ANY. THIS INFORMATION IS A DISCLOSURE AND IS NOT INTENDED TO BE PART OF ANY CONTRACT BETWEEN THE BUYER AND SELLER.

Seller __is __is not occupying the property.

A. The subject property has the items checked below (read across):

__Range   __Oven   __Microwave
__Dishwasher   __Trash Compactor   __Garbage Disposal
__Washer/Dryer Hookups   __Window Screens   __Rain Gutters
__Burglar Alarms   __Smoke Detector(s)   __Fire Alarm
__T.V. Antenna   __Satellite Dish   __Intercom
__Central Heating   __Central Air Cndtng.   __Evaporator Cooler(s)
__Wall/Window Air Cndtng.   __Sprinklers   __Public Sewer System
__Septic Tank   __Sump Pump   __Water Softener
__Patio/Decking   __Built-in Barbeque   __Gazebo
__Sauna   __Pool   __Spa__Hot Tub
__Security Gate(s)   __Garage Door Opener(s)   __Number Remote Controls

Garage: __Attached   __Not Attached   __Carport
Pool/Spa Heater: __Gas   __Solar   __Electric
Water Heater: __Gas   __Private Utility or
Water Supply: __City   __Well
Gas Supply: __Utility   __Bottled   Other _____

Exhaust Fan(s) in _____ 220 Volt Wiring in _____ Fireplace(s) in _____ Gas Starter _____
Roof(s): Type: _____ Age: _____ (approx.)
Other: _____
Are there, to the best of your (Seller's) knowledge, any of the above that are not in operating condition? __Yes __No. If yes, then describe.
(Attach additional sheets if necessary.): _____
_____
_____

__Interior Walls __Ceilings __Floors __Exterior Walls __Insulation __Roof(s) __Windows __Doors __Foundation __Slab(s) __Driveways __Sidewalks __Walls/Fences __Electrical Systems __Plumbing/Sewers/Septics __Other Structural Components (Describe: _____

_____

If any of the above is checked, explain. (Attach additional sheets if necessary): _____
_____
_____

B. Are you (Seller) aware of any significant defects/malfunctions in any of the following? __Yes __No. If yes, check appropriate space(s) below.

C. Are you (Seller) aware of any of the following:

1. Features of the property shared in common with adjoining landowners, such as walls, fences, and driveways, whose use or responsibility for maintenance may have an effect on the subject property .... __Yes __No
2. Any encroachments, easements or similar matters that may affect your interest in the subject property .... __Yes __No

3. Room additions, structural modifications, or other alterations or repairs made without necessary permits .... ___Yes ___No

4. Room additions, structural modifications, or other alterations or repairs not in compliance with building codes .... ___Yes ___No

5. Landfill (compacted or otherwise) on the property or any portion thereof .... ___Yes ___No

6. Any settling from any cause, or slippage, sliding, or other soil problems ...... ___Yes ___No

7. Flooding, drainage or grading problems.................................. ___Yes ___No

8. Major damage to the property or any of the structures from fire, earthquake, floods, or landslides .... ___Yes ___No

9. Any zoning violations, nonconforming uses, violations of "setback" requirements .... ___Yes ___No

10. Neighborhood noise problems or other nuisances .... ___Yes ___No

11. CC&R's or other deed restrictions or obligations .... ___Yes ___No

12. Homeowners' Association which has any authority over the subject property .... ___Yes ___No

13. Any "common area" (facilities such as pools, tennis courts, walkways, or other areas co-owned in undivided interest with others)................ ___Yes ___No

14. Any notices of abatement or citations against the property .... ___Yes ___No

15. Any lawsuits against the seller threatening to or affecting this real property .... ___Yes ___No

If the answer to any of these is yes, explain. (Attach additional sheets if necessary.): _____
_____
_____
_____

Seller certifies that the information herein is true and correct to the best of the Seller's knowledge as of the date signed by the Seller.

Seller _____
Date _____

Seller _____
Date _____

III
AGENTS INSPECTION DISCLOSURE

(Please Print)

IV
AGENTS INSPECTION DISCLOSURE

(To be completed only if the agent who has obtained the offer is other than the agent above.)

THE UNDERSIGNED, BASED ON A REASONABLY COMPETENT AND DILIGENT VISUAL INSPECTION OF THE ACCESSIBLE AREAS OF THE PROPERTY, STATES THE FOLLOWING:

(Please Print)

V

BUYER(S) AND SELLER(S) MAY WISH TO OBTAIN PROFESSIONAL ADVICE AND/OR INSPECTIONS OF THE PROPERTY AND TO PROVIDE FOR APPROPRIATE PROVISIONS IN A CONTRACT BETWEEN BUYER AND SELLER(S) WITH RESPECT TO ANY ADVICE/INSPECTIONS/DEFECTS.

(To be completed only if the seller is represented by an agent in this transaction.)

THE UNDERSIGNED, BASED ON THE ABOVE INQUIRY OF THE SELLER(S) AS TO THE CONDITION OF THE PROPERTY AND BASED ON A REASONABLY COMPETENT AND DILIGENT

VISUAL INSPECTION OF THE ACCESSIBLE AREAS OF THE PROPERTY IN CONJUNCTION WITH THAT INQUIRY, STATES THE FOLLOWING: _____
_____
_____

Agent (Broker
Representing Seller) _____ By _____ Date
_____
(Associate Licensee
or Broker-Signature)

_____
_____
_____
_____

Agent (Broker
obtaining the Offer) _____ By _____ Date
_____
(Associate Licensee
or Broker-Signature)

I/WE ACKNOWLEDGE RECEIPT OF A COPY OF THIS STATEMENT.

Seller _____ Date _____ Buyer
_____ Date _____
Seller _____ Date _____ Buyer
_____ Date _____

Agent (Broker
Representing Seller) _____ By _____ Date
_____
(Associate Licensee
or Broker-Signature)

Agent (Broker
obtaining the Offer) _____ By _____ Date
_____
(Associate Licensee
or Broker-Signature)

A REAL ESTATE BROKER IS QUALIFIED TO ADVISE ON REAL ESTATE. IF YOU DESIRE LEGAL ADVICE, CONSULT YOUR ATTORNEY.

SPECIAL STUDIES ZONE DISCLOSURE

The real property at _____,
_____ County, California, lies within a special studies zone designated
by the California Department of Geology.

This disclosure is made under Public Resources Code § 2621.9.

_____   _____, 19____
Seller

I acknowledge that I have received a copy of this disclosure form.

_____   _____, 19____
Buyer

CREDIT INFORMATION

Name: _____

Soc. Sec. No. _____

Home phone: _____

Work phone: _____

Address: _____

_____

[ ] own   [ ] rent for $_____/mo. from _____

Phone:_____

Previous address if less than 2 years at current address:

_____

_____

Name, address and phone of employer:

_____

_____

_____

Title: _____

How long with employer: _____

If less than 2 years, name, address and phone of previous employer:

_____

_____

_____

Title: _____

How long with employer: _____

If less than 2 years, name, address and phone of previous employer:

_____

_____

_____

Title: _____

How long with employer: _____

Current monthly gross income: $ _____

Creditors (include holders of credit card and charge accounts):

Name   Address   Account Number

_____

_____

_____

_____

_____

_____

Other credit references:

_____

_____

_____

Assets:

1. Checking and savings accounts

   Bank   Address
   _____   _____ $_____
   _____   _____ $_____
   _____   _____ $_____
   _____   _____ $_____

2. Stocks and bonds

   _____ $_____
   _____ $_____
   _____ $_____
   _____ $_____

3. Real estate _____

   Market value: $_____   Mortgages/liens: $_____   Net equity: $_____

4. Vehicles (make, year and market value)

   _____ $_____
   _____ $_____

5. Business

   _____ $_____
   _____ $_____

6. Other

   _____ $_____
   _____ $_____

Total assets $_____

Liabilities:		Unpaid Balance	Monthly Payment
1. Vehicle loans	_____	$_____	$_____
2. Real estate loans	_____	$_____	$_____
3. Spousal/child support	_____	$_____	$_____
4. Other	_____	$_____	$_____

Total $ _____   Monthly total $ _____

   We authorize _____ to verify our deposits with all banks, savings
and loan associations, credit unions, and stockbrokers listed above. We further authorize
_____ to receive any and all information about our credit from credit-
reporting agencies and to verify employment with the employers listed above.

_____   _____ , 19 ___

_____   _____ , 19 ___

OFFER TO PURCHASE REAL PROPERTY

Property address:

_____.

_____, Buyer(s),

herein offer to _____, Seller(s)

to purchase the property described above, on the terms set out below.

1. Purchase Price and Down Payment

_____ DOLLARS to be paid as follows:

Down payment of $_____, in cash, to be paid into escrow on or before close of escrow.

Deposits as specified in Section 2 below.

Balance of purchase price to be paid on or before close of escrow.

2. Deposit

A deposit of $_____, in the form of a _____ check made out to _____, is submitted with this offer. The check will be held by the Seller uncashed until and unless this offer is accepted, and will be returned to the Buyer if this offer is not accepted. If this offer is accepted, the check will be deposited with the escrow holder.

This deposit will be increased to a total of $_____ upon removal of all contingencies in this contract or not later than _____, 19__, whichever is earlier.

3. Liquidated Damages

If Buyer defaults on this contract, Seller shall be released from Seller's obligations under this contract and, by signing their initials here, Buyer _____ and Seller _____ agree that Seller shall keep all deposits, up to an amount equal to three percent (3%) of the purchase price stated above.

4. Dispute Resolution

Disputes arising from this contract shall be settled:

    [ ] by binding arbitration under the rules of the American Arbitration Association.
    [ ] according to the laws of California.

5. Attorney's Fees

If litigation or arbitration arises from this contract, the prevailing party shall be reimbursed by the other party for reasonable attorney's fees and court or arbitration costs.

6. Contingencies

This offer is conditioned upon the following:

[ ] Submittal to Seller of Buyer's written approval of the following inspection reports, indicating Buyer's acceptance of the physical condition of the property, by _____, 19___. Buyer shall have the following inspections of the property made, at Buyer's expense.

    [ ] Inspection by a licensed Pest Control Operator
    [ ] Inspection by a licensed General Contractor as to the physical condition of the property in general, including, but not necessarily limited to, heating and plumbing, electrical systems, solar energy systems, roof and condition of appliances included in this transaction
    [ ] Inspection by a licensed Plumbing Contractor
    [ ] Inspection by a licensed Roofing Contractor
    [ ] Inspection by a licensed Energy Conservation Inspector in accordance with local ordinances
    [ ] Inspection by a geologist registered with the State of California
    [ ] Other _____

[ ] Buyer's obtaining of financing as specified in Section 13 below, by _____, 19___.

[ ] Written consent of the present lender(s), within _____ days of acceptance of this offer, to Buyer's assumption of any existing loans on the property.

[ ] Receipt of, and approval by Buyer of preliminary title report within _____ days of acceptance of this offer.

[ ] At close of escrow, title to the property is to be clear of all liens and encumbrances of record except those listed in the preliminary title report.

[ ] Sale of Buyer's current residence at _____ in _____, _____ County, State of _____ not later than _____, 19___.

If Buyer, after making a good-faith effort, cannot remove in writing the above contingencies by the dates specified, this contract shall become void, and all deposits shall be returned to Buyer.

7. Escrow

Title insurance company selected by Buyer and Seller is:
_____

Escrow company selected by Buyer and Seller is:
_____.

Buyer and Seller agree to execute escrow instructions by _____, 19___ .Buyer and Seller agree that deed shall be recorded in favor of Buyer and all net proceeds of sale distributed to Seller no later than _____, 19___.

8. Prorations

Seller shall be responsible for payment of Seller's prorated share of real estate taxes accrued until recordation of the deed.

Buyer agrees to assume non-callable assessment bond liens (i.e., those which cannot be paid off early by the Seller) as follows: _____.

9. Possession

Seller shall deliver physical possession of property to Buyer
      [] at close of escrow.
      [] no later than _____ days after the close of escrow.

If Seller continues to occupy the property after close of escrow, Seller shall pay to Buyer $_____ for each such day.

10. Fixtures

All fixtures, including built-in appliances, electrical, plumbing, light and hearing fixtures, garage door openers, attached carpets and other floor coverings, and window shades or blinds, are included in the sale except:

_____
_____.

11. Personal Property

The following items of personal property are included in this transaction:

_____
_____.

12. Risk of Damage to Property

If, before Buyer has received title to the property or possession of the property, the premises of the property are substantially damaged by fire, flood, earthquake or other cause, Buyer shall be relieved of any obligation to buy the property and shall have all deposits returned to him. When Buyer receives title to or possession of the property, Buyer assumes sole responsibility for the physical condition of the property.

Seller is responsible for maintaining fire insurance on the property until the date of recordation of the deed.

13. Buyer's Financing

Buyer shall, by the date specified in the financing contingency of Clause 6, provide Seller with written evidence of having obtained financing as described below:

First Loan:

$_____ Amount of loan amortized over not less than _____ years.

$_____ Maximum amount of monthly loan payment including principal, interest and, if applicable, private mortgage insurance (PMI), but not including taxes or insurance on the property (e.g., fire insurance), during the first year of the loan agreement.

> [ ] Conventional (non-subsidized)
> [ ] Owner financing
> [ ] VA   [ ] FHA   [ ] Cal-Vet
> [ ] Other: _____

> [ ] _____% fixed rate **or**

> [ ] _____% beginning rate on an adjustable rate loan, with the highest possible rate not to exceed _____% and rate to be adjusted not more frequently than _____.

Loan origination fee (points) of not more than _____% of the loan amount and application. Appraisal fees to total not more than $_____, with no balloon payment unless stated below: _____.

Second Loan:

$_____ Amount of loan amortized over not less than _____ years.

$_____ Maximum amount of monthly loan payment including principal, interest and, if applicable, private mortgage insurance (PMI), but not including taxes or insurance on the property (e.g., fire insurance), during the first year of the loan agreement.

> [ ] Conventional (non-subsidized)
> [ ] Owner financing
> [ ] Other: _____

> [ ] _____% fixed rate **or**

> [ ] _____% beginning rate on an adjustable rate loan, with the highest possible rate not to exceed _____% and rate to be adjusted not more frequently than _____.

Loan origination fee (points) of not more than _____% of the loan amount and application. Appraisal fees to total not more than $_____, with no balloon payment unless stated below: _____.

Third Loan:

$_____ Amount of loan amortized over not less than _____ years.

$_____ Maximum amount of monthly loan payment including principal, interest and, if applicable, private mortgage insurance (PMI), but not including taxes or insurance on the property (e.g., fire insurance), during the first year of the loan agreement.

    [ ] Conventional (non-subsidized)
    [ ] Owner financing
    [ ] Other: _____

    [ ] _____% fixed rate **or**

    [ ] _____% beginning rate on an adjustable rate loan, with the highest possible rate not to exceed _____% and rate to be adjusted not more frequently than _____:

Loan origination fee (points) of not more than _____% of the loan amount and application. Appraisal fees to total not more than $_____, with no balloon payment unless stated below: _____.

Subsidized Loans:

If any of the above loans involves a state or federal government agency, the Buyer shall provide to the Seller, within ten (10) business days of acceptance of this offer, copies of any documents pertinent to Buyer's eligibility for the loan(s), e.g.:

    [ ] DD-1 for Cal-Vet
    [ ] Certificate of Eligibility for VA
    [ ] Other:_____

14. Expenses of Sale

Expenses of sale shall be paid for as follows:

Buyer	Seller	Both equally	
[ ]	[ ]	[ ]	Escrow fees
[ ]	[ ]	[ ]	Title search
[ ]	[ ]	[ ]	CLTA policy for Buyer
[ ]	[ ]	[ ]	ALTA extended policy for lender(s)
[ ]	[ ]	[ ]	Documentary transfer tax
			Recording and Notary fees
[ ]	[ ]	[ ]	Grant deed
[ ]	[ ]	[ ]	Reconveyance of existing trust deed
[ ]	[ ]	[ ]	Trust deed(s)

15. Seller's Disclosures

Buyer acknowledges receipt from Seller of

[ ] Seller's Real Estate Transfer Disclosure Statement (Cal. Civ. Code § 1102) dated
_____, 19___.

[ ] Other inspection reports obtained by Seller, as follows:

Type	Preparer	Date

[ ] Documents set out in Civil Code § 1368 relating to condominiums and other common interest developments.

[ ] Documents containing all conditions, covenants, and restrictions that affect the property.

16. Time is of the Essence

Time is of the essence in this transaction.

17. Duration of Offer

This offer is submitted to the Seller by the Buyer on _____, 19___ at
_____.M., Pacific Time, and will be considered revoked if not accepted by
Seller in writing by _____.M. on _____, 19___,
or if Buyer communicates in writing to Seller, prior to notification of acceptance of this offer by
Seller, Buyer's revocation of this offer.

18. Commission to Brokers

Seller shall pay only those broker's commissions for which Seller has separately contracted in writing with a broker licensed by the California Commissioner of Real Estate.

If Buyer or Seller wishes advice concerning the legal or tax aspects of this transaction, Buyer or Seller shall separately contract and pay for it.

19. Credit Information

Buyer shall deliver to Seller, within _____ days of submittal of this offer, information showing Buyer's financial condition on a form provided by Seller. Seller shall keep the statement confidential. Buyer will also authorize disclosure to Seller of credit information about Buyer from credit card and charge account holders, banks, savings and loan associations, credit unions and brokerages where Buyer has accounts, and from credit-reporting agencies.

20. Entire Agreement

This document represents the entire agreement between Buyer and Seller. Any modifications or amendments to this contract shall be made in writing, signed and dated by both parties.

21. Foreign Investors

If Seller is a foreign person as defined in the Foreign Investment in Real Property Act, Buyer shall, absent a specific exemption, have withheld in escrow ten percent (10 %) of the gross sale price of the property. Buyer and Seller shall execute and provide the escrow holder specified in Clause 7 above with all documentation required by the Act.

22. Rent Control

The property [ ] is [ ] is not located in a city or county subject to local rent control. A rent control ordinance may restrict the rent that can be charged for this property.

23. Transfer Requirements

Local and state law may require certain disclosures, inspections, modifications or repairs before transfer of the property, including (but not limited to):

Disclosure that property is located in a Special Flood Hazard Area as set forth on a Federal Emergency Management Agency "Flood Insurance Rate Map" or "Flood Hazard Boundary Map."

Smoke detector(s) installed and operational.

Local energy efficiency ordinance requirements met.

Disclosure that property is in a special studies (earthquake) area.

Payment of local anti-speculation taxes.

Other: _____
_____
_____

Seller shall take responsibility for complying with all such applicable requirements except:
_____
_____

24. Seller's Right to Accept Backup Offers

Seller may enter into subsequent contracts with other persons for sale of the property. Any such contracts shall be contingent on the termination of the contract between Buyer and Seller. Seller shall notify all other offerors of the existence (though not necessarily the terms) of this offer.

25. Seller's Right to Demand Removal of Contingencies

If, any time at least two weeks from the date Buyer and Seller enter into a contract for purchase of the property, Seller gives Buyer a written demand to remove all contingencies in Clause 6 of this contract concerning inspection reports and/or the Buyer's ability to arrange financing and/or get approval for assumption of loans, and/or the Buyer's ability to sell an existing residence, Buyer shall have ninety-six (96) hours from receipt of the demand if personally delivered (or five days from the date of mailing, if the demand is mailed by certified mail) in which to remove all these contingencies. If Buyer cannot do so, then this contract shall be terminated immediately, Buyer and Seller shall sign a mutual release, and all deposits shall be returned to Buyer.

26. Other Terms and Conditions

_____

_____

_____

_____

27. Notice to Backup Offeror(s) [To be completed only if Buyer is a backup offeror]

Buyer is aware that Seller has entered into contracts for the sale of the property with:

_____

_____

_____

_____

_____

and that Seller's acceptance of Buyer's offer is contingent upon the contracts with the above persons no longer being in force, either by default on the part of the above offeror(s) or because the above offeror(s) cannot remove contingencies as provided for in their contract(s).

28. Buyer's Signature

Buyer has read and understands Clauses 1-27 of this contract, which constitute the entire offer Buyer hereby makes to Seller.

Buyer(s) signature(s)

_____   Date:_____, 19___

_____   Time:_____M.

29. Acceptance By Seller(s)

Seller(s)' accept(s) this offer as stated.

Seller(s)' signature(s):

_____   Date:_____, 19___

_____   Time:_____M.

ADDITION TO REAL PROPERTY
PURCHASE CONTRACT

The material set out below is hereby made a part of the contract dated
_____,19 _____ between _____
_____, Buyer(s) and _____
_____ , Seller(s) to purchase real property
located at _____
_____.

Read, understood, and agreed to by:

_____   _____
Signature of Buyer   Date

_____   _____
Signature of Seller   Date

DEPOSIT RECEIPT

_____, Seller(s) of the property
located at _____
_____ in _____, California, hereby
acknowledge receipt from _____, Offeror(s) of the sum
of $_____ in the form of a cashier's check payable to _____
_____.

This check will be held by the Seller uncashed until and unless Offeror's offer is
accepted, and will be returned to the Offeror if this offer is not accepted.

Signed _____

       _____

Date   _____ , 19 _____

ACCEPTANCE OF PURCHASE OFFER

_____, the owner(s) of the
property at _____
_____in the city of _____,
county of _____, California, hereby accept the offer
to purchase the property made on _____, 19__, by
_____.

Signed _____

_____ , Sellers

Date _____ , 19 _____

SHORT FORM COUNTER-OFFER

_____, Seller(s) of the real
property at _____,
_____, California, accept(s) the offer to purchase the
property dated _____,19 _____ made by
_____,with the following
exceptions:

_____   _____, 19___, ___.M.

_____   _____, 19___, ___.M.

COUNTER-OFFER TO PURCHASE REAL PROPERTY

Property address:

_____ .
_____, Seller(s),
herein make a counter-offer to the _____, 19____ offer of
_____, Buyer(s)
to purchase the property described above.

1. Purchase Price and Down Payment

_____ DOLLARS to be paid as follows:

Down payment of $_____, in cash, to be paid into escrow
on or before close of escrow.

Deposits as specified in Section 2 below.

Balance of purchase price to be paid on or before close of escrow.

2. Deposit

Buyer [ ] has submitted [ ] will submit, upon acceptance of this counter-offer to Seller a
deposit of $_____, in the form of a _____ check made out to
_____. If this counter-offer is accepted, the check will be
deposited with the escrow holder.

Buyer's deposit will be increased to a total of $_____ upon removal of all
contingencies in this contract or not later than _____, 19__, whichever is earlier.

3. Liquidated Damages

**If Buyer defaults on this contract, Seller shall be released from Seller's obligations under this
contract and, by signing their initials here, Buyer _____ and Seller
_____ agree that Seller shall keep all deposits, up to an amount equal to
three percent (3%) of the purchase price stated above.**

4. Dispute Resolution

Disputes arising from this contract shall be settled:

    [ ] by binding arbitration under the rules of the American Arbitration Association.
    [ ] according to the laws of California.

5. Attorney's Fees

If litigation or arbitration arises from this contract, the prevailing party shall be reimbursed by the
other party for reasonable attorney's fees and court or arbitration costs.

6. Contingencies

This counter-offer is conditioned upon the following:

[ ] Submittal to Seller of Buyer's written approval of the following inspection reports, indicating Buyer's acceptance of the physical condition of the property, by _____, 19__. Buyer shall have the following inspections of the property made, at Buyer's expense.

    [ ] Inspection by a licensed Pest Control Operator
    [ ] Inspection by a licensed General Contractor as to the physical condition of the property in general, including, but not necessarily limited to, heating and plumbing, electrical systems, solar energy systems, roof and condition of appliances included in this transaction
    [ ] Inspection by a licensed Plumbing Contractor
    [ ] Inspection by a licensed Roofing Contractor
    [ ] Inspection by a licensed Energy Conservation Inspector in accordance with local ordinances
    [ ] Inspection by a geologist registered with the State of California
    [ ] Other _____

[ ] Buyer's obtaining of financing as specified in Section 13 below, by _____, 19__.

[ ] Written consent of the present lender(s), within _____ days of acceptance of this offer, to Buyer's assumption of any existing loans on the property.

[ ] Receipt of, and approval by Buyer of preliminary title report within _____ days of acceptance of this offer.

[ ] At close of escrow, title to the property is to be clear of all liens and encumbrances of record except those listed in the preliminary title report.

[ ] Sale of Buyer's current residence at _____ in _____, _____ County, State of _____ not later than _____, 19__.

If Buyer, after making a good-faith effort, cannot remove in writing the above contingencies by the dates specified, this contract shall become void, and all deposits shall be returned to Buyer.

7. Escrow

Title insurance company selected by Buyer and Seller is:
_____

Escrow company selected by Buyer and Seller is:
_____.

Buyer and Seller agree to execute escrow instructions by _____, 19___ .Buyer and Seller agree that deed shall be recorded in favor of Buyer and all net proceeds of sale distributed to Seller no later than _____, 19__.

8. Prorations

Seller shall be responsible for payment of Seller's prorated share of real estate taxes accrued until recordation of the deed.

Buyer agrees to assume non-callable assessment bond liens (i.e., those which cannot be paid off early by the Seller) as follows: _____.

9. Possession

Seller shall deliver physical possession of property to Buyer
       [] at close of escrow.
       [] no later than _____ days after the close of escrow.

If Seller continues to occupy the property after close of escrow, Seller shall pay to Buyer $_____ for each such day.

10. Fixtures

All fixtures, including built-in appliances, electrical, plumbing, light and hearing fixtures, garage door openers, attached carpets and other floor coverings, and window shades or blinds, are included in the sale except:

_____
_____.

11. Personal Property

The following items of personal property are included in this transaction:

_____
_____.

12. Risk of Damage to Property

If, before Buyer has received title to the property or possession of the property, the premises of the property are substantially damaged by fire, flood, earthquake or other cause, Buyer shall be relieved of any obligation to buy the property and shall have all deposits returned to him. When Buyer receives title to or possession of the property, Buyer assumes sole responsibility for the physical condition of the property.

Seller is responsible for maintaining fire insurance on the property until the date of recordation of the deed.

13. Buyer's Financing

Buyer shall, by the date specified in the financing contingency of Clause 6, provide Seller with written evidence of having obtained financing as described below:

First Loan:

$_____ Amount of loan amortized over not less than _____ years.

$_____ Maximum amount of monthly loan payment including principal, interest and, if applicable, private mortgage insurance (PMI), but not including taxes or insurance on the property (e.g., fire insurance), during the first year of the loan agreement.

    [ ] Conventional (non-subsidized)
    [ ] Owner financing
    [ ] VA   [ ] FHA   [ ] Cal-Vet
    [ ] Other: _____

    [ ] _____% fixed rate **or**

    [ ] _____% beginning rate on an adjustable rate loan, with the highest possible rate not to exceed _____% and rate to be adjusted not more frequently than _____.

Loan origination fee (points) of not more than _____% of the loan amount and application. Appraisal fees to total not more than $_____, with no balloon payment unless stated below: _____.

Second Loan:

$_____ Amount of loan amortized over not less than _____ years.

$_____ Maximum amount of monthly loan payment including principal, interest and, if applicable, private mortgage insurance (PMI), but not including taxes or insurance on the property (e.g., fire insurance), during the first year of the loan agreement.

    [ ] Conventional (non-subsidized)
    [ ] Owner financing
    [ ] Other: _____

    [ ] _____% fixed rate **or**

    [ ] _____% beginning rate on an adjustable rate loan, with the highest possible rate not to exceed _____% and rate to be adjusted not more frequently than _____.

Loan origination fee (points) of not more than _____% of the loan amount and application. Appraisal fees to total not more than $_____, with no balloon payment unless stated below: _____.

Third Loan:

$_____ Amount of loan amortized over not less than _____ years.

$_____ Maximum amount of monthly loan payment including principal, interest and, if applicable, private mortgage insurance (PMI), but not including taxes or insurance on the property (e.g., fire insurance), during the first year of the loan agreement.

    [ ] Conventional (non-subsidized)
    [ ] Owner financing
    [ ] Other: _____

    [ ] _____% fixed rate **or**

    [ ] _____% beginning rate on an adjustable rate loan, with the highest possible rate not to exceed _____% and rate to be adjusted not more frequently than _____.

Loan origination fee (points) of not more than _____% of the loan amount and application. Appraisal fees to total not more than $_____, with no balloon payment unless stated below: _____.

Subsidized Loans:

If any of the above loans involves a state or federal government agency, the Buyer shall provide to the Seller, within ten (10) business days of acceptance of this offer, copies of any documents pertinent to Buyer's eligibility for the loan(s), e.g.:

    [ ] DD-1 for Cal-Vet
    [ ] Certificate of Eligibility for VA
    [ ] Other:_____

14. Expenses of Sale

Expenses of sale shall be paid for as follows:

Buyer	Seller	Both equally	
[ ]	[ ]	[ ]	Escrow fees
[ ]	[ ]	[ ]	Title search
[ ]	[ ]	[ ]	CLTA policy for Buyer
[ ]	[ ]	[ ]	ALTA extended policy for lender(s)
[ ]	[ ]	[ ]	Documentary transfer tax
			Recording and Notary fees
[ ]	[ ]	[ ]	Grant deed
[ ]	[ ]	[ ]	Reconveyance of existing trust deed
[ ]	[ ]	[ ]	Trust deed(s)

15. Seller's Disclosures

Buyer acknowledges receipt from Seller of

[ ]   Seller's Real Estate Transfer Disclosure Statement (Cal. Civ. Code § 1102) dated
_____, 19___.

[ ]   Other inspection reports obtained by Seller, as follows:

Type   Preparer   Date

_____

_____

_____

_____

_____

[ ]   Documents set out in Civil Code § 1368 relating to condominiums and other common interest developments.

[ ]   Documents containing all conditions, covenants, and restrictions that affect the property.

16. Time is of the Essence

Time is of the essence in this transaction.

17. Duration of Counter-Offer

This counter-offer is submitted to the Buyer by the Seller on _____,
19___ at _____.M., Pacific Time, and will be considered revoked if not
accepted by Buyer in writing by _____.M. on _____, 19___,
or if Seller communicates in writing to Buyer, prior to notification of acceptance of this counter-offer by Buyer, Seller's revocation of this counter-offer.

18. Commission to Brokers

Seller shall pay only those broker's commissions for which Seller has separately contracted in writing with a broker licensed by the California Commissioner of Real Estate.

If Buyer or Seller wishes advice concerning the legal or tax aspects of this transaction, Buyer or Seller shall separately contract and pay for it.

19. Credit Information

Buyer shall deliver to Seller, within _____ days of submittal of this counter-offer , information showing Buyer's financial condition on a form provided by Seller. Seller shall keep the statement confidential. Buyer will also authorize disclosure to Seller of credit information about Buyer from credit card and charge account holders, banks, savings and loan associations, credit unions and brokerages where Buyer has accounts, and from credit-reporting agencies.

20. Entire Agreement

This document represents the entire agreement between Buyer and Seller. Any modifications or amendments to this contract shall be made in writing, signed and dated by both parties.

21. Foreign Investors

If Seller is a foreign person as defined in the Foreign Investment in Real Property Act, Buyer shall, absent a specific exemption, have withheld in escrow ten percent (10 %) of the gross sale price of the property. Buyer and Seller shall execute and provide the escrow holder specified in Clause 7 above with all documentation required by the Act.

22. Rent Control

The property [ ] is [ ] is not located in a city or county subject to local rent control. A rent control ordinance may restrict the rent that can be charged for this property.

23. Transfer Requirements

Local and state law may require certain disclosures, inspections, modifications or repairs before transfer of the property, including (but not limited to):

Disclosure that property is located in a Special Flood Hazard Area as set forth on a Federal Emergency Management Agency "Flood Insurance Rate Map" or "Flood Hazard Boundary Map."

Smoke detector(s) installed and operational.

Local energy efficiency ordinance requirements met.

Disclosure that property is in a special studies (earthquake) area.

Payment of local anti-speculation taxes.

Other: _____
_____
_____

Seller shall take responsibility for complying with all such applicable requirements except:
_____
_____

24. Seller's Right to Accept Backup Offers

Seller reserves the right to enter into subsequent contracts with other persons for sale of the property. Any such contracts shall be contingent on the termination of the contract between Buyer and Seller. Seller shall notify all subsequent offerors of the existence (though not necessarily the terms) of the contract between Buyer and Seller.

25. Seller's Right to Demand Removal of Contingencies

If, any time at least two weeks from the date that Buyer and Seller enter into a contract for purchase of the property, Seller gives Buyer a written demand to remove all contingencies in Clause 6 of this contract concerning inspection reports and/or the Buyer's ability to arrange financing and/or get approval for assumption of loans, and/or the Buyer's ability to sell an existing residence, Buyer shall have ninety-six (96) hours from receipt of the demand if personally delivered (or five days from the date of mailing, if the demand is mailed by certified mail) in which to remove all these contingencies. If Buyer cannot do so, then this contract shall be terminated immediately, Buyer and Seller shall sign a mutual release, and all deposits shall be returned to Buyer.

26. Other Terms and Conditions

_____
_____
_____

27. Notice to Backup Offeror(s) [To be completed only if Buyer is a backup offeror]

Buyer is aware that Seller has entered into contracts for the sale of the property with:

_____
_____
_____
_____

and that Seller's counter-offer is contingent upon the contracts with the above persons no longer being in force, either by default on the part of the above offeror(s) or because the above offeror(s) cannot remove contingencies as provided for in their contract(s).

28. Seller's Signature

Seller has read and understands Clauses 1-27 of this contract, which constitute the entire counter-offer Seller hereby makes to Buyer.

Seller(s)' signature(s)

_____   Date:_____, 19____

_____   Time:_____M.

29. Acceptance By Buyer(s)

Buyer(s)' accept(s) this offer as stated.

Buyer(s)' signature(s):

_____   Date:_____, 19____

_____   Time:_____M.

COUNTER-OFFER REVOCATION

_____

_____, the seller(s) of the property at

_____ in

_____, California, hereby revoke the counter-offer made to

_____ on

_____, 19_____, and hereby authorize escrow holder(s)
to return to buyer(s) any deposit funds tendered by buyer(s).

Signed   _____

                 _____ , Seller(s)

             on _____, 19_____, _____. M.

Deposit
Received By   _____

                 _____ , Buyer(s)

             on _____, 19_____, _____. M.

CONTINGENCY RELEASE

_____, Buyer(s) of
the property at _____
_____, _____, California, hereby remove
the following contingencies from the purchase contract dated
_____, 19___.

    If this release is based on accepting any inspection report, a copy of the report signed by the Buyer(s), is attached.

    Buyer(s) release Seller(s) from liability for any physical defects disclosed by the attached report(s).

_____   _____

_____   _____
Buyer(s)   Seller(s)

_____, 19 ____   _____, 19 ____

SELLER'S DEMAND FOR REMOVAL OF CONTINGENCIES

Under the terms of the contract dated _____ , 19 ___ between

_____ , Seller(s), and

_____ , Buyer(s), for

purchase of the real property at_____ , California,

Seller(s) hereby demand(s) that Buyer(s) remove the following contingencies specified in Clause

6 of the contract:

☐ ninety-six (96) hours from receipt of this demand (personally delivered) or

☐ five days from mailing of this demand by certified mail.

If Buyer(s) does not remove these contingencies within the time specified, the contract shall

become void, and all deposits shall be promptly returned to Buyer(s) upon Buyer(s)' execution of

a release, releasing Buyer(s) and Seller(s) from all obligation under the contract.

_____ _____ , 19 ___
Seller

Personally delivered: _____ , 19 ___, _____ _ M.

Mailed by certified mail: _____ , 19 ___

REAL ESTATE PURCHASE CONTRACT RELEASE

_____ , Seller(s), and

_____ , Buyer(s), hereby

execute this mutual release, releasing all our legal rights with respect to the contract dated

_____ for sale of the real property at _____

_____ , and declaring the contract void and of no effect.

Each of us expressly releases the others, their heirs, insurers and legal representatives,

from all claims known or unknown to us that have arisen or may arise from the contract.

In executing this release we intend to bind our spouses, heirs, legal representatives,

assigns, and anyone else claiming under us, in addition to ourselves. None of us has assigned to

another party a claim arising from the contract.

Buyer(s) acknowledge(s) that Seller(s) has returned to Buyer(s) or directed the escrow

holder to return all deposits made by Buyer(s) in connection with the contract.

Signatures: Date:

_____   _____
Seller

_____   _____
Seller

_____   _____
Buyer

_____   _____
Buyer

About the Author

George Devine is a licensed real estate broker and a widely respected educator in the real estate field. He holds a B.A. from the University of San Francisco and an M.A. from Marquette University, and has pursued additional studies at San Francisco State University, Seton Hall University, Fordham University, New York University and the University of California at Berkeley. Currently, he is an instructor in the real estate sales and broker license preparation classes, college level classes, and continuing education classes offered by Anthony Schools of Northern California. He was also the author and principal instructor of a course on San Francisco Rent Control Law for New Technologies Institute. He has also served on the faculties of the University of San Francisco, Seton Hall University, Marquette University, Manhattan College and St. John's University.

For several years, George Devine wrote the popular "Real Estate Handbook" column in the weekly *Real Estate Guide* section of the San Francisco *Progress.* In addition to being an active broker he serves as a consultant to private parties and members of the legal profession concerning the practicalities of real estate transactions in California.

Business and Finance

How To Form Your Own Corporation
By attorney Mancuso. Provides all the forms, Bylaws, Articles, minutes of meeting, stock certificates and instructions necessary to form your small profit corporation. Includes a thorough discussion of the practical and legal aspects of incorporation, including the tax consequences.

California Edition	$24.95
Texas Edition	$21.95
New York Edition	$19.95
Florida Edition	$19.95

The Non-Profit Corporation Handbook
By attorney Mancuso. Includes all the forms, Bylaws, Articles, minutes, and instructions you need to form a non-profit corporation. Step-by-step instructions on how to choose a name, draft Articles and Bylaws, attain favorable tax status. Thorough information on federal tax exemptions, which groups outside of California will find particularly useful.

California only $24.95

The California Professional Corporation Handbook
By attorneys Mancuso and Honigsberg. In California a number of professions must fulfill special requirements when forming a corporation. Among them are lawyers, dentists, doctors and other health professionals, accountants and certain social workers. This book contains detailed information on the special requirements of every profession and all the forms and instructions necessary to form a professional corporation.

California only $29.95

Marketing Without Advertising
A creative and practical guide that shows small businesspersons how to avoid wasting money on advertising. The authors, experienced business consultants, show how to implement an ongoing marketing plan to tell potential and current customers that yours is a quality business worth trusting, recommending and coming back to.

National Edition $14.00

Billpayers' Rights
By attorney Warner. Complete information on bankruptcy, student loans, wage attachments, dealing with bill collectors and collection agencies, credit cards, car repossessions, homesteads, child support and much more.

California only $12.95

Chapter 13: The Federal Plan to Repay Your Debts
By attorney Kosel. This book allows an individual to develop and carry out a feasible plan to pay most of his/her debts over a three-year period. Chapter 13 is an alternative to straight bankruptcy and yet it still means the end of creditor harassment, wage attachments and other collection efforts. Comes complete with all necessary forms and worksheets.

National Edition $14.95

The Partnership Book
By attorneys Clifford and Warner. When two or more people join to start a small business, one of the most basic needs is to establish a solid, legal partnership agreement. This book supplies a number of sample agreements which you can use as is. Buy-out clauses, unequal sharing of assets, and limited partnerships are all discussed in detail.

National Edition $18.95

Bankruptcy: Do-It-Yourself
By attorney Kosel. Tells you exactly what bankruptcy is all about and how it affects your credit rating, property and debts, with complete details on property you can keep under the state and federal exempt property rules. Shows you step-by-step how to do it yourself; comes with all necessary forms and instructions.

National Edition $15.95

Small Time Operator
By Bernard Kamoroff, C.P.A.. Shows you how to start and operate your small business, keep your books, pay your taxes and stay out of trouble. Comes complete with a year's supply of ledgers and worksheets designed especially for small businesses, and contains invaluable information on permits, licenses, financing, loans, insurance, bank accounts, etc. Published by Bell Springs.

National Edition $10.95

Start-Up Money: How to Finance Your Small Business
By Michael McKeever. For anyone about to start a business or revamp an existing one, this book shows how to write a business plan, draft a loan package and find sources of small business finance.

National Edition $12.95

The Independent Paralegal's Handbook: How to Provide Legal Services Without Going to Jail
More and more nonlawyers are opening legal typing services to help people prepare their own papers for divorce, bankruptcy, incorporation, eviction, etc. Called independent paralegals, these legal pioneers pose much the same challenge to the legal establishment as midwives do to conventional medicine. Written by Nolo Press co-founder Ralph Warner, who established one of the first divorce typing services in 1973, this controversial book is sure to become the bible of the new movement aimed at delivering routine legal services to the public at a reasonable price.

National Edition $12.95

Estate Planning, Wills & Probate

Plan Your Estate: Wills, Probate Avoidance, Trusts and Taxes
By attorney Clifford. Comprehensive information on making a will, alternatives to probate, planning to limit inheritance and estate taxes, living trusts, and providing for family and friends. Explains new California statutory will and includes actual forms.

California Edition $15.95

Nolo's Simple Will Book

By attorney Denis Clifford. This book will show you how to draft a will without a lawyer in any state except Louisiana. Covers all the basics, including what to do about children, whom you can designate to carry out your wishes, and how to comply with the technical legal requirements of each state. Includes examples and many alternative clauses from which to choose.
National Edition $14.95

WillWriter—a software/book package

By Legisoft. Use your computer to prepare and update your own valid will. A manual provides help in areas such as tax planning and probate avoidance. Runs on Apple II+, IIe, IIc, the Mac, Commodore and the IBM PC (and most PC compatibles).
National Edition $49.95

How to Settle A Simple Estate

Forms and instructions necessary to settle a California resident's estate after death. This book deals with joint tenancy and community property transfers as well as showing you how to actually probate an estate, step-by-step. The book is aimed at the executor, administrator or family member who will have the actual responsibility to settle the estate.
California Edition $19.95

Family and Friends

How to Do Your Own Divorce

By attorney Sherman. This is the original "do-your-own-law" book. It contains tearout copies of all the court forms required for an uncontested dissolution, as well as instructions for certain special forms.
California Edition $14.95
Texas Edition $12.95

Annulment: Your Chance to Remarry Within the Catholic Church

By attorney Zwack. (Harper & Row). This is the only book that explains fully in lay terms the grounds and procedures by which Roman Catholics who have undergone civil divorces can also have their former marriages annulled by the Church.
National Edition $5.95

The Living Together Kit

By attorneys Ihara and Warner. A legal guide for unmarried couples with information about buying or sharing property, the Marvin decision, paternity statements, medical emergencies and tax consequences. Contains a sample will and Living Together Contract.
National Edition $14.95

California Marriage and Divorce Law

By attorneys Ihara and Warner. This book contains invaluable information for married couples and those considering marriage or remarriage on community and separate property, names, debts, children, buying a house, etc. Includes prenuptial contracts, a simple will, probate avoidance information and an explanation of gift and inheritance taxes. Discusses "secret marriage" and "common law" marriage.
California only $14.95

Social Security, Medicare & Pensions: The Sourcebook for Older Americans

By attorney Matthews. The most comprehensive resource tool on the income, rights and benefits of Americans over 55. Includes detailed information on social security, retirement rights, Medicare, Medicaid, supplemental security income, private pensions, age discrimination, as well as a thorough explanation of the new social security legislation.
National Edition $14.95

How to Modify & Collect Child Support in California

By attorneys Matthews, Segal and Willis. California court awards for child support have radically increased in the last two years. This book contains the forms and instructions to obtain the benefits of this change without a lawyer and collect support directly from a person's wages or benefits, if necessary.
California only $17.95

A Legal Guide for Lesbian/Gay Couples

By attorneys Curry and Clifford. Here is a book that deals specifically with legal matters of lesbian and gay couples: raising children (custody, support, living with a lover), buying property together, wills, etc. and comes complete with sample contracts and agreements.
National Edition $17.95

How to Adopt Your Stepchild

By Frank Zagone. Shows you how to prepare all the legal forms; includes information on how to get the consent of the natural parent and how to conduct an "abandonment" proceeding. Discusses appearing in court and making changes in birth certificates.
California only $17.95

The Power of Attorney Book

By attorney Clifford. Covers the process which allows you to arrange for someone else to protect your rights and property should you become incapable of doing so. Discusses the advantages and drawbacks and gives complete instructions for establishing a power of attorney yourself.
National Edition $15.95

How to Change Your Name

By attorneys Loeb and Brown. Changing one's name is a very simple procedure. Using this book, you can file the necessary papers yourself, saving $200 to $300 in attorney's fees. Comes complete with all forms and instructions for the court petition method or ths simpler usage method.
California only $14.95

Your Family Records: How to Preserve Personal, Financial and Legal History

By Pladsen and attorney Clifford. Helps you organize and record all sorts of items that will affect you and your family when death or disability occur, e.g., where to find your will and deed to the house. Includes information about probate avoidance, joint ownership of property and genealogical research. Space is provided for financial and legal records.
National Edition $14.95

Landlord/Tenant

Tenants' Rights
By attorneys Moskovitz, Warner and Sherman. Discusses everything tenants need to know in order to protect themselves: getting deposits returned, breaking a lease, getting repairs made, using Small Claims Court, dealing with an unscrupulous landlord, forming a tenants' organization, etc. Sample Fair-to-Tenants lease, rental agreements, and unlawful detainer answer forms.
California Edition $14.95

The Landlord's Law Book: Rights and Responsibilities
By attorney Brown. Now, for the first time, there is an accessible, easy to understand law book written specifically for landlords. Covers the areas of discrimination, insurance, tenants' privacy, leases, security deposits, rent control, liability, and rent with-holding.
California only $19.95

The Landlord's Law Book: Evictions
By attorneys David Brown and Ralph Warner. This is the most comprehensive manual available on how to do each step of an eviction, and the only one to deal with rent control cities and contested evictions including how to represent yourself in court if necessary. All the required forms, with directions on how to complete and file them, are included. Vol. 1 covers Rights and Responsibilites.
California only $19.95

Landlording
By Leigh Robinson (Express Press). Written for the conscientious landlord or landlady, this compre-hensive guide discusses maintenance and repairs, getting good tenants, how to avoid evictions, record keeping and taxes.
National Edition $17.95

Real Estate

All About Escrow
(Express Press) By Sandy Gadow. This book gives you a good understanding of what your escrow officer should be doing for you. Includes advice about inspections, financing, condominiums and cooperatives.
National Edition $10.95

The Buyer's Guide: Inspecting a Home or Income Property
By Jim Yuen, a professional housing inspector. A realistic and practical approach to inspecting residential and income property. Designed for home owners, buyers, sellers and real estate personnel.
National Edition $15.95

Homebuyers: Lambs to the Slaughter
By attorney Bashinsky (Menasha Ridge Press). Written by a lawyer/broker, this book describes how sellers, agents, lenders and lawyers are out to fleece you, the buyer, and advises how to protect your interests.
National Edition $12.95

For Sale By Owner
By George Divine. The average Cailfornia home sold for $130,000 in 1986. That meant the average seller paid $7800 in broker's commissions. This book will show you how to sell your own home and save the money. All the background information and legal technicalities are included to help you do the job yourself and with confidence.
California Edition $24.95

Homestead Your House
By attorney Warner. Under the California Homestead Act, you can file a Declaration of Homestead and thus protect your home from being sold to satisfy most debts. This book explains this simple and inexpensive procedure and includes all the forms and instructions. Contains information on exemptions for mobile homes and houseboats.
California only $8.95

Copyrights & Patents

Legal Care for Your Software
By attorney Remer. Shows the software programmer how to protect his/her work through the use of trade secret, trademark, copyright, patent and, most especially, contractual laws and agreements. This book is full of forms and instructions that give programmers the hands-on information they need.
International Edition $24.95

Intellectual Property Law Dictionary
By attorney Elias. "Intellectual Property" includes ideas, creations and inventions. The Dictionary is designed for inventors, authors, programmers, journalists, scientists and business people who must understand how the law affects the ownership and control of new ideas and technologies. Divided into sections on: Trade Secrets, Copyrights, Trademarks, Patents and Contracts. More than a dictionary, it places terms in context as well as defines them.
National Edition $17.95

How to Copyright Software
By attorney Salone. Shows the serious programmer or software developer how to protect his or her programs through the legal device of copyright.
International Edition $24.95

Patent It Yourself
By attorney Pressman. Complete instructions on how to do a patent search and file for a patent in the U.S. Also covers how to choose the appropriate form of protection (copyright, trademark, trade secret, etc.), how to evaluate salability of inventions, patent prosecution, marketing, use of the patent, foreign filing, licensing, etc. Tearout forms are included
National Edition $24.95

Researching the Law

Legal Research: How to Find and Understand the Law

By attorney Elias. A hands-on guide to unraveling the mysteries of the law library. For paralegals, law students, consumer activists, legal secretaries, business and media people. Shows exactly how to find laws relating to specific cases or legal questions, interpret statutes and regulations, find and research cases, understand case citations and Shepardize them.

National Edition $14.95

California Civil Code

(West Publishing) Statutes covering a wide variety of topics, rights and duties in the landlord/tenant relationship, marriage and divorce, contracts, transfers of real estate, consumer credit, power of attorney, and trusts.

California only $16.50

California Code of Civil Procedure

(West Publishing) Statutes governing most judicial and administrative procedures: unlawful detainer (eviction) proceedings, small claims actions, homestead procedures, wage garnishments, recording of liens, statutes of limitation, court procedures, arbitration, and appeals.

California only $16.50

Rules and Tools

Make Your Own Contract

By attorney Elias. Provides tear-out contracts, with instructions, for non-commercial use. Covers lending money, selling or leasing personal property (e.g., cars, boats), leasing and storing items (with friends, neighbors), doing home repairs, and making deposits to hold personal property pending final payment. Includes an appendix listing all the contracts found in Nolo books.

National Edition $12.95

The People's Law Review

Edited by Ralph Warner. This is the first compendium of people's law resources ever published. Contains articles on mediation and the new "non-adversary" mediation centers, information on selfhelp law programs and centers (for tenants, artists, battered women, the disabled, etc.); and articles dealing with many common legal problems which show people how to do-it-themselves.

National Edition $8.95

Author Law

By attorney Bunnin and Beren. A comprehensive explanation of the legal rights of authors. Covers contracts with publishers of books and periodicals, with samples provided. Explains the legal responsibilities between coauthors and with agents, and how to do your own copyright. Discusses royalties, negotiations, libel and invasion of privacy. Includes a glossary of publishing terms.

National Edition $14.95

The Criminal Records Book

By attorney Siegel. Takes you step-by-step through the procedures available to get your records sealed, destroyed or changed. Detailed discussion on your criminal record what it is, how it can harm you, how to correct inaccuracies, marijuana possession records and juvenile court records.

California only $14.95

Everybody's Guide to Small Claims Court

By attorney Warner. Guides you step-by-step through the Small Claims procedure, providing practical information on how to evaluate your case, file and serve papers, prepare and present your case, and, most important, how to collect when you win. Separate chapters focus on common situations (landlord-tenant, automobile sales and repair, etc.).

National Edition $10.95
California Edition $12.95

Media Law: A Legal Handbook for the Working Journalist

By attorney Galvin. This is a practical legal guide for the working journalist (TV, radio and print) and those who desire a better understanding of how the law and journalism intersect. It informs you about censorship, libel and invasion of privacy; how to gain access to public records, including using the Freedom of Information Act; entry to public meetings and courtrooms; dealing with gag orders.

National Edition $14.95

Fight Your Ticket

By attorney Brown. A comprehensive manual on how to fight your traffic ticket. Radar, drunk driving, preparing for court, arguing your case to a judge, cross-examining witnesses are all covered.

California only $12.95

How to Become a United States Citizen

By Sally Abel. Detailed explanation of the naturalization process. Includes step-by-step instructions from filing for naturalization to the final oath of allegiance. Includes a study guide on U.S. history and government. Text is written in both English and Spanish.

National Edition $9.95

Draft, Registration and The Law

How it works, what to do, advice and strategies.

California only $9.95

Murder on the Air

By Ralph Warner and Toni Ihara. An unconventional murder mystery set in Berkeley, California. When a noted environmentalist and anti-nuclear activist is killed at a local radio station, the Berkeley violent crime squad swings into action. James Rivers, an unplugged lawyer, and Sara Tamura, Berkeley's first female murder squad detective, lead the chase. The action is fast, furious and fun. $5.95

29 Reasons Not to Go to Law School

A humorous and irreverent look at the dubious pleasures of going to law school. By attorneys Ihara and Warner, with contributions by fellow lawyers and illustrations by Mari Stein. $6.95

nolo

self-help law books

Order Form

Quantity	Title	Unit Price	Total

Prices subject to change

___Please send me a catalogue

Tax: (CA only; San Mateo, LA, & Bart Counties, 6 1/2%, Santa Clara 7%, all others, 6%)

Subtotal_____

Tax_____

Postage & Handling_____

Total _____

Postage & Handling:

No. of Books	Postage & Handling
1	$1.50
2-3	$2.00
4-5	$2.50

Over 5, add 5% of total before tax

Please allow 3-5 weeks for delivery. For faster service, add $1 for UPS delivery (no P.O. boxes, please).

Name_____

Address_____

for

_____

_____VISA   _____Mastercard

#_____ exp._____

Signature_____

Phone (   )_____

ORDERS: Credit card information or a check may be sent to NOLO Press, 950 Parker St., Berkeley,CA 94710
Use your credit card and call our **800 lines**

for faster service:
Orders <u>only</u>: **US: 800-992-NOLO**
CA: 800-446-NOLO
(M-F, 9:00 - 5:00 PDT)

For general information call (415)549-1976

or

Send a check only to NOLO Distributing, Box Box 544, Occidental, CA 955465